The Handbook of
Chinese
Horoscopes

Theodora Lau was born in Shanghai, China, and now lives in Hong Kong. She is married and has two children. This is her first book.

The Handbook of
Chinese
Horoscopes

By
Theodora
Lau

Calligraphy
by Kenneth Lau

ARROW BOOKS

Arrow Books Limited
17-21 Conway Street, London W1P 6JD

An imprint of the Hutchinson Publishing Group

London Melbourne Sydney Auckland
Johannesburg and agencies
throughout the world

First published in Great Britain
by the Souvenir Press Ltd 1979
Arrow edition 1981
Reprinted 1981 (twice), 1982, 1983 and 1984

Printed and bound in Great Britain by
Anchor Brendon Ltd, Tiptree, Essex

ISBN 0 09 924690 2

For: J & M and Perfect Understanding

Contents

INTRODUCTION   1

The Twelve Animal Signs or Earth Branches   1
The Years of the Lunar Signs from 1900 to 1995   9
The Exact Lunar Years from 1900 to 1995   9
The Twelve Signs and Their Hours   12
The Twenty-four Segments of the Lunar Agricultural Almanac   12
The Signs in General   14
The Yin and the Yang   15
The Five Elements   17
The Elements and You   22
Compatibility Among the Signs   26
Incompatibility Among the Signs   28
Conclusion   29

CHAPTER 1: THE RAT   31

The Rat Sign   32
The Year of the Rat   33
The Rat Personality   33
The Rat Child   37
The Five Types of Rats   37
The Rat and His Ascendants   40
How the Rat Fares in Different Years   41
Compatibility Table for the Rat   42
Famous Persons Born in the Year of the Rat   44

CHAPTER 2: THE OX   45

The Ox Sign   46
The Year of the Ox   47

The Ox Personality   47
The Ox Child   51
The Five Types of Oxen   52
The Ox and His Ascendants   55
How the Ox Fares in Different Years   56
Compatibility Table for the Ox   57
Famous Persons Born in the Year of the Ox   59

CHAPTER 3: THE TIGER   61

The Tiger Sign   62
The Year of the Tiger   63
The Tiger Personality   63
The Tiger Child   67
The Five Types of Tigers   68
The Tiger and His Ascendants   71
How the Tiger Fares in Different Years   72
Compatibility Table for the Tiger   73
Famous Persons Born in the Year of the Tiger   75

CHAPTER 4: THE RABBIT   77

The Rabbit Sign   78
The Year of the Rabbit   79
The Rabbit Personality   79
The Rabbit Child   84
The Five Types of Rabbits   85
The Rabbit and His Ascendants   88
How the Rabbit Fares in Different Years   89
Compatibility Table for the Rabbit   90
Famous Persons Born in the Year of the Rabbit   92

CHAPTER 5: THE DRAGON   93

The Dragon Sign   94
The Year of the Dragon   95
The Dragon Personality   95
The Dragon Child   100
The Five Types of Dragons   101
The Dragon and His Ascendants   104

How the Dragon Fares in Different Years   106
Compatibility Table for the Dragon   107
Famous Persons Born in the Year of the Dragon   109

CHAPTER 6: THE SNAKE   111

The Snake Sign   112
The Year of the Snake   113
The Snake Personality   113
The Snake Child   118
The Five Types of Snakes   119
The Snake and His Ascendants   121
Compatibility Table for the Snake   123
How the Snake Fares in Different Years   124
Famous Persons Born in the Year of the Snake   126

CHAPTER 7: THE HORSE   127

The Horse Sign   128
The Year of the Horse   129
The Horse Personality   129
The Horse Child   134
The Five Types of Horses   135
The Horse and His Ascendants   138
How the Horse Fares in Different Years   139
Compatibility Table for the Horse   140
Famous Persons Born in the Year of the Horse   142

CHAPTER 8: THE SHEEP   143

The Sheep Sign   144
The Year of the Sheep   145
The Sheep Personality   145
The Sheep Child   150
The Five Types of Sheep   151
The Sheep and His Ascendants   153
Compatibility Table for the Sheep   155
How the Sheep Fares in Different Years   156
Famous Persons Born in the Year of the Sheep   158

CHAPTER 9: THE MONKEY — 159

The Monkey Sign — 160
The Year of the Monkey — 161
The Monkey Personality — 161
The Monkey Child — 167
The Five Types of Monkeys — 168
The Monkey and His Ascendants — 171
How the Monkey Fares in Different Years — 172
Compatibility Table for the Monkey — 173
Famous Persons Born in the Year of the Monkey — 175

CHAPTER 10: THE ROOSTER — 177

The Rooster Sign — 178
The Year of the Rooster — 179
The Rooster Personality — 180
The Rooster Child — 186
The Five Types of Roosters — 188
The Rooster and His Ascendants — 190
How the Rooster Fares in Different Years — 192
Compatibility Table for the Rooster — 193
Famous Persons Born in the Year of the Rooster — 195

CHAPTER 11: THE DOG — 197

The Dog Sign — 198
The Year of the Dog — 199
The Dog Personality — 200
The Dog Child — 204
The Five Types of Dogs — 205
The Dog and His Ascendants — 208
Compatibility Table for the Dog — 209
How the Dog Fares in Different Years — 210
Famous Persons Born in the Year of the Dog — 212

CHAPTER 12: THE BOAR: — 213

The Boar Sign — 214
The Year of the Boar — 215

The Boar Personality   215
The Boar Child   220
The Five Types of Boars   221
The Boar and His Ascendants   224
How the Boar Fares in Different Years   225
Compatibility Table for the Boar   226
Famous Persons Born in the Year of the Boar   228

CHAPTER 13: THE 144 MARRIAGE COMBINATIONS

229

CHAPTER 14: WHEN SUN SIGNS MEET MOON SIGNS: THE 144 COMBINATIONS

271

A Note about the Calligraphy

The calligraphy heading each chapter is free-form calligraphy, written with a brush, which simply gives the direct translation of each animal's name in Chinese. That is, the Rat is given the Chinese character for Rat and not the character which means the first Earth Branch, symbolizing the Rat's place in the Chinese Zodiac.

INTRODUCTION

Introduction

THE TWELVE ANIMAL SIGNS OR EARTH BRANCHES

The Chinese lunar calendar is the longest chronological record in history, dating from 2637 B.C. when the Emperor Huang Ti introduced the first cycle of this zodiac in the 61st year of his reign. A complete cycle takes 60 years and is made up of five simple cycles of 12 years each. The 77th cycle started on February 5, 1924, and will end on February 1, 1984. Twelve animals were assigned to each of the 12 years when, according to legend, the Lord Buddha summoned all the animals to come to him before he departed from Earth. Only twelve came to bid him farewell. As a reward he named a year after each one in the order that it arrived. First came the Rat, then the Ox, the Tiger, Rabbit, Dragon, Snake, Horse, Sheep, Monkey, Rooster, Dog and Boar. Thus, we have the twelve animal signs of today. The animal ruling the year in which you were born exercises a profound influence on your life. As the Chinese say, "This is the animal that hides in your heart."

During the complete 60-year cycle each of the animal signs (sometimes also referred to as the twelve Earth Branches) is combined with the five main elements: Wood, ruled by the planet Jupiter; Fire, by Mars; Earth, by Saturn; Metal or Gold, by the Planet Venus; and Water, by Mercury. These five elements are further split into magnetic poles, positive and negative, which the Chinese call the Yin and Yang, respectively.

In the lunar calendar, the day begins at 11 P.M. and the twenty-four hours are divided into twelve sections of two hours each. Each section is ruled by one of the animal signs. As in Western astrology, the sign which rules the time of birth is the ascendant and shapes the personality, too. Its influence can be very strong. For example, an aggressive Rat person may prove to have been born between 3 and 5 A.M., the hours of the Tiger; on the other hand, a quiet Rat person was probably born between 9 to 11 A.M., the hours governed by the cool influence of the Snake.

Like their Western counterparts, the twelve Earth Branches are divided into active and passive sides. The Rat, Tiger, Dragon, Horse, Monkey and Dog belong to the positive stem, while the Ox, Rabbit, Snake, Sheep, Rooster and Boar are the negative signs.

Aside from the element of its year (which changes continuously), each of the twelve Earth Branches has a fixed element and season.

The following table depicts these as well as the positive and negative stems:

Stem	Sign	North (Winter)	East (Spring)	South (Summer)	West (Autumn)
−	BOAR	Water			
+	RAT	Water			
−	OX	Water			
+	TIGER		Wood		
−	RABBIT		Wood		
+	DRAGON		Wood		
−	SNAKE			Fire	
+	HORSE			Fire	
−	SHEEP			Fire	
+	MONKEY				Metal
−	ROOSTER				Metal
+	DOG				Metal

The Earth element is not present in the chart as it is reasoned by Chinese sages that Earth is symbolically composed of the four other elements and therefore cannot be appointed to any one of the twelve lunar signs. Some Chinese fortune-tellers take one representative from each of the other elements, the Ox from Water, the Dragon from Wood, the Sheep from Fire, and the Dog from Metal and appoint Earth as their secondary element. Other soothsayers insist that the presence of all the four other elements in one's natal chart creates the missing Earth element.

The year of the Rat is said to bring bounty, that of the Ox, responsibility and hard work. People born in the Sheep's year are said to "eat paper," a popular Oriental term for wasting money. The Snake-born are reputed to be enchanting and beautiful—but also cold and ruthless.

There are some years which, because of the element with which they are combined, are dreaded by all. One such year is that of the Fire Horse. When it last came, in 1967, there were many voluntary abortions in Asia and the birth rate dropped precipitously for the year, proving that Orientals still believe that children, especially females, born in the year of the Fire Horse will bring disaster to their families and future spouses. Most people in Asia have inhibitions about having Fire Horse children the same way a Westerner would about walking under a ladder or crossing the path of a black cat—even though he might swear that it is all a bunch of nonsense. One thing is true: Fire Horses do stand out quite dramatically, but there is no reason why they couldn't gain recognition for good deeds rather than bad ones.

Although the Western calendar based on the movements of the sun is more consistent and easier to follow, the lunar calendar of the East is more accurate in registering the changes in seasons and the growth of all life in the universe. Chinese farmers used the calendar as an almanac for the most favorable days each year to sow and reap their crops. And long before modern science developed ways to forecast the weather, the Chinese relied heavily on the horoscope to predict their rains. This holds true even at the present time. We will find that if the natural element of a year is Water then there will be either an abundance of water or destructive floods, depending on whether the influence is linked to the positive or negative side of the element. In addition, the calendar was consulted for such things as the most auspicious day to visit the barber, start building a home, marry, and of course, for the numerous Chinese festivals. An authentic lunar calendar contains all the Do's and Don't's for each day of the year, down to the most favorable and unfavorable hours of each day. (Coincidentally, a woman's normal menstrual cycle is the length of one lunar month.) This complete calendar-almanac is still published yearly in Hong Kong and Taiwan; it requires the knowledge of a special code to interpret it, but no self-respecting fortune-teller will be found without it.

The lunar year is divided into twelve months of 29½ days. Every two and a half years, an intercalary month is added to adjust the calendar. The intercalary month is consecutively interposed from the

2nd to the 11th months of the lunar year. The addition of this month every third year produces the Lunar Leap Year. For easy reference, the beginning of each lunar month is the date of the New Moon marked on the Western calendar.

You may be interested to know that on the first day of Spring, as indicated by the lunar calendar, a freshly laid egg can be made to stand erect on its base. Try it: I know this has to be seen to be believed. In Hong Kong, this day is called the Lap Chun. In the Gregorian calendar, the first day of Spring always falls on the 4th or 5th day of February. In 1979, Lap Chun falls on February 4th; in 1980, February 5th, in 1981, February 4th. In the lunar calendar its position always varies. Certain lunar years may have two Lap Chuns while other lunar years may have no Lap Chuns at all (when Chinese New Year starts after February 5th and ends before the first day of Spring in the succeeding year). Chinese soothsayers consider a year without a Lap Chun as a "blind" year, as it did not "see" the first day of Spring, and such years are generally not auspicious for getting married.

In this book, you must study the animal of the year in which you were born, the lunar sign that ruled the hour of birth, the Moon sign that corresponds to your Sun sign (see page 12), the element of the year of birth and the fixed element of your animal sign. By integrating these factors, their attributes and the effects of positive and negative forces and all the possible combinations and variations, you will discover—if you don't already know—what hides in your heart, and the hearts of others. Not only will you then understand your own total self, but you should be able to predict what you can expect from your personal and professional relationships, as well as from a given year.

Take, for example, 1976, the year of the positive Fire Dragon, which visited a great many natural calamities on the world: major earthquakes in China, tidal waves in the Philippines, volcanic eruptions, etc. But aside from the destructive forces of Fire, this Dragon year was also considered very lucky as it had two Lap Chuns. It was an extremely good year to get married or start a business. We see this Dragon year, as always, proving lucky for the Rat, Dragon and Monkey people. Jimmy Carter, a Rat, rose from anonymity to the Presidency. Walter Mondale, his running mate, a Dragon, was one of the most compatible choices a Rat person could make, and consequently the Rat-Dragon team proved unbeatable. One also has to take into consideration the country of this event. America, born 1776, is ruled by the Monkey sign; it is therefore a country in which Rat and Dragon natives do well.

1977 was the year of the negative Fire Snake and since the Snake's natural or fixed element is also fire, this double Fire year saw much fighting; numerous small wars and international conflicts broke out and it brought drought to many parts of the world. Kidnapping, hijacking and terrorist attacks also had their heyday. However, the Snake is also a sign of progress and advancement. The disastrous excesses of this year were balanced by equally positive results in commercial and industrial fields. The Sadat-Begin talks initiated this year also reflected the Snake's influence and his prowess in negotiating delicate political issues.

As misunderstanding and misrepresentations abound when Snake meets Monkey, America was beset by monetary problems. Her balance of payments were not healthy and her currency weak when traded against other currencies. It was also a trying time for President Carter and all Rat natives. The euphoria and optimism of the previous Dragon year had evaporated and they were faced with many unpleasantries and harsh realities that had to be dealt with in the Snake's presence. As suspicion is often cast on Monkeys during Snake years, the U.S. made little advancement in her diplomatic endeavors and her sincere efforts toward political settlements were misinterpreted.

1978 was the year of the positive Earth Horse. The Horse's natural element is Fire and he is a Yang (+) sign. This was also a blind year, as Chinese New Year started after the first day of Spring and ended before the Lap Chun of 1979. The stable Earth element of this year curbed destructive inclinations, and 1978 was a mellow year with fewer crises and upheavals than there would be in a Metal or Fire Horse year. This year also saw the end of the drought brought on by the two previous Fire years.

The record snowfall that heralded the arrival of the Horse brought more than enough water for the parched farmlands. This Earth year was particularly good for agriculture as the Chinese lunar almanac shows the picture of a farmer with his trousers rolled up (meaning he would wade through flooded rice paddies) and leading a fat, robust Spring Ox which symbolizes a year of plenty ahead. When the farmer is depicted with wooden clogs, it indicates a year of little water; when he wears only straw slippers and leads a thin, hungry-looking Spring Ox, it signifies a lean year of drought and crop failures.

World economies had a good chance to stabilize or recover in 1978 since the Earth element fosters growth and prosperity. Overall, this was a difficult year for the Rats unless they happened to be born in a Wood year, because Earth can be controlled by Wood.

1979 is the year of the negative Earth Sheep. The Sheep's fixed element is also Fire but he is a Yin (-) sign. This year also has two Lap Chuns, one at the beginning and one at the end. An auspicious year of many blessings. A calm and progressive year although the Sheep's reign tends to bring out too much sensitivity and lack of decisiveness. Yet, the Sheep is still viewed as a lucky sign in the sense that he could bring about peace and prosperity without too much hard work on our part. Enemies will try not to provoke outright confrontations with each other and matters can be settled to a reasonable degree of satisfaction. Earth- and wood-related industries will see the biggest gains while steel and other metal-based trade will suffer setbacks. If your sign's natural element or the element ruling the year or your birth is Earth or Wood, you are in luck, too.

1980 is the Metal Monkey's year, a positive year which will certainly knock out the doldrums caused by the Sheep of '79. A strong, assertive kind of year that will strive to leave its mark on the pages of history. The Monkey will put commerce back in full swing; mergers, new inventions and successful coalitions will distinguish its year. Because the Monkey's natural element is also Metal, this double Metal year will not be without conflicts caused through overambitiousness. Many countries will display surges of high aspiration and even the man on the street will not be beyond taking on extra risks and loving it.

The metal of this year could be a bright silver coin as money is easily generated during the Monkey's time, or, on the dark side of things, it could also be a metal sword when conflicts and distrust caused mainly by greediness arise. On the world scene, economic, social and diplomatic intercourse will be very active. Russia, the Fire Snake, will experience unsettling times in the year of the Monkey and she will be drawn into many disputes caused by her lack of faith or mistrust.

1981 brings in the year of the resolute Metal Rooster. The Rooster is also a metal sign and this unyielding double metal combination will cause a lot of problems, especially monetary ones caused by too much optimism. It will be far from dull and under the Rooster's exacting rule we may have to pay a high price for our progress and success this year. This will also be another blind year. (The next blind year after this one will be in 1986, the Fire Tiger.)

Of course, the above are but very general predictions for the whole world. Each country will be affected in a different way, based on its birth sign. China, for example, was formed anew in 1949, the year of the Earth Ox. And, true to form, she has progressed largely through her own hard work and the total dedication of her people. So governed by the sign of the Ox, China will have different fortunes under any given year than say France, 1958 (the 5th Republic), a Dog; or Canada, 1867 (British North American Act), a Rabbit; or colorful Hong Kong, born 1842 (Treaty of Nanking), a Tiger.

I have written this book with the hope that it will help preserve the fast-fading folklore of Chinese horoscopes, which has endured through countless generations but is no longer popular or even encouraged in the China of today. It has been compiled from Chinese books, popular sayings, legends and mythology, interpretations of modern-day Chinese fortune-tellers as well as my own theories and observations. I also hope it will serve to bring you new insights about yourself and the people around you. It may enable you to find it easier to understand the occasional crankiness of your Dog boss, the change-able and capricious mind of a Horse client, the domineering but expansive ways of a Dragon friend or the serene but sceptical nature of a Snake-born.

You may be surprised to find that your local handyman, who is capable of fixing everything, was indeed born in the year of the dexterous Monkey, and that your slow, sure and conservative banker just happens to belong to the year of the reliable Ox. Again, you may be more patient with that annoying associate who is always the first to complain and cry wolf, when you discover she was born in the year of the Sheep. And you may laugh to learn that the fellow in your office who wears those atrocious ties will have been born in the year of the flamboyant Rooster.

It may shed light on why you dislike certain people, while with others you have an almost instant rapport. You will find the signs you will be most or least likely to be compatible with. But again, please bear in mind that there are bound to be exceptions depending on the sign that influences the time of your birth and the sign governing the month of your birth, too.

The section on how each sign fares in different years, as well as the marriage combinations and the compatibility tables, was written to serve as a general guide, with the supposition that we are dealing with pure or strongly dominant lunar signs. A Snake born during the hours of the Snake is a "pure" sign. A Dragon born during the hours of the Rabbit will most likely maintain his more "dominant" Dragon characteristics. But a Sheep born during the hours of the Tiger may display the "stronger" Tiger traits of his ascendant sign, and be compatible with a Dog, which would normally not be the case according to the compatibility tables. As a result, when consulting the marriage combinations and compatibility tables, it is important to keep in mind that other factors in the horoscope may affect the relationship between two signs. For instance, most people display a strong affinity for persons born in their ascendant sign, even if it is the sign most incompatible with their own birth sign. Thus, a Boar lady born during the hours of the Snake may get along very well with Snake persons, who would normally be anathema to a Boar.

When a person is born during the hours of the sign most incompatible with his birth sign, it is often very difficult (even for the most experienced fortune-reader) to predict what traits will be most likely to come to the fore in him. Take, for instance, a Rooster born during the hours of the Rabbit. He may turn out to be an extremely shy Rooster secretly harboring grand designs and lofty ambitions, or a loquacious one who is shrewd, diplomatic and strictly noncommittal in spite of all the noise he makes. Needless to say, such people are usually complicated in nature and volatile in temperament. A sure way to determine which sign dominates such a person is to observe the lunar signs of the people he prefers to work with or finds himself attracted to.

Here is an example of how to analyze the three most important animal signs in a person's life. We can take a subject born on:

July 4, 1946 at 12 A.M.	*Degree of Importance*
His birth sign is: Dog (year—1946)	1st
His ascendant is: Rat (time—12 A.M.)	2nd
His month of birth is governed by: Cancer or the Sheep	3rd

Looking first at the subject's birth sign, we can say that he will be most compatible with a Tiger, Horse or Rabbit. But because of his ascendant sign, the Rat, we can also deduce that this Dog will have an affinity for Rat people and may also get on well with Monkey and the otherwise unlikely Dragon natives. If his ascendant sign tends to dominate his personality, this Dog may even shun the Horse (normally an excellent partner for the Dog) because his ascendant sign, the Rat, is most incompatible with Horses.

To discover how being born in the month of the Sheep will shape the subject's personality, please read the chapter on the Sheep and consult page 284, "Cancerian Dog," of Chapter 14: "When Sun Signs Meet Moon Signs."

In the context of the Chinese lunar cycles, the charming Western custom of naming children after paternal or maternal grandparents is more meaningful and appropriate than one would realize. For if the grandparent is sixty years older than his namesake, then the lunar calendar will have come full cycle; both will have been born under the same animal sign and under the influence of the same element.

Perhaps after reading this book, you may believe enough to listen to the wise words of the Snake, look for sympathy from the gentle Sheep, go along with the clever schemes of the Monkey, have fun with the ever youthful and carefree Horse, rely on the Rabbit's unerring diplomacy or depend on the strength of the indomitable Dragon. And you may get your way by humoring the critical Rooster, reasoning with the Dog, going into battle with the optimistic Tiger or bargaining with the indefatigable Rat.

THE YEARS OF THE LUNAR SIGNS FROM 1900 TO 1995

RAT	1900	1912	1924	1936	1948	1960	1972	1984
OX	1901	1913	1925	1937	1949	1961	1973	1985
TIGER	1902	1914	1926	1938	1950	1962	1974	1986
RABBIT	1903	1915	1927	1939	1951	1963	1975	1987
DRAGON	1904	1916	1928	1940	1952	1964	1976	1988
SNAKE	1905	1917	1929	1941	1953	1965	1977	1989
HORSE	1906	1918	1930	1942	1954	1966	1978	1990
SHEEP	1907	1919	1931	1943	1955	1967	1979	1991
MONKEY	1908	1920	1932	1944	1956	1968	1980	1992
ROOSTER	1909	1921	1933	1945	1957	1969	1981	1993
DOG	1910	1922	1934	1946	1958	1970	1982	1994
BOAR	1911	1923	1935	1947	1959	1971	1983	1995

Note: Please check your exact birth date against the more detailed listing that follows, since the years overlap.

THE EXACT LUNAR YEARS FROM 1900 TO 1995

Sign		Element	
Rat	January 31, 1900 to February 18, 1901	Metal	(+)
Ox	February 19, 1901 to February 7, 1902	Metal	(−)
Tiger	February 8, 1902 to January 28, 1903	Water	(+)
Rabbit	January 29, 1903 to February 15, 1904	Water	(−)
Dragon	February 16, 1904 to February 3, 1905	Wood	(+)
Snake	February 4, 1905 to January 24, 1906	Wood	(−)
Horse	January 25, 1906 to February 12, 1907	Fire	(+)
Sheep	February 13, 1907 to February 1, 1908	Fire	(−)
Monkey	February 2, 1908 to January 21, 1909	Earth	(+)
Rooster	January 22, 1909 to February 9, 1910	Earth	(−)
Dog	February 10, 1910 to January 29, 1911	Metal	(+)
Boar	January 30, 1911 to February 17, 1912	Metal	(−)
Rat	February 18, 1912 to February 5, 1913	Water	(+)
Ox	February 6, 1913 to January 25, 1914	Water	(−)
Tiger	January 26, 1914 to February 13, 1915	Wood	(+)
Rabbit	February 14, 1915 to February 2, 1916	Wood	(−)
Dragon	February 3, 1916 to January 22, 1917	Fire	(+)
Snake	January 23, 1917 to February 10, 1918	Fire	(−)
Horse	February 11, 1918 to January 31, 1919	Earth	(+)
Sheep	February 1, 1919 to February 19, 1920	Earth	(−)
Monkey	February 20, 1920 to February 7, 1921	Metal	(+)
Rooster	February 8, 1921 to January 27, 1922	Metal	(−)
Dog	January 28, 1922 to February 15, 1923	Water	(+)
Boar	February 16, 1923 to February 4, 1924	Water	(−)
Rat	February 5, 1924 to January 24, 1925 GERRY	Wood	(+)
Ox	January 25, 1925 to February 12, 1926	Wood	(−)
Tiger	February 13, 1926 to February 1, 1927	Fire	(+)
Rabbit	February 2, 1927 to January 22, 1928	Fire	(−)
Dragon	January 23, 1928 to February 9, 1929	Earth	(+)
Snake	February 10, 1929 to January 29, 1930	Earth	(−)
Horse	January 30, 1930 to February 16, 1931	Metal	(+)
Sheep	February 17, 1931 to February 5, 1932 Bob	Metal	(−)
Monkey	February 6, 1932 to January 25, 1933	Water	(+)
Rooster	January 26, 1933 to February 13, 1934 − ME	Water	(−)
Dog	February 14, 1934 to February 3, 1935	Wood	(+)
Boar	February 4, 1935 to January 23, 1936	Wood	(−)
Rat	January 24, 1936 to February 10, 1937	Fire	(+)
Ox	February 11, 1937 to January 30, 1938	Fire	(−)
Tiger	January 31, 1938 to February 18, 1939	Earth	(+)
Rabbit	February 19, 1939 to February 7, 1940	Earth	(−)
Dragon	February 8, 1940 to January 26, 1941	Metal	(+)

Snake	January 27, 1941 to February 14, 1942	Metal	(−)
Horse	February 15, 1942 to February 4, 1943	Water	(+)
Sheep	February 5, 1943 to January 24, 1944	Water	(−)
Monkey	January 25, 1944 to February 12, 1945	Wood	(+)
Rooster	February 13, 1945 to February 1, 1946	Wood	(−)
Dog	February 2, 1946 to January 21, 1947	Fire	(+)
Boar	January 22, 1947 to February 9, 1948	Fire	(−)
Rat	February 10, 1948 to January 28, 1949	Earth	(+)
Ox	January 29, 1949 to February 16, 1950	Earth	(−)
Tiger	February 17, 1950 to February 5, 1951	Metal	(+)
Rabbit	February 6, 1951 to January 26, 1952	Metal	(−)
Dragon	January 27, 1952 to February 13, 1953	Water	(+)
Snake	February 14, 1953 to February 2, 1954	Water	(−)
Horse	February 3, 1954 to January 23, 1955	Wood	(+)
Sheep	January 24, 1955 to February 11, 1956	Wood	(−)
Monkey	February 12, 1956 to January 30, 1957	Fire	(+)
Rooster	January 31, 1957 to February 17, 1958	Fire	(−)
Dog	February 18, 1958 to February 7, 1959	Earth	(+)
Boar	February 8, 1959 to January 27, 1960	Earth	(−)
Rat	January 28, 1960 to February 14, 1961	Metal	(+)
Ox	February 15, 1961 to February 4, 1962	Metal	(−)
Tiger	February 5, 1962 to January 24, 1963	Water	(+)
Rabbit	January 25, 1963 to February 12, 1964	Water	(−)
Dragon	February 13, 1964 to February 1, 1965	Wood	(+)
Snake	February 2, 1965 to January 20, 1966	Wood	(−)
Horse	January 21, 1966 to February 8, 1967	Fire	(+)
Sheep	February 9, 1967 to January 29, 1968	Fire	(−)
Monkey	January 30, 1968 to February 16, 1969	Earth	(+)
Rooster	February 17, 1969 to February 5, 1970	Earth	(−)
Dog	February 6, 1970 to January 26, 1971	Metal	(+)
Boar	January 27, 1971 to January 15, 1972	Metal	(−)
Rat	January 16, 1972 to February 2, 1973	Water	(+)
Ox	February 3, 1973 to January 22, 1974	Water	(−)
Tiger	January 23, 1974 to February 10, 1975	Wood	(+)
Rabbit	February 11, 1975 to January 30, 1976	Wood	(−)
Dragon	January 31, 1976 to February 17, 1977	Fire	(+)
Snake	February 18, 1977 to February 6, 1978	Fire	(−)
Horse	February 7, 1978 to January 27, 1979	Earth	(+)
Sheep	January 28, 1979 to February 15, 1980	Earth	(−)
Monkey	February 16, 1980 to February 4, 1981	Metal	(+)
Rooster	February 5, 1981 to January 24, 1982	Metal	(−)
Dog	January 25, 1982 to February 12, 1983	Water	(+)
Boar	February 13, 1983 to February 1, 1984	Water	(−)

Rat	February 2, 1984 to February 19, 1985	Wood	(+)
Ox	February 20, 1985 to February 8, 1986 — *LAUREN*	Wood	(–)
Tiger	February 9, 1986 to January 28, 1987	Fire	(+)
Rabbit	January 29, 1987 to February 16, 1988	Fire	(–)
Dragon	February 17, 1988 to February 5, 1989	Earth	(+)
Snake	February 6, 1989 to January 26, 1990	Earth	(–)
Horse	January 27, 1990 to February 14, 1991	Metal	(+)
Sheep	February 15, 1991 to February 3, 1992	Metal	(–)
Monkey	February 4, 1992 to January 22, 1993	Water	(+)
Rooster	January 23, 1993 to February 9, 1994	Water	(–)
Dog	February 10, 1994 to January 30, 1995	Wood	(+)
Boar	January 31, 1995 to February 18, 1996	Wood	(–)

Year texts taken from the Chinese Ten Thousand Years (Perpetual) Lunar Calendar.

THE TWELVE SIGNS AND THEIR HOURS

11 P.M. to 1 A.M.—Hours ruled by the Rat
1 A.M. to 3 A.M.—Hours ruled by the Ox
3 A.M. to 5 A.M.—Hours ruled by the Tiger
5 A.M. to 7 A.M.—Hours ruled by the Rabbit
7 A.M. to 9 A.M.—Hours ruled by the Dragon
9 A.M. to 11 A.M.—Hours ruled by the Snake
11 A.M. to 1 P.M.—Hours ruled by the Horse
1 P.M. to 3 P.M.—Hours ruled by the Sheep
3 P.M. to 5 P.M.—Hours ruled by the Monkey
5 P.M. to 7 P.M.—Hours ruled by the Rooster
7 P.M. to 9 P.M.—Hours ruled by the Dog
9 P.M. to 11 P.M.—Hours ruled by the Boar

THE TWENTY-FOUR SEGMENTS OF THE LUNAR AGRICULTURAL ALMANAC

Have you ever wondered why Western astrological signs fall on odd days of the month instead of simply on the 1st or 30th? Looking into the lunar calendar, I found that it is divided into twenty-four sections which were originally used as a guide for agriculture. In matching the closest dates of these twenty-four sections or stems with the Western calendar, one finds that they coincide with the twelve astrological signs of the West. The twelve animal signs are also assigned a month in this calendar, so we can match East with West.

Closest Dates on Western Calendar	English Translation of Chinese Terms	Western SUN SIGN	Eastern MOON SIGN
Jan. 21 to Feb. 5 Feb. 5 to Feb. 19	Severe Cold Spring Begins	AQUARIUS (Jan. 21–Feb. 19)	TIGER
Feb. 19 to Mar. 5 Mar. 5 to Mar. 20	Rain Waters Excited Insects	PISCES (Feb. 20–Mar. 20)	RABBIT
Mar. 20 to Apr. 5 Apr. 5 to Apr. 20	Vernal Equinox+ Clear and Bright	ARIES (Mar. 21–Apr. 19)	DRAGON
Apr. 20 to May 5 May 5 to May 20	Grain Rains Come Summer Begins	TAURUS (Apr. 20–May 20)	SNAKE
May 20 to Jun. 6 Jun. 6 to Jun. 21	Grain Fills Grain in Ear	GEMINI (May 21–Jun. 21)	HORSE
Jun. 21 to Jul. 7 Jul. 7 to Jul. 22	Summer Solstice++ Moderate Heat	CANCER (Jun. 22–Jul. 21)	SHEEP
Jul. 22 to Aug. 7 Aug. 7 to Aug. 22	Great Heat Autumn Begins	LEO (Jul. 22–Aug. 21)	MONKEY
Aug. 22 to Sept. 8 Sept. 8 to Sept. 23	Limit of Heat White Dew	VIRGO (Aug. 22–Sept. 22)	ROOSTER
Sept. 23 to Oct. 8 Oct. 8 to Oct. 23	Autumn Equinox+ Cold Dew	LIBRA (Sept. 23–Oct. 22)	DOG
Oct. 23 to Nov. 7 Nov. 7 to Nov. 22	Hoarfrost Descends Winter Commences	SCORPIO (Oct. 23–Nov. 21)	BOAR
Nov. 22 to Dec. 7 Dec. 7 to Dec. 21	Little Snow Great Snow	SAGITTARIUS (Nov. 22–Dec. 21)	RAT
Dec. 21 to Jan. 6 Jan. 6 to Jan. 21	Winter Solstice++ Little Cold	CAPRICORN (Dec. 22–Jan. 20)	OX

+Equinox—When the sun crosses the equator and day and night are of equal length.
++Solstice—When the sun is farthest from the equator and appears to stand still. Summer solstice begins with the longest day and Winter solstice starts with the longest night.

THE SIGNS IN GENERAL

Since the twelve animal signs or Earth Branches are also each assigned a month in the lunar calendar, we can match a Western zodiac sign with its Eastern counterpart.

Thus, since the month of December is dominated by the Rat, we link him with the sanquine Sagittarius personality. The Ox in January has solid Capricorn as his other self, while the felicitous Tiger in February has many similar traits with Aquarius. The Rabbit and Pisces cohabitate the month of March just as the Dragon and Aries are linked in April. Taurus in May coincides with the Snake, and Gemini in June could well speak for the Horse. After that, we find Cancer and the Sheep having much more in common than just sharing the month of July. Leo and the Monkey take control of August, and Virgo couldn't be better classed than with the Rooster of September. Libra definitely strikes a balance with his friend, the Dog, and lastly, the deeply devoted signs of Scorpio and the Boar are joined in the month of November.

Like their Western Counterparts, the Moon signs are distinguished by certain identifying features.

Here you will find the effervescent, practical and self-assured qualities of the Rooster/Virgo and Horse/Gemini girls as well as the bubbling, attractive and popular charm of the well-groomed Monkey/Leo and Tiger/Aquarius ladies.

You can similarly identify the warm, earthy and appealing beauty of the Dog/Libra and the Rat/Sagittarius women or be enticed by the sophisticated and hypnotic allure of the Snake/Taurus females.

Then, no doubt, it will be easy to spot the ultrafeminine and whimsical damsels in distress: the Sheep/Cancer and the Rabbit/Pisces, with their scented handkerchiefs dabbing away tears that could melt the hardest hearts.

Next, you could come face to face with the inimitable Dragon lady herself, Aries, who will need no help at all as she is entirely in control and fully aware of her awesome powers.

Perhaps last but not least, the quiet, capable and well-mannered Ox/Capricorn or Boar/Scorpio girls will appeal to you.

For the men, how could one possibly miss the high-powered Rooster in full regalia—busy pecking away at the opposition—or the successful and dynamic Dragon with his feats of endurance and dedication. One can rest assured knowing that the Ox is duty bound and in full command of his quarters while the honest, forthright Boar, the perfect boy scout, will be helping out his neighbor or organizing social functions. The faithful and anxious Dog is waving his union card and defending home and country, while the single-minded, lusty Snake is totally immersed in making his latest female conquest or financial merger.

Behind the scenes, the aesthetic and sensitive Sheep and Rabbit gentlemen are quietly dictating the latest modes in fashion or the direction of the arts.

Not to be ignored or outdone in any way, you will perceive the combustible Tiger, straining at his leash, and the dashing and debonair Horse in tune with every beat.

The likeable but crafty Rat is busy checking and increasing his bank account while the ingenious Monkey is having great fun solving the most baffling problems and conjuring up new tricks of his own.

THE YIN AND THE YANG

Since ancient times the Chinese have ascribed the source of all movement of matter and the life force to the constant, equilibrating pull of the negative and positive sides of energy, which they call the Yin and Yang.

The Yin and Yang are embodied in the Chinese symbol for the T'ai Chi:

Yang, or Day   Yin, or Night

This circle (or egg, as others see it) is used to symbolize the origin of life. Yang signifies birth or the day, Yin death or night. Because the two portions of the T'ai Chi balance each other perfectly, the symbol is also referred to as the "Ultimate Principle of all matter."

In Oriental art, medicine and philosophy, everything is classified under these two stems. To maintain harmony and order in the universe and within the body, is to keep the Yin and Yang constantly in delicate balance. Chaos and disharmony abound when their even pull is disturbed in any way. Like opposite poles of a magnet, the Yin will attract a Yang, but will repel another Yin force.

For the purposes of Chinese horoscope reading, it should be noted that the Yin or Yang only repels the similar negative or positive stem directly opposite its polarity. If you refer to the incompatibility circle on page 28, you will see that all the conflicting signs belong to the same stem. Only if the animal signs are directly across from each other is there any repelling action. In the triangles of affinity (page 27) you can see how three positive or negative signs can be harmonious when they are 120° away from one another.

Applying the Yin and Yang principle to the five elements in the horoscope may be a more complicated matter. For instance, the positive stem of Wood is a fir tree, the negative is the flexible bamboo. The positive stem of Fire may be a forest fire, the negative could be the flame of a lamp or candle that emits beneficial light. The positive of the Earth element, a hill; the negative, a valley. The positive of Metal, a gong or weapon; the negative, a cooking pot or coin. The positive stem of Water, a wave; the negative, still water.

The "negative" here should not be taken in a pejorative sense as it does not mean something bad or undesirable in this context. Both the positive (Yang) and negative (Yin) forces have their good and bad aspects. For instance, a person born under a positive sign will find himself more effective when he proceeds in active ways. It would be "negative" (in the pejorative sense) for him to proceed in a passive way. Similarly, a person born under a negative sign is at his best when he behaves in a passive or nonaggressive manner. The first is compelled to be a doer and innovator, the second excels as a thinker and negotiator. Generally, Yang people are more spontaneous, Yin people more reflective and intuitive.

In the Chinese system of casting fortunes, the Yin and Yang will appear alternately with the same element in combination with the twelve animal signs. Thus, the Yang (+) will be paired off with the

Fire element first in, let us say, the year of the Rat (1936). Immediately following, in the year of the Ox (1937), the Yin (−) force will have its turn to be combined with the same element, Fire, to balance off the Yang Force.

We therefore find that there will be only six changes of elements in a normal twelve-year cycle, because each element must appear twice, once in its positive state and once in its negative state.

THE FIVE ELEMENTS

A fundamental part of Oriental philosophy is the interrelationships among the five basic elements. These are divided into Conducive and Controlling interrelationships, and are as follows:

CONDUCIVE

From Metal we get Water

Metal is usually represented by the Chinese character for gold, but in this context, the metal could mean a vessel or container for holding water, so we can say that metal traps water. In another sense, metal is the only element that will change into a liquid when heated.

From Water we get Wood

Water here means the rain or dew that makes plant life flourish, thus producing wood in the process.

From Wood we get Fire

Fire cannot exist by itself but is produced by burning wood. Also, fire is generated in rubbing together two pieces of wood.

From Fire we get Earth

Symbolically fire reduces everything to ashes, which becomes part of the earth again.

From Earth we get Metal

All metal has to be extracted from the earth.

CONTROLLING

The entire universe is composed of these five elements. They are interdependent and each is controlled by another. Hence we find that:

Metal is controlled by Fire

Metal can only be melted and forged with great heat.

Fire is controlled by Water

Nothing will put out a fire as fast as water.

Water is controlled by Earth

We dig canals in the earth to irrigate fields or build dikes to keep out or absorb water.

Earth is controlled by Wood

Trees and their roots hold the soil together and get their nourishment from the earth.

Wood is controlled by Metal

Even the largest tree can be felled by the metal blade of an axe.

Under this philosophy, we see that no one element can be called the strongest or weakest. Like the Yin and Yang they are forever dependent on one another and are equal. They are linked by the chain of life that brings about their very existence, and there is no power struggle. Each has its own place and function.

Even in the human body, these five elements maintain their reciprocal relationship. In Chinese medicine and acupuncture, the elements rule the five major organs of the body. Metal is linked to the lungs, Fire controls our heart, Water is associated with the kidneys, Earth is for the spleen and pancreas and Wood is identified with the Liver.

So when a Chinese doctor, herbalist or acupuncturist treats an illness, he has to keep these relationships in mind. For example, when the Earth (pancreas) is affected, the Metal (lungs) is weakened, too. If the Water (kidney) malfunctions, then it cannot produce its counterpart, Wood. And therefore the Wood organ, the liver, will begin to deteriorate.

METAL ELEMENT

People born in the years controlled by the Metal element will be as rigid and resolute in expression as their particular signs will permit. They are guided by strong feelings and will pursue their objectives with intensity and little hesitation. Sustained by their ambitions, they are capable of prolonged effort to get what they want. They are very success-oriented and unwavering in their determination.

These persons are not easily swayed or influenced to change course once they have decided on it, even by hardships, drawbacks and initial failures. Whatever constancy and perseverance their native lunar signs contain will be greatly enhanced by the Metal element. But they do have trouble letting go when situations are no longer feasible and can be unreasonably stubborn and unadaptable in their fixity of mind.

They prefer to sort out and solve their problems alone and will not appreciate interference or unsolicited assistance. They map out their own destinies, clear their own paths and visualize their own goals without outside help.

Although they may look inflexible and coldly self-reliant, persons ruled by Metal can conduct electricity; their strong impulses and generative powers will be felt by all they come in contact with, thereby bringing about the changes and transformations they desire.

They have strong monetary and accumulative instincts and will use these traits to support their independent spirits and their strong tastes for luxury, opulence and power.

To be totally effective, however, they must learn to compromise and not to be overly insistent on always having their own way. Often, they are unbending and opinionated and will break off a good relationship because others do not heed their wishes or conform readily to their will.

WATER ELEMENT

Persons born in a year dominated by the Water element have a better than average ability to communicate and to advance their ideas by influencing the thoughts of others. Other people's minds are their vessels and help carry their creative ideas into positive action. They are basically ruled by sympathetic vibrations and convey their feelings and emotions to the best degree that their native animal sign will permit.

They have a knack for noticing things that will become important and can accurately gauge future potentials. They set things into the orbit they desire by prodding and utilizing the talents and resources of others. However, they know how to be unobtrusive in their persistence and will never make others feel they are being imposed upon. In this manner, like their element, Water, they will be able to wear away the strongest rocks of opposition by their silent but constant efforts. Because these people would rather infiltrate than dominate, they will know how, when and whom to approach on a given subject. They have the talent for making people desire what they themselves desire, thus achieving their goals in a sure but indirect way. They like to propel instead of compel others into motion.

Because of their basic awareness and flexibility, they are fluid like their element. In their negative states, such people tend to be too conciliatory and will take the easiest route open to them. At their worst, they will be inconstant and passive and lean too much on others for support. Thus, they sabotage their basic abilities for accomplishing goals. To succeed, they must be more assertive and use their immense power of persuasion to turn their plans into reality. Others would be wise to be guided by their intuitions.

WOOD ELEMENT

People born under the auspices of the Wood element value their ethics; they have high morals and a good deal of self-confidence. They know the intrinsic value of things and their interests are wide and varied. Their expansive and cooperative natures will allow them to do things on a grand scale. They possess executive personalities because they can apportion and separate matters into the right categories and work orders. Their progressiveness and generosity enable them to take on large projects, long-term or sizable developments or expensive scientific studies—definitely not one-man ventures.

They have the ability to convince others to merge and join forces with them. They branch out rapidly and diversify into many fields whenever possible, as they advocate constant growth and renewal. They know how to share whatever rewards they reap by collective efforts with all those who justly deserve a piece of the corporate pie. Their innate goodwill and compassionate understanding of how others think and operate will raise them to very fortunate positions. They will find support and finances whenever and wherever they have need of them, for people will have faith in their ability to turn information and ideas into profit.

Their chief shortcoming is that they tend to bite off more than they can chew and push things to a breaking point. They may not be able to finish what they start if they spread their resources too thin. Their plans could then turn sour or they may drift from one project to another without satisfactory results.

FIRE ELEMENT

Persons born in a year ruled by the Fire element will display above-average qualities of leadership; they are decisive and sure of themselves. They have the maximum capacity allowed by their particular sign to motivate people and bring ideas into fruition because they will be more aggressive and positive than other natives of their particular sign. Loving adventure and innovation, they will tend to take on bright new ideas readily and try to dominate others with their creativeness and originality. They do not fear risks and like to keep on the move and to explore new horizons.

They are the doers—given to dynamic action and speech. However, they must keep a close rein on their emotions as their ambition and forcefulness may amplify their selfishness and make them inconsiderate and impatient when their wishes are not gratified. The more a Fire person tries to achieve his ends by force or violence, the more he will encounter opposition and danger.

They have all the prerequisites to produce winners of the highest caliber provided they are sympathetic to the views of others and hear everyone out before taking action. They should cultivate the qualities of a good listener and curb their impulsive tendencies. Many of these people also tend to be too outspoken for their own good.

Like their element, Fire, they constantly draw others to their warmth and brilliance and they can greatly benefit those who seek their company. But fire persons can also turn destructive and cause a good deal of damage when they fail to control and direct their energies properly.

EARTH ELEMENT

People born under signs influenced by the Earth element are more concerned with functional and practical aspirations. They have excellent deductive powers and like solid and reliable pursuits on which to expend their energy. With their foresight and capacity for organization, they are effective planners and administrators. They will put whatever resources they find to optimum use and are wise and prudent in financial affairs as well as holding on to their own money. They are intelligent and most objective in directing others toward realizing well-plotted goals.

They are generally enterprising in a serious and methodical manner and can organize and run businesses that require a firm hand. They make excellent managers and are good at reinforcing or building a solid foundation for any industry, trade or government. These are people who will substantiate their findings and have sound reasons for everything they do. While they may move slowly, they proceed toward good and lasting results.

People belonging to this particular element like to keep things in their proper perspective and are conservative by nature. They rarely exaggerate their findings, calculations and expectations. They will give you their undiluted views and present the true picture of a situation without any retouching, modifications or frills. Their most common faults will be their lack of imagination, overprotectiveness of their own interests and unadventurous outlook on life.

However, they can be expected to shoulder their responsibilities admirably and can discipline themselves.

THE ELEMENTS AND YOU

The element of your lunar sign, the year of your birth, as well as the time, month and country of birth, will exercise their influence on your life.

Based on the elements, if you want to know how a particular year will suit you, we could take for example the year 1980 (Metal Monkey) and make a study of how the element of this year fares with your native elements. Let's say you are a Fire Rooster (1957). On page 192 of "How the Rooster Fares in Different Years," you will note that as a Rooster, you are predicted to fare badly in a Monkey's year. However, since the element of this particular year is Metal, you can gauge that you will be able to control or conquer your problems in 1980 and emerge much better than forecasted. This is because your birth element of Fire is able to conquer this year's element. If, however, this year happens to be that of a Water Monkey, then you can deduce that you may fare even worse than predicted, as neither the Monkey sign nor the Water element are conducive to the Fire Rooster.

In our birth chart or life's formula as I shall call it, there is a series of five elements, and their effect on our lives will have the following descending order of importance:

1. Element of the year of birth
2. Element of your animal sign
3. Element of the hour of birth
4. Element of the month of birth
5. Element of the country of birth

To give a concrete example, we shall take a person born in America, on March 30, 1949, between 9 and 11 A.M.

Element of this person's year of birth (1949)	= Earth
Fixed element of his animal sign (Ox)	= Water
Fixed element of his hour of birth (Snake)	= Fire
Fixed element of the month of birth (Aries, which corresponds to the Dragon)	= Wood
Fixed element of the country of birth (Monkey)	= Metal

Looking at this person's life formula, we see him having all the five elements. Most of us, however, may end up lacking one or more of the elements, while having a concentration of one or two others. Of course, the idea is that the more elements one possesses in his birth chart, the less susceptible he is to harm or opposition from the other elements. As you have seen from the explanation on page 17, each of the five elements has power over one other element, while its influence can be cancelled out by the element that it cannot conquer.

The presence of elements can be used to predetermine our areas of work, helping us in choosing the right careers and goods to deal in.

If the elements dominating your life fall mainly into the Metal category, you will then be most successful when dealing with Wood and its by-products, as Metal conquers Wood. The lumber business, paper products, furniture, architecture, etc., should be excellent fields for you. Water and its related industries will likewise be beneficial since Metal is conducive to Water. Next, Metal industries such as mining, steel, automobile and aircraft manufacture, jewelry, canned food, etc., should also provide little conflict. To work in any other field will not exactly be like courting disaster, but if you should persist in working with Fire when your elements are Metal-based, then you may not find the same degree of success or ease of achievement. Earth-related fields will also cause you conflict.

Now, if we take a look at someone with a majority of Fire elements in his life's formula, it can be assumed that he will be happy in fields related to Wood and Metal industries. Fire-related industries should also provide no hindrance, but a person with a lot of Fire in his chart will have no one to blame if he insists on a Water-based profession and literally gets soaked in the process. The Earth element will also limit him to a certain degree and he may find progress slow or difficult in its related fields.

If Water features strongly on your overall chart, you will be able to deal successfully with Fire and Wood merchandise, as Water can control Fire and produce Wood. Likewise, this person will also be at home in his own Water-related professions, but may be unable to find easy success in Earth-related fields as Earth controls Water. Metal will also hinder him to certain degrees. Professions which involve person-to-person contact, public relations, psychology, public speaking and the like should be associated with Water as the human body is made up mainly of water.

If Earth should happen to be the strong element in your life, then Water and Metal-related professions will provide you with the easiest route to financial gain, job satisfaction and success. Fire could be a good second choice; you should avoid dealing in Wood as Earth is controlled by Wood.

Finally, if all your elements lean heavily toward Wood, then you should deal in Earth and Water-related industries, which dominate agriculture, foodstuffs (except dried), dairy products and real estate. I know of a Wood Ox who tried his hand at everything and then made his fortune dealing in real estate financing. Should your dominant element be Wood, it goes without saying that all Wood-related fields will not impede your progress while Fire could harm you to some extent and Metal will definitely hurt your element.

The following table should provide the general guidelines as to which fields each element will be best in:

Element	Main Conflict	Some Conflict	No Conflict	Successful
Metal	Fire	Earth	Metal	Water, Wood
Fire	Water	Earth	Fire	Wood, Metal
Water	Earth	Metal	Water	Fire, Wood
Earth	Wood	Fire	Earth	Water, Metal
Wood	Metal	Fire	Wood	Earth, Water

By looking at the above, you can appreciate how the five vital elements influence our life's composition and can now understand the Chinese system of name choosing that lends a helping hand in reshaping destiny.

The Chinese remedy for element deficiencies is simply to add the missing or weak elements into the writing of a child's given names. Thus, they believe that a person's fate can be altered or bad luck neutralized by the placing of strong emphasis on certain characters in his name.

To this day, elders of any good Chinese family must spend countless hours deliberating on the name for a new family member. They visit fortune-tellers and numerology experts, consult tables and books and take many other facts into consideration to ensure that they come up with not only the best possible name but the best way in which to write it. If, for example, Fire is missing from a child's life composition, then the Chinese character for Fire must be carefully incorporated into his name, with a balance of rhythm, sound, number of strokes and meaning, in an all-out effort to supply him with what he needs to bring him a step closer to perfection—or balance.

For those who do not understand the writing of Chinese characters, it must be explained that words and names are characters made up of other characters or radicals (a symbol that is something of an abbreviation of characters). So one Chinese character, such as the name of a person or place, will embody several other characters but still retain its own distinct meaning and identity.

Of course, it will not be very practical for a Westerner to change his name, much less incorporate such words as Fire or Metal into the writing of it. He must therefore find other ways to correct his element deficiencies.

To counteract the lack of Metal, he could simply wear gold or silver jewelry. Wood can be replaced by carrying a wooden charm or beads, or by having a lot of plant life in his home or office. Likewise, the Earth element can be provided by the same method or strengthened by wearing gemstones derived from hardened Earth or rock. If a person needs the Water element to balance off the others, he could choose a residence near a lake or by the coast. Failing this, he could also keep an aquarium or other small bodies of water in his home or office. Missing Fire can be represented by the use of lights, candles or other forms of electricity, or by carrying a small mirror on one's person as mirrors reflect sunlight and can produce Fire. Precious stones with red or orange colors are also believed to impart warmth or fire.

Last but not least, people who are lacking a certain element should always try to pick associates or partners strong in that missing element. Such relationships have a higher degree of success.

COMPATIBILITY AMONG THE SIGNS

Each of the twelve lunar signs in the Chinese cycle is appointed a compass point. Signs that form a triangle as shown in the affinity illustration make the best and most enduring unions.

The first triangle consists of the positive doers—the Rat, Dragon and Monkey. They are the performance and progress-oriented signs, adept at handling matters with initiative and innovation. Self-starters, they will initiate action, clear their paths of uncertainty and hesitation and forge fearlessly ahead. Restless and short-tempered when hindered or unoccupied, they are ruled by dynamic energy and ambition. They are the melting pot for ideas. They team up beautifully in any order as they possess a common modus operandi and can appreciate each other's ways of thinking.

The second triangle is made up of the most purposeful and steadfast signs. The Ox, Snake and Rooster are the dutiful and dedicated fighters who strive to achieve great heights and conquer by their constancy and unfailing determination. These three are fixed in their views and given to thought and systematic planning. They are the most intellectual signs of the cycle. They depend on their own assessment of facts and figures and give little credence to hearsay evidence. They are most likely to comply with the dictates of their heads rather than their hearts. Slow and sure in their movements, they like to act indepen-

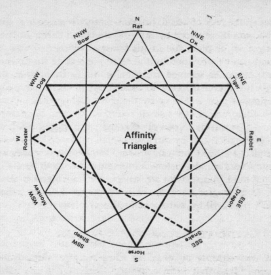

dently. They will invariably seek each other out and can intermarry and intermingle most successfully.

The third triangle is formed by the Tiger, the Horse and the Dog. These signs seek to serve humanity, promote universal understanding and heighten communications. They are made for personal contact and will develop strong bonds with their fellow human beings. They relate well to society as they are basically honest and open and motivated by idealism. Unorthodox at times but always honorable in intent, this trio act more on impulse and heed their inner conscience. They provide their own counsel and inspire others to action by their high-spirited and aggressive personalities. Extroverted, energetic and defiant against adversity and injustice, they will get along fabulously together.

The fourth and last triangle is made up of the emotionally guided signs of the Rabbit, the Sheep and the Boar. These three signs are mainly concerned with their senses and what they can appreciate with them. They are expressive, intuitive and eloquent in aesthetic and artistic ways. They excel in the finer arts, are more diplomatic and compassionate and have generally calmer natures than other lunar signs. Dependent on others for stimulation and leadership, they are flexible because they are sympathetically tuned in to the vibrations of their environment. These three signs are drawn toward beauty and the higher aspects of love. They will extol the virtues of peaceful coexistence with their fellowmen. No doubt, these three animals will provide each other with excellent company and share the same basic philosophies.

INCOMPATIBILITY AMONG THE SIGNS

Signs directly opposite each other, as illustrated in the wheel below, are in direct conflict and will make the most incompatible matches.

Thus, we find that the Rat will encounter his biggest clashes with someone born in the year of the Horse, as well as the other way around. The Ox will be pitted against his chief rival, the Sheep, and vice versa. The Tiger's main adversary, right across from him, will be the Monkey; and the Rabbit will never see eye to eye with the Rooster, who on the other hand will be equally exasperated by the Rabbit's reticence. The Dragon and the Dog will have great difficulty getting

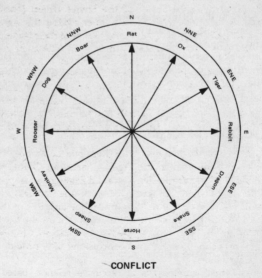

CONFLICT

along peacefully and the Snake and the Boar will not tolerate each other and will opt to go their separate paths.

Signs that do not appear directly opposite each other and are not found together within the Triangle of Affinity will be compatible in varying degrees.

CONCLUSION

The Moon, being the closest heavenly body to Earth, has shown its many visible powers to mankind since the dawn of civilization. Its magnetic pull has ruled the rising and ebbing ocean tides as well as all other bodies of water. The Chinese culture has built itself firmly around the lunar influence, believing it to affect humans so immensely because our bodies consist of three-quarters liquid. Likewise, plants and animals are subject to its all-encompassing force.

Would it be too farfetched, therefore, to speculate that even nations will be beneficially or adversely affected, depending on whether they were born under a good or a bad moon? Will the year in which a country is formed have a great bearing on its place in history?

Will the furtive Fire Snake of the Soviet Union (born with the Bolshevik Revolution of 1917) be forever eyeing the American Fire Monkey with distrust—and vice versa? What of their leaders? Will Fire Horse Brezhnev and Wood Rat Carter get on with each other or will they have difficulties in communications? Is it a coincidence that peaceful and fortunate Canada (born under the sign of the Rabbit) has Pierre Trudeau, a Sheep, for her Prime Minister? What about Israel, born 1948, the Earth Rat? Can she always count on the help and support of her friend, the American Fire Monkey? Israel has so far had two Dog leaders to guard her shaky frontiers, Golda Meir and Itzhak Rabin.

Was it by chance that the Fifth Republic of France, 1958 (Dog), should choose the charismatic Tiger, Charles de Gaulle, to head its government? Its present leader, Giscard d'Estaing also happens to be a Tiger. Is Japan largely progressive, work-oriented and chauvinistic because it was born anew in 1945, under the auspices of the Rooster? What of Great Britain's fortune in the reign of a monarch who ascended the throne in 1952, year of the Water Dragon? Chinese fortune-telling leaves us to draw our own conclusions, after providing us with the necessary tools.

It is said that astrology is an accurate science, based on fixed formulas and mathematical calculations. Likewise, lunar horoscopes are equally exacting and scientifically evolved.

Yet I hasten to add that in the Orient, it is also considered an art form: the art of recognizing relevant facts in whatever disguises they may appear or be expressed in. The Chinese sages of old and the fortune-tellers of today liken themselves to medical diagnosticians of the present, probing, searching and forever interpreting telltale signs of what the future may hold.

The ancient Chinese method of chance reading is never dogmatic or fatalistic. We are never made to feel hemmed in by our weaknesses nor inhibited by our deficiencies. Rather, we are encouraged to exploit our resources in varied and imaginative ways.

Having trouble dealing with the Dragon? Get a Monkey or Rat to be your interpreter. Unable to understand the mystical Snake and his mysterious moves? Ask the outgoing Rooster for an appropriate translation. Impatient with the retiring ways of the Rabbit? Send a good-hearted Sheep as your ambassador of goodwill. Vexed by the fiery temper of the Tiger? Ally yourself to a Horse or a Dog for good measure.

Thus, Chinese horoscopes, instead of restricting us, teach us how to plot new courses if our present methods of approach do not meet with success, and how to circumvent the circumstances of birth and other barriers and reach our goals by taking new routes. As they instruct us in self-analysis and in knowing what to expect from situations, we will be able at worst to face, at best to solve, the problems we are most fated to encounter.

Chapter 1
The Rat

I am the self-proclaimed acquisitor.
I am a link yet I function as
    a complete unit.
I aim at encompassing heights
And strike my target
Sure and steady.
Life is one joyous journey for me.
Each search must end with a new quest.
I am progress, exploration and insight.
I am the womb of activity.

I AM THE RAT.

THE RAT SIGN

Chinese name for the Rat: SHU
Ranking order: First
Hours ruled by the Rat: 11 P.M. to 1 A.M.
Direction of its sign: Directly North
Season and principle month: Winter—December
Corresponds to the Western sign: Sagittarius
Fixed element: Water
Stem: Positive

THE LUNAR YEARS OF THE RAT IN THE WESTERN CALENDAR

Starting Dates	Ending Dates	Element
January 31, 1900	February 18, 1901	Metal
February 18, 1912	February 5, 1913	Water
February 5, 1924	January 24, 1925	Wood
January 24, 1936	February 10, 1937	Fire
February 10, 1948	January 28, 1949	Earth
January 28, 1960	February 14, 1961	Metal
February 15, 1972	February 2, 1973	Water
February 2, 1984	February 19, 1985	Wood

If you were born on the day before the start of the lunar year of the Rat, e.g., January 30, 1900, you belong to the animal sign before the Rat—which is the Boar.

If you were born on the day after the lunar year of the Rat, e.g., February 19, 1901, then you belong to the sign following that of the Rat—the Ox.

THE YEAR OF THE RAT

The Rat year is a year of plenty, bringing opportunity and good prospects. It will be marked by speculation and fluctuations in the prices of commodities and the stock market; the world economy in general will boom. Business will be on the upswing, fortunes can be made and it will be an easy time to accumulate wealth. However, this is also the time to make long-term investment plans as the bonanza the year of the Rat brings will serve to see us through the bleak years that may follow. All ventures begun at this time will be successful if one prepares well. But do not take chances or unnecessary risks: the year of the Rat is still ruled by the cold of winter and the darkness of night. Those who speculate indiscriminately and overextend themselves will come to a sad reckoning.

On the whole, this will be a happier year than most: free from explosive events and wars and with far less catastrophes than, say, the years of the Tiger or the Dragon.

Nonetheless, it will be spicy. It promises a lot of bickering, bargaining and petty arguments that will do little harm. A congenial time that will find most of us socializing and enjoying ourselves.

THE RAT PERSONALITY

The charm of the Rat personality is as universally known and loved as the Walt Disney character, Mickey Mouse. He could be forthright and honest but in such a disarming manner that you find yourself at a disadvantage.

Remarkably easy to get along with, hard working and thrifty, he will be generous only to those he is inordinately fond of, so if you get an expensive gift from him, you should certainly rate yourself high in his esteem. However, in spite of his penny-pinching ways, he will never be found wanting for admirers as he emits such fantastic appeal.

On the surface, a Rat person may appear reserved, but this is not so. He is never as quiet as he may look. Actually, he is easily agitated but is able to maintain his self-control, which explains why he is so popular and has a multitude of friends.

The Rat person is usually a bright, happy and sociable personality. Occasionally, you may come across a supercritical or grouchy, fault-finding one. But on the whole, he enjoys parties and other large gatherings. He will endeavor to join exclusive clubs and as a rule can always be found in a close circle of friends or fellow conspirators. He likes getting involved and is very outgoing.

The Rat really cherishes his friends, associates and family relations; at times he gets entangled with other people's lives and affairs because he can't easily rid himself of strong emotional attachments once he has made them. Still, one can never be exactly sure of how and where he stands. His capacity to love can only be overruled by his shrewdness and love of money.

A Rat boss may demonstrate great concern about whether his employees are getting enough exercise or eating a balanced diet. In his heart, he sincerely cares about their welfare; he will visit them when they are sick and make their problems his problems, yet when it comes to giving them that well-deserved raise in salary, he will hedge and be a little stingy. A lot of arm twisting and collective bargaining is needed when it comes to parting a Rat from his money.

The Rat lady may continually amaze you by being a model of frugality. She is forever distributing old clothes, recycling toys, buying or selling secondhand items, stretching meals, leftovers and the family budget until they could positively scream. However, she may not care to apply these same rigid standards when dealing with her precious offspring. If her children know how to get around her, she will find it hard to deny them anything. Rat people are rarely tightwads where their families are concerned.

At times, the Rat is decidely clannish. Maybe there is some truth about safety in numbers. He never worries about having another mouth to feed and may allow his relatives, in-laws, friends, etc., to stick around his home and live off him. Why? Because the crafty Rat will always be able to find something for them to do to earn their keep. Laggards, professional bums and freeloaders will all get put to work swiftly in his household. Charity has its limits. Trust the efficient Rat.

The Rat native keeps his secrets well but he can be an expert at weeding other people's gardens where confidences are concerned. He has few qualms about using vital information gathered or capitalizing on the mistakes of others. After all, you certainly don't expect him to ignore the knock of opportunity, especially when he has had his ear glued to the door so much of the time.

As much as he likes to keep his feelings to himself, one can always tell when he is upset as he tends to become edgy, curt and impertinent. Some are just absolute nags. Since the Rat person is also active and most industrious, he is irritated most by idleness and waste.

On his negative side, the Rat person loves to gossip, criticize, compare, carp and bargain—usually over unimportant issues. He buys things he does not really need and is always taken in by bargains. Maybe it is his accumulative urge. Mementos, souvenirs and hoards of sentimental junk will be found tucked away in his room and in his heart. He also has the tendency to be the neighborhood's busybody, though more often than not, his intentions are good.

The Rat is reputed to make an excellent writer and this is not surprising at all. He makes it a point to know practically everything about everyone in town. He keeps tabs, has an uncanny eye for detail, a good memory and is incredibly inquisitive.

The native of this year will be successful in whatever he chooses to do because like his sign, the Rat, he will adapt himself to the situation at hand. He has the ability to cope with difficulties and is at his best during a crisis. Levelheaded and alert, he possesses keen intuition, foresight and business acumen. Adversity merely serves to sharpen his wits and he is always busy cooking up some scheme.

There is no need to worry about the Rat's safety as he always checks out the back door before entering any transaction. This is in case he has to make a quick or untimely exit from the scene. Self-preservation is high on his list of priorities and he usually takes the path with the least repercussions. If you want to get out of trouble fast, follow the Rat's course. He has a built-in alarm and defense mechanism that rarely fails.

His stumbling block is overambition. He tries to do too much too soon and as a result scatters his energies. If he can avoid doing this and perseveres in finishing what he's started, a person of this sign will end up wealthy, which is just as well, as the Rat loves money!

Although the Rat is equipped with an inborn ability to sense danger and therefore should know when to stop, he often has great difficulty in relying on his own sound judgment because he simply cannot pass up bargains and so-called "good deals." Alas, he ends up falling into the same old trap. He will have no problems in life if only he can conquer his greed and quit while he is ahead. In his lifetime, the covetous Rat has to suffer at least one large financial blow before he learns that avarice does not pay off. However, it is most unlikely to find a poor Rat native, and if you do, well, with his resourcefulness, you can bet he will not remain poor for long. It will be totally out of character if he hasn't got a nest egg hidden away somewhere.

Being the true sentimentalist of the Chinese cycle, the Rat is not only deeply attached to his children but to his elders as well. Parents with children born in this year can be sure that they will be well regarded and cared for by them. Unlike the Dragon child, who may demand perfection of his parents, the Rat youngster will have infinite trust in his parents, cater to their needs and overlook their shortcomings.

Aside from doting on their children and husbands, the Rat mother revels in the fact that she is a superb homemaker. She will follow her husband's career development like his campaign manager, drive the children to piano, ballet and violin lessons and take on so much social activity that your head would spin. A husband belonging to this sign, on the other hand, can be found helping out with household chores and will like to spend his holidays and weekends with the family.

The time of birth plays an important role in the Rat's way of life. Needless to say, one born in the evening will have a more hectic and strenuous life (night Rats have to scurry around constantly in search for food) than his brother born during the quiet of the day.

The Rat person will be attracted to the people of the Ox sign, whom he finds strong, reliable and appreciative of the devotion he has to offer. Equally compatible with the Rat will be the mighty people of the Dragon year. He will also find the Snake attractive and intelligent, and may make a suitable alliance with him. He is captivated by power and brilliance, so the Rat will always fall for the irresistible Monkey. He agrees with the clever Monkey's way of doing things and the Monkey, on the other hand, will be overjoyed to find the Rat on his own cunning wavelength. Tiger, Dog, Boar or another Rat person will have no trouble teaming up with a Rat.

He will come into many conflicts with persons born in the Horse sign. The Horse is just too independent and changeable for the clannish Rat. It would also be unwise for him to marry the Rooster. The Rooster, being the intrepid dreamer, will exasperate the practical Rat no end. A marriage with the Sheep is also questionable; the indulgent Sheep will probably squander the Rat's hard-earned savings.

THE RAT CHILD

A child born in the year of the Rat will be sweet and loving. He may be shy, but inwardly he is fiercely competitive. Often, he resorts to crying to get more attention and usually clings to one or two people with whom he identifies. Although he has a charming disposition, he is possessive of parents and friends and jealous of attention given to others.

He will talk early. He likes to eat (mention of his favorite foods always makes him light up) and he takes an early interest in cooking and other household chores. Being affectionate and demonstrative, he will not like being left alone. He will enjoy group play, can concentrate on detailed work and make friends easily. You can depend on him to keep things tidy or at least know where they are.

The Rat child will start to show his calculating nature very early in life. He will insist that he get the bigger half of the apple, exactly the same number of cookies as his older brother (preferably more, but under no circumstances less). It will be hard to cheat him on anything. He learns fast and never misses a trick. He takes regular stock of his possessions—so don't try to give away any of his old toys thinking he won't miss it. Then again, if you consult him, be prepared for a struggle as the selfish little Rat won't part with anything easily.

With younger children, the Rat child will tend to be motherly; at his worst, he will boss them around mercilessly. Given the proper encouragement, he will be ambitious in school. He will be most eager to participate in anything that stimulates his sharp mental powers.

The vivacious Rat will be an avid reader. He will learn the importance of the written word early and be able to express himself well. Many of the world's greatest writers and historians were born in the year of the Rat.

THE FIVE TYPES OF RATS

METAL RAT—1840, 1900, 1960

This type of Rat is most likely to be idealistic in thought, vivid in speech and actions and intensely emotional. He may cover up his feelings by presenting himself as a happy and charming personality. In reality, he is easily moved to jealousy, anger, selfishness and possessiveness.

His outlook will be based on what his senses can appreciate. He loves money but will not hoard it and won't mind spending if he can get good value and quality. He knows how to invest wisely. He will not be as romantic as the Rats of the other elements but could be sensual and moralistic at the same time.

He likes to impress and his home will be as splendidly decorated as he can afford. He loves drama and pageantry and has classic tastes. He will probably be athletically inclined. If he curbs his domineering tendencies, he will succeed in making himself known and liked by all the right people. Basically, he is a Rat who will advance himself by getting into influential circles.

WATER RAT—1852, 1912, 1972

This type of Rat is more concerned with mental exercise, the intricacies of the thinking process. His insight is excellent and he relates well to people of all levels. He will be respected and able to promote his talents because of his accommodating and understanding nature. He is traditional and conservative in his behavior, preferring to swim with the tide rather than fight it. Still, he is calculating and shrewd. A person born under this combination will manifest all the qualities needed to wield influence in areas he deems important. He is aware of other people's likes and dislikes and knows how to please those in a position to help him. However, he may not be too discriminating and tends to speak to anyone who cares to listen. This might get him into trouble.

Drawn to the acquisition of knowledge and the written word, and being adept at putting down his thoughts on paper, this Rat will work to further his own education and will never want to stop learning.

WOOD RAT—1864, 1924, 1984

A progressive, success-oriented and very amicable type of Rat, he will try to explore everything and will find good use for almost anything he comes across. He has a very good comprehension of how the System works, and he can make it work for himself. He is farsighted and always concerned about finding out the whys and the wherefores. Although he is egotistic, he makes himself agreeable and is quite thoughtful of others because he seeks their admiration and approval.

He has his principles and knows what he wants. He is strict with priorities, but he can be flexible in order to achieve his aims. He loves security and is always worried about his future, which is one reason why he works so hard.

Outwardly, he exudes self-confidence and know-how and is probably very professional about what he does and a good talker. He can promote ideas and projects capably and will have little difficulties in drumming up support for his ventures.

FIRE RAT—1876, 1936, 1996

This is a chivalrous and dynamic Rat who loves getting involved in all sorts of activities and never tires of embarking on new campaigns for justice and a better deal. He loves travel and fashionable clothes and is open and aggressive by nature. This could also be a more generous type of Rat.

Although he is energetic and idealistic, he lacks a sense of diplomacy and may be too blunt at times to win the support he requires. A not too well-disciplined fellow, he will follow the dictates of his heart more often than his head. As much as he is devoted to his home and family, he may still take off whenever he feels too hemmed in and head for the open country.

He is independent and very, very competitive. But since he will not be content to maintain a simple middle-of-the-road existence, his fortunes may change often and sometimes quite drastically if he is too impatient.

EARTH RAT—1888, 1948, 2008

This type of rat will mature early; for him happiness and contentment is found in order, discipline and security. He will strive to develop his positive traits and be recognized for his talents. He is very realistic and not at all given to flashy dreams and expectations.

He likes to maintain good relations with everyone and prefers to work in one place or job for a long time where he will have good and loyal friends. He can zero in on one subject at a time and is thorough in his work. On the darker side, he can also be too achievement conscious, self-righteous and intolerant with others, especially if he is in too much of a rush to get things done exactly to his specifications.

He cares a great deal for his reputation and public image, but is warm and protective toward those he loves. He has high material standards and is always comparing his degree of success with his contemporaries. This type could become overpractical and stingy with money.

He never gambles and rarely takes chances. As a result, this Rat's fortunes will increase slowly but surely. He sticks to proven rules and modes of operation and usually expects those who work with him to do the same.

THE RAT AND HIS ASCENDANTS

Born During the Hours of the Rat – 11 P.M. to 1 A.M.

Supercharming but also a bit conceited. Wonderful homebody and a good writer.

Born During the Hours of the Ox – 1 A.M. to 3 A.M.

Slow plodding Rat with a serious outlook. Still dominated by Rat's appealing ways but his gambler instincts are curtailed by the Ox's caution.

Born During the Hours of the Tiger – 3 A.M. to 5 A.M.

Aggressive and bossy, an overachiever. All will be well if he can save his money—which the Tiger in him will resent.

Born During the Hours of the Rabbit – 5 A.M. to 7 A.M.

May be docile and soft-spoken but his calculating ways will be increased. The charm of the Rat coupled with the Rabbit's astuteness will be hard to defeat.

Born During the Hours of the Dragon – 7 A.M. to 9 A.M.

Rat with expansive ways and a very large heart, sometimes too large for his purse. He will give you a loan and regret it afterward. The Dragon's strong will and the Rat's money-making talents will make him very successful in business.

Born During the Hours of the Snake – 9 A.M. to 11 A.M.

Will have hoards of admirers. He will worm his way into your pocket as well as your heart. The Snake in him makes him wary of hidden dangers. He is a bit sly.

Born During the Hours of the Horse – 11 A.M. to 1 P.M.

Dashing but daring Rat who will take many risks in life. The fickle-minded ways of the Horse may also make his love life turbulent. He will either be riding high on a wave of success or on the brink of bankruptcy.

Born During the Hours of the Sheep — 1 P.M. to 3 P.M.

Too sentimental. However, you may find his money-grubbing ways greatly tempered by good taste and refinement. Since both signs here are opportunistic, he will be adept at currying favors from those in power.

Born During the Hours of the Monkey — 3 P.M. to 5 P.M.

Very enterprising combination. He knows every trick in the book and won't hesitate to use it. With the Monkey's influence, he is less sentimental and will also have a fantastic sense of humor.

Born During the Hours of the Rooster — 5 P.M. to 7 P.M.

Extra intelligent and capable. But, oh so smug! The Rat in him is busy saving money while the Rooster side comes up with grand designs on how to spend it. He could redeem himself by applying all his administrative qualities to running a business with someone else's money.

Born During the Hours of the Dog — 7 P.M. to 9 P.M.

The Dog in him tries to be fair-minded and unprejudiced, while the Rat's basic craving for wealth is gnawing away at the Dog's noble conscience. Still, this combination could turn out a writer of great authority or a journalist-/philosopher with an acid pen.

Born During the Hours of the Boar — 9 P.M. to 11 P.M.

This Rat will hate carrying the Boar's scruples inside him. It makes him hesitate when he could take advantage of ideal situations. He may end up being a do-gooder who gets no thanks unless he gets smart.

HOW THE RAT FARES IN DIFFERENT YEARS

Year of RAT

A prosperous year for the Rat native. He can look forward to a promotion or boost in career. Few small illnesses worry him this year and he can make unexpected achievement and monetary gains.

Year of OX

A fairly good year. The Rat's gains will not be substantial but it will still be a bright and happy time for his family and he will benefit indirectly from the good fortune of others. He could find stress in his work area and more responsibilities than usual.

Year of TIGER

A moderately fair year. This year is unsafe for speculation and the Rat will be

COMPATIBILITY TABLE FOR THE RAT

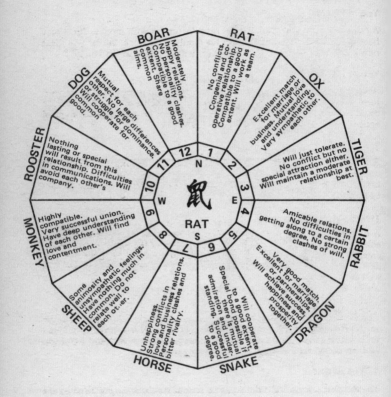

BOAR — Moderately happy relations. No personality clashes. Compatible to a good extent. Share common aims.

RAT — No conflicts. Operative and co-operative relationship. Compatible to a good extent. Will work as a team.

OX — Excellent match for marriage or business. Mutual love and understanding. Very sympathetic to each other.

DOG — Mutual respect for each other. No large differences. No struggle for dominance. Will cooperate for common good.

TIGER — Will just tolerate. No conflict but no special attraction either. Will maintain a moderate relationship at best.

ROOSTER — Nothing lasting or special will result from this relationship. Difficulties in communications. Will avoid each other's company.

RABBIT — Amicable relations. No difficulties in getting along to a certain degree. No strong clashes of will.

MONKEY — Highly compatible. Very successful union. Have deep understanding of each other. Will find love and contentment.

DRAGON — Very good match. Excellent for marriage or partnerships. Will achieve success, happiness and prosperity together.

SHEEP — Some animosity and unsympathetic feelings. Have nothing much in common. Do not relate well to each other.

SNAKE — Will cooperate to a good extent. Special bond possible if there is mutual admiration and understanding. Successful to a good degree.

HORSE — Unhappiness. Strong conflicts in love and business relations. Personality clashes and bitter rivalry.

Center: 鼠 **RAT**

N, E, S, W

12 1 2 3 4 5 6 7 8 9 10 11

involved in some misunderstanding or be forced to take actions th
against his better judgment. He could feel some loneliness or sadness a
death of some family member or close associate. The Rat may also be
required to travel more than usual.

Year of RABBIT

A calm and quiet year. Still, the Rat must be careful with money. There may
be some misunderstandings within his family or at work, but he will make
new contacts in business. New members will be added to his family.

Year of DRAGON

A very good year. Excellent business and romantic prospects. The Rat will
have a smooth time with financial gains or promotions. But while the Rat
could be recognized for his achievements this year, he must also be on guard
against newfound friends who tend to use him.

Year of SNAKE

A mixed year. The Rat has to be very careful in making investments or
important decisions. A big illness or some loss of money will cast gloom over
him. His luck will turn for the better toward the end of the year and he may
be able to recoup some losses.

Year of the HORSE

A difficult time is in store for the Rat. He has to be very conservative in
assessments or business commitments as the year of the Horse forces him to 1990
entertain, waste money or become engaged in lawsuits. He may run into
debt or be unable to get back money due him. Love affairs may not turn out
well at this time.

Year of SHEEP

The Rat's finances make a recovery this year and there are some achievements career-wise. However, his plans cannot all be realized without
encountering changes or some small upheaval. He will be able to discover
and take advantage of previously unseen opportunities.

Year of MONKEY

The Rat will enjoy a fruitful year as no serious troubles are predicted on the
home or business front. He will receive more good news than bad. However,
he should avoid breaking friendships or partnerships at this time to avoid
future repercussions.

Year of ROOSTER

Celebrations are in store for the Rat. New partnerships or a marriage in the family. A very hectic time as good things could happen overnight. Due to his busy schedule and many commitments, the Rat must be on guard against infections, cuts, bruises and overwork.

Year of DOG

A less pleasant year for the Rat native. Misfortunes will come in threes. He may receive bad news while traveling and be unable to influence or change the course of things he does not like. He worries too much this year as many unsettled issues occupy his mind. A time for him to be patient and prudent.

Year of BOAR

Not much progress to be made in business or investments. A time for the Rat to consolidate. Friends and family members make excessive demands on his time and money. If not careful, his illnesses could develop complications. In place of illness, he could lose some money or personal belonging.

FAMOUS PERSONS BORN IN THE YEAR OF THE RAT

Metal
Adlai Stevenson
Lucretia Borgia

Water
James Callaghan
Pope John Paul

Wood
Wm. Shakespeare
James Baldwin
George Sand
Jimmy Carter
Sidney Poitier
Doris Day
Marlon Brando

Fire
Charlotte Brontë
Mozart
Karim Aga Khan
Pablo Casals
Yves St. Laurent

Earth
Leo Tolstoy
Jules Verne
Maurice Chevalier
Prince Charles
Peggy Fleming

Chapter 2
The Ox

Mine is the stabilizing force
That perpetuates the cycle of life.
I stand immobile against the
Test of adversity,
Resolute and unimpeachable.
I seek to serve integrity,
To bear the burdens of righteousness.
I abide by the laws of nature—
Patiently pushing the wheel of Fate.
Thus, I shall weave my destiny.

I AM THE OX.

THE OX SIGN

Chinese name for the Ox: NIÚ
Ranking order: Second
Hours ruled by the Ox: 1 A.M. to 3 A.M.
Direction of its sign: North-Northeast
Season and principal month: Winter—January
Corresponds to the Western sign: Capricorn
Fixed elements: Water
Stem: Negative

THE LUNAR YEARS OF THE OX IN THE WESTERN CALENDAR

Starting Dates	Ending Dates	Element
February 19, 1901	February 7, 1902	Metal
February 6, 1913	January 25, 1914	Water
January 25, 1925	February 12, 1926	Wood
February 11, 1937	January 30, 1938	Fire
January 29, 1949	February 16, 1950	Earth
February 15, 1961	February 4, 1962	Metal
February 3, 1973	January 22, 1974	Water
February 20, 1985	February 8, 1986	Wood

If you were born on the day before the lunar year of the Ox, e.g.,
February 18, 1901, you belong to the animal sign before the Ox—
which is the Rat.If you were born on the day after the lunar year of the
Ox, e.g., February 8, 1902, then you belong to the sign following that of
the Ox—the Tiger.

THE YEAR OF THE OX

We will feel the yoke of responsibility coming down on us this year. No success can be achieved without conscientious efforts. The trials and tribulations the Ox year brings will be mainly on the homefront. It is a good time to settle domestic affairs and put your house in order.

Way-out fashions, abstract art forms and newfangled notions will be given an impassive stare by the phlegmatic Ox, while politics and diplomacy will simply be treated with indifference. Better stick to routine and support conservative policies. Frivolities are out!

This year will no doubt bear fruit, but the motto is: "No work, no pay!" Time waits for no man; if we are too lazy to sow then we can blame no one if we have nothing to reap. We will find a great many things requiring our attention, and the list of what needs to be done will seem endless. The Spartan influence of the Ox will be a constantly cracking whip over our heads. Better to apply oneself diligently than waste time arguing with the authorities. They will prevail, as the year of the Ox favors discipline.

Most conflicts this year will arise more from a lack of communication and refusal to give in on small technicalities than anything else. But hang on and be patient. Everything will be sorted out and we will be rewarded for our efforts—so long as we remember to do things the conventional way. This is no time for tricky shortcuts.

For the rebels, it may be worthwhile to point out that although the stoical Ox is soft-spoken, he carries a big stick, and this is his year.

THE OX PERSONALITY

The Ox or the Buffalo sign symbolizes prosperity through fortitude and hard work. A person born during this year will be dependable, calm and methodical. A patient and tireless worker, he sticks to routine and conventions. Although he is generally fair-minded and a good listener, it is difficult to make him change his views as he is stubborn and often has strong prejudices.

Still, because of his steady and trustworthy character, the Ox person will be entrusted with positions of authority and responsibility. He will not fall short where duty calls. As a matter of fact, he should be careful not to get carried away.

Beneath his somewhat modest but neat appearance, the Ox shields a resolute and logical mind. His intelligence and dexterity is hidden by the reticent and undemonstrative front. But in spite of being basically an introvert, his forceful nature can turn him into a commanding and eloquent speaker when the occasion arises. In times of turmoil, his presence of mind, refusal to be intimidated and innate self-confidence will restore order. He walks with his head held high.

A person born under this particular sign is systematic. He adheres to fixed patterns and has great respect for tradition. In fact, he tends to do exactly what is expected of him and is so predictable that he may be unfairly criticized for a lack of imagination. But the dutiful Ox knows that only through doing things in their proper order can he hope to achieve lasting success. His is the uncluttered mind. You won't find him muddling through life depending on his luck to pull him through. What people born under the other signs may accomplish by guile and wit, the Ox-born will by sheer tenacity and dedication. You can rely on his promises; once he gives his word, he will stick by it. Public opinion means little to him. He will apply himself wholeheartedly to whatever task he is doing and finish the job. He detests loose ends.

The Ox can be terribly naive about affairs of the heart. He cannot fully comprehend the entrapments of love, much less employ enticing strategy and other allures to plead his romantic cause. Don't expect lyric poetry and moonlight serenades from him. He just doesn't have the right chemistry for these sort of things. Even his presents are likely to be strong and durable wares: unpretentious and long lasting.

Because they are traditionalists, the Ox man and woman will also be inclined to long courtships. It takes time for them to develop intimate relationships. They are slow to warm up and reveal their true feelings. The Ox man may be a knight of the most distinguished order, a gentleman of the highest caliber, but he can turn into a fumbling, tongued-tied lad when it comes to wooing his fair maiden.

But if you marry him and place your trust squarely on his shoulders, he will never disappoint you; he will stick by you faithfully all his life. You never need worry about the rent or the bills getting paid. He may not keep you in diamonds and furs but life will be as comfortable as he can make it and you will never be in need.

If you have the good fortune to marry an Ox lady, you sure picked the no-nonsense type of girl. She'll starch your collar just the way your mother does it, fold your newspaper neatly on the breakfast table every day without fail and poach your eggs to perfection. Even that "good morning" kiss may seem like nothing more than a dutiful peck now and then. But if you think of her as being boring or too set in her ways, consider this. She is neat and punctual. You will never go through married life without clean shirts or holes in your socks or having to eat burnt dinners. Honest, hard-working and above reproach, she will make an ideal wife. The checkbook will be balanced and your joint account never overdrawn. It's up to you to liven up her life and take the lead. After all, the Ox person usually performs more than his or her share. A lot of wonderful things come wrapped in plain brown paper. The Ox is one of them. Don't ever belittle the packaging. He is worth his weight in gold.

Aside from his many sterling qualities, the Ox person is also known to nurture grievances far too long. He has a long and exacting memory, and injuries can be registered down to their last detail.

Where other signs such as the Tiger, Rooster or Rat may complain vehemently when they are upset and the Sheep and Rabbit will sulk and become morose, the Ox will react by plunging himself into hard work to alleviate his misery and tension. If severely disappointed in love, he may bury himself in his work forever and lead a solitary existence instead of running the risk of ever being humiliated or rejected again.

The Ox will insist on settling his accounts. Debts will be paid to the last decimal point. If he owes you something he will never forgive himself if he doesn't show his gratitude in a tangible way. No profuse but empty phrases of appreciation from him. He considers flowery words and lavish flattery uncouth and beneath his dignity. But won't it come as a surprise to you when you find out that that gruff fellow, who barely managed to mumble a "Thank you," left you something in his will? Well, that's a typical Ox gesture for you. If anyone's actions speak louder than his words—his do.

Beware of the Ox's legendary patience, because when an Ox person loses his temper, he is really something to reckon with. It could be a terrifying experience. There will be no reasoning with him: he will act like a bull and attack anyone in his path. The only advisable thing to do is to get out of his way until he cools off. By and large, however, he is seldom given to such taxing display of fireworks unless he finds his situation truly unbearable.

At home, his word is law. He knows how to give orders as well as follow them. And he expects his directives to be carried out to the letter. He has a materialistic outlook on life, and although he may be inordinately fond and proud of his family, he demands a lot from them, too. He will use the yardstick of success and personal achievement to measure his love for them. Even though he is not easily moved by emotions, he is a good provider and is capable of great sacrifices for his family's welfare. When and where it really counts, he will not let them down.

An Ox person will always be an asset to his firm and family. He has no reason to feel insecure himself as he will be well cared for all his life. Reason dictates that one so valuable should not be left to fend for himself.

The Ox born during the day will be more aggressive and active compared to the quiet night ox. Similarly, the winter Ox will have more trying times and a leaner life than the summer Ox.

The native of this lunar sign is a down-to-earth type and will follow his head rather than his heart. So if you want to win your case, appeal to his reason and intelligence. Make a list of the pros and cons and support every request with pertinent and reliable data. Sentiments alone rarely make him change his mind. He also has a remarkable constitution and does not get sick easily. Proud and uncompromising, the Ox is disdainful of weakness in others. If he can learn to cultivate more humor and compassion, he will be much happier.

A natural-born leader and disciplinarian, he tends to be too rigid. Likely to be a self-made man, he staunchly believes everyone should pull his own weight—and no hedging about it either. At his worst, the Ox is unapproachable, inflexible and narrow-minded. His lack of tact and consideration for others coupled with a militant view of life at times could make him unsuitable for positions involving public relations, diplomacy and finesse. However, he is respected and liked for his basic honesty, unpretentiousness and steadfast principles. He inspires loyalty in all his subordinates, as no task is beneath him.

As mentioned earlier, the Ox person is not one who will go for the shortcuts. His quiet dignity and strong morals will prevent him from resorting to unfair means to achieve his goals. He will dislike asking others for help. As a matter of fact, he is so self-reliant, that you may have to beg him to accept a service.

The Ox-born has dynastic tendencies. Careful and conscientious, he builds things to last. This sturdiness in his genes will extend to his offspring and generations to come even if they are not born under the same sign. His excellent character makes him an empire builder. He will take all precautions to ensure the prosperity and survival of his lineage.

As the paterfamilias, he will lay down the laws pontifically and stand for no youthful rebellion. He builds his life around his home, his work and his country and will always prefer long-term, stable investments. Being a strict creature of habit, he is no gambler: risks and razor-thin margins unnerve him because they endanger his deep-felt need for security.

Of all the twelve signs, the colorful Rooster will bring the sunshine into the Ox's orderly life and make a splendid partner for him. Both have high respect for authority, admire efficiency and possess strong dedication to duty. These common attributes will unite them. Equally well suited will be the affectionate Rat or the wise Snake, both of whom will care deeply for the worthy Ox. Dragon, Rabbit, Ox, Horse, Boar and Monkey will also be compatible to a lesser degree with the Ox. But the Dog may find him too bland and criticize his lack of humor; the Ox himself will not care too much for the company of the capricious Sheep or the rebellious Tiger native, who in turn will resent his regimentation.

Whatever happens, one can be sure that the success enjoyed by the Ox will have been earned by his own merits. In short, the strong and disciplined Ox does not expect and will not be getting any free rides in life. This stalwart fellow will emerge a winner through his own efforts and no one should be more deserving.

THE OX CHILD

This child will not be a crybaby. He is unusually tough and can endure hardship. A rugged individualist, he tends to begin speaking late and would rather settle arguments with his fists. Stubborn and unyielding, he can turn the house upside down when he puts his mind to it. He is not the fussy type but will be adamant about the few concessions he demands. One of them will be his privacy.

He won't resent discipline and in fact will welcome your fixing a schedule for him. He may insist on having his meals served at the same time each day but he will not be particular about food. He thrives on regularity; knowing where everything is and what is expected of him will give him a sense of security. A girl born under this sign will go for order and neatness at home.

The Ox youngster enjoys taking charge when mother or teacher is away and is stern and unsympathetic to offenders. He can and usually will give you an unbiased opinion, as he is not easily influenced or taken in by flattery. Instead of bribing or begging him to do something unpleasant, it will be more effective to simply tell him, "It is an order!" He is not argumentative by nature but you must gain his respect before he will obey you.

He relishes teaching younger children and will show remarkable patience and perseverance in waiting for what he wants. Being the strong, silent type, he may not readily reveal his feelings. He can be deeply hurt and no one may even suspect it, because the Ox child is a very private person. Although he may put up a blunt, strong-willed and loyal front, the Ox is terribly naive about the realities of life. He needs to be protected in this respect and he will rely heavily on moral support from his parents, teachers and family.

At school, he may be an exemplary student as he is not one to lock horns with the authorities. His serious and no-nonsense outlook on life makes him avoid joking or clowning around. He should be encouraged to express his emotions and develop his sense of humor.

Above all, he will be reliable and responsible. He will win the respect of his elders as well as his peers. The Ox child will be an outstanding example of both an excellent leader and follower and perform his duties well.

THE FIVE TYPES OF OXEN

METAL OX—1901, 1961, 2021

This type of Ox will have strong clashes of will with people, even his superiors, who do not agree with his views. He expresses himself clearly, intensely and resolutely and can never be accused of being vague about what he wants. He will stick to his guns at all cost; when necessary he can be quite eloquent—and he will use all his abilities to the full when he wants to forge ahead.

He is not very affectionate by nature but could have scholarly inclinations and be a lover of classical music and art. He has a strong sense of responsibility and can be relied upon to keep his word, which shouldn't be too difficult as he or she will be a person of few words.

At times, he tends to force issues; he can become a one-man army when he is obsessed with succeeding in his objectives. He can become a fanatic about them. Tough and arrogant, he does not know the word "failure." A person of remarkable stamina, he will require little rest or diversion. He won't mind working around the clock if that is what it takes to get things done. He can be narrow-minded and vengeful when he doesn't get his way.

WATER OX—1853, 1913, 1973

This is a more realistic than idealistic type of Ox. Patient, practical and unrelentingly ambitious, he possesses a shrewd mind and a keen sense of values. He puts things to their proper use and has many notable contributions to make because he knows how to bide his time and organize his activities.

This Ox will be more reasonable and flexible and is open to suggestions, although he may still not approve of change or unconventional methods being introduced into his life. But he is not as stern as other Oxen and will not be too unhappy if asked to bend to the wind. He is primarily concerned about improving his status and security and will uphold law and order in everything he undertakes.

He will make his mark by working well with others and can steer his own course without any difficulty, provided he does not get too rigid or demand too much from others. He can concentrate on more than one goal at a time and can wear out and wait out the opposition by this methodical calmness, patience and determination.

WOOD OX—1865, 1925, 1985

This type of Ox is less rigid and at least conscious if not considerate of other people's emotions. He reacts more quickly than others of his sign and is likely to be more graceful socially. He will be admired for his integrity and ethics. He is fair and impartial although his lunar animal sign draws him toward conservatism. He understands and operates within a fixed social system and will be a much better showman than the Oxen of the other elements.

Given the chance and motivation, he will embrace new and progressive views; he is less stubborn and able to concede to majority rule.

He could climb to great heights, amassing wealth and achieving prominence, if he can succeed in founding and developing sizable industrial outfits. He has strong drive and will exploit his potentials to the maximum. He understands the importance of coexistence and will link his ambitions to a larger order of things. He is capable of teamwork and is likely to be corporate-minded.

FIRE OX—1877, 1937, 1997

This Ox is a combustible performer and the type most drawn to power and importance. His native sense of control is reinforced but so is his strong temper. As a result, he can be more forceful and proud than the other Oxen, with the exception of the quiet Metal Ox. He is materialistic and may have a superiority complex. Consequently, he tends to eliminate persons or things he considers useless or inappropriate without attempting to assess their true worth. He is objective and outspoken and can be too harsh to those who dare oppose him.

The Fire element here could turn his hard-working tendencies toward the military—or even all-out war against his opponents. He tends to overestimate his abilities and may show little patience or consideration for the feelings of others. Otherwise, he is basically honest and a fair person who does not like to take advantage of others if he can avoid it. His family will benefit most from his labors as he is apt to be very protective to his loved ones and will see to it that they are always well provided for.

EARTH OX—1889, 1949, 2009

This is an enduring although less creative type of Ox who is always faithful to his duties. He knows his limitations and realizes his imperfections quite young in life. He will shine in any career he decides to undertake as he is practical, industrious and prepared to pay the price demanded for success. He contributes his share willingly and will favor practical and worthy endeavors. He looks for security and stability and will work efficiently with these two master goals in mind.

Although he may not be sensitive or very emotional by nature, he is capable of sincere and lasting affection and will be loyal and steadfast to his loved ones and his principles.

He fights for constant advancement of his station in life and will endure difficulties and suffering without complaint. Purposeful and determined, this Ox will go far; it will be hard to push him back because he will never surrender captured ground. He may be the slowest but is the surest of all the Oxen.

THE OX AND HIS ASCENDANTS

Born During the Hours of the Rat — 11 P.M. to 1 A.M.

An Ox with a touch of real sentiment. The Rat's charm softens him and he is more flexible and communicative. Still, he never forgets an injury or how to count his pennies.

Born During the Hours of the Ox — 1 A.M. to 3 A.M.

Master sergeant type. Put one toe out of line and he will chop it off. Gifted with extraordinary self-control and dedication. Not much can be said for his humor or imagination.

Born During the Hours of the Tiger — 3 A.M. to 5 A.M.

Captivating Ox with a lively personality. He certainly won't be soft-spoken or shy. By the way, watch out for his infamous temper.

Born During the Hours of the Rabbit — 5 A.M. to 7 A.M.

You still won't get this Ox to change his opinion about you, but at least he will be diplomatic and discreet. A genteel Ox who will collect art and antiques and is not fond of strenuous work.

Born During the Hours of the Dragon — 7 A.M. to 9 A.M.

Great strength and power to achieve his ambitions. It is a pity he is so inflexible and opinionated; otherwise he could have so much more.

Born During the Hours of the Snake — 9 A.M. to 11 A.M.

This combination consists of two secretive signs who are adverse to taking advice. He could be a loner with a cunning side to his nature.

Born During the Hours of the Horse — 11 A.M. to 1 P.M.

A happier Ox with some of the fancy ways of the Horse. Who knows, he may even love to dance. However, the mercurial Horse in him could steer him away from his steadfast goals.

Born During the Hours of the Sheep — 1 P.M. to 3 P.M.

An artistic Ox with a tender side to his personality. Will be more lenient and receptive. He is business-minded and will have the sense to make money out of his talents.

Born During the Hours of the Monkey — 3 P.M. to 5 P.M.

A shrewd but jovial Ox who just won't take his problems too seriously. With the Monkey's influence, he won't have to. He always has a card up his sleeve.

Born During the Hours of the Rooster — 5 P.M. to 7 P.M.

Dynamic and dutiful. He will argue a lot before taking action and uses colorful rhetoric instead of just his fists. Something of a cross between the soldier and the preacher.

Born During the Hours of the Dog — 7 P.M. to 9 P.M.

A severe moralist who could be utterly boring if not saved by the Dog's even temperament. Well, at least he won't be too prejudiced and will give you a fair hearing at the court-martial. Good luck!

Born During the Hours of the Boar — 9 P.M. to 11 P.M.

An affectionate Ox although he is still demanding and conservative. He lacks the needed conviction to press issues at times. His hard-working qualities will be equally matched by the Boar's love of good food.

HOW THE OX FARES IN DIFFERENT YEARS

Year of RAT

A smooth and prosperous time for the Ox. Luck will favor his undertakings, and all his previous troubles tend to fade away. He gains recognition in his work and could assume new posts of importance. Celebrations can be expected at home.

Year of OX

A good year although the Ox's plans may suffer delays and small difficulties may crop up unexpectedly. An auspicious time for marriage or new partnerships. Children will be born into his family or he will be spending more time with youngsters. His problems will not be large this year but he can expect some unwelcome traveling or entertaining.

Year of TIGER

A difficult time. The Ox will meet opposition from many sources but will be able to conquer or persevere through his hardships. He must be patient and not be disappointed if results are not immediately visible. A time for the Ox person to reassess his position. He must not take unnecessary risks or drastic measures during the reign of the Tiger.

57

COMPATIBILITY TABLE FOR THE OX

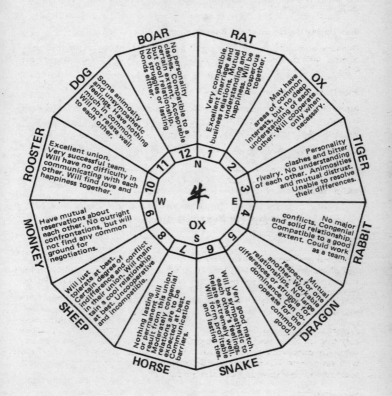

Year of RABBIT

A fair year for the Ox although he still has many loose ends to tie up and other problems to settle. He could still lose on some investments or fail to collect debts owed to him. His health is protected although he may experience some sorrow at the death of someone close to him. Progress is steady.

Year of DRAGON

A moderate year as many changes and unexpected troubles keep the Ox busy. Plans will be realized but not as quickly as he wishes. He will have to work hard although he will come in contact with helpful and influential people.

Year of SNAKE

Good times predicted for the Ox person. He will find it easy to make money. Things are all within his reach this year. On the darker side, he may suffer from a misunderstanding with some associate or find that some friend betrays his confidence. All his problems can be resolved if he is open to discussion.

Year of HORSE

An unsettled year for the Ox. Unhappy love or financial affairs beset him and he could have financial setbacks or be involved in accidents. Illness can also cause unexpected delays and make him unable to honor his commitments. Darkest clouds should pass by autumn. A time for him to consolidate or make conservative estimates.

Year of SHEEP

Not much progress can be expected this year although the Ox receives good news to boost his confidence. No illness or serious quarrels and his home life will be relatively peaceful. However, he should not be overoptimistic as he could lose some money he thought he has gained or lose something he cannot even talk about.

Year of MONKEY

A lucky and prosperous year for the Ox. He will be feted or sought after by important people. Good tidings in his family or a new job or promotion could await him. New ventures or partnerships can be foreseen.

Year of ROOSTER

The Ox will have a moderately happy time and will still enjoy success although he could experience one strange or unlikely incident this year. He should be on the watchout for some foreclosure in property or being swindled by a friend.

Year of DOG

Although problems seem large this year, they will turn out to be less serious than they look. The Ox will have a fairly good time, as expected complications do not develop and his path is cleared of obstacles and opposition. He may have to suffer temporary separation from a loved one or his family. Forced traveling or entertaining is indicated.

Year of BOAR

A busy time in store for the Ox native. He will not net much results to show for his conscientious efforts, but he should not fret as he will make valuable contacts for later use. A mixed year for the Ox, as family troubles and some friction at work may disturb him. On the whole, he will fare quite well as the numerous problems that beset him will be little ones.

FAMOUS PERSONS BORN IN THE YEAR OF THE OX

Metal
Walt Disney
Emperor Hirohito
Eisaku Sato

Water
Richard Nixon
Gerald Ford
Archbishop Makarios
Willy Brandt
Vincent van Gogh
Carlo Ponti

Wood
Gore Vidal
Sammy Davis Jr.
Peter Sellers
Richard Burton
Margaret Thatcher
Melina Mercouri

Fire
Robert Redford
Vanessa Redgrave
Dustin Hoffman
Boris Spassky

Earth
Adolf Hitler
Nehru
Charlie Chaplin

Chapter 3
The Tiger

I am the delightful Paradox.
All the world is my stage.
I set new trails ablaze;
I seek the unattainable,
And try the untried.
I dance to life's music
In gay abandon.
Come with me on my carousel rides.
See the myriad of colors,
The flickering lights.
All hail me the unparalleled performer.

I AM THE TIGER.

THE TIGER SIGN

Chinese name for the Tiger: HU
Ranking order: Third
Hours ruled by the Tiger: 3 A.M. to 5 A.M.
Direction of its sign: East-Northeast
Season and principal month: Winter—February
Corresponds to the Western sign: Aquarius
Fixed element: Wood
Stem: Positive

THE LUNAR YEARS OF THE TIGER IN THE WESTERN CALENDAR

Starting Dates	Ending Dates	Element
February 8, 1902	January 28, 1903	Water
January 26, 1914	February 13, 1915	Wood
February 13, 1926	February 1, 1927	Fire
January 31, 1938	February 18, 1939	Earth
February 17, 1950	February 5, 1951	Metal
February 5, 1962	January 24, 1963	Water
January 23, 1974	February 10, 1975	Wood
February 9, 1986	January 28, 1987	Fire

If you were born on the day before the start of the lunar year of the Tiger, e.g., February 7, 1902, you belong to the animal sign before the Tiger—which is the Ox.

If you were born on the day after the lunar year of the Tiger, e.g., January 29, 1903, then you belong to the sign following that of the Tiger—the Rabbit.

THE YEAR OF THE TIGER

This is definitely an explosive year. It usually begins with a bang and ends with a whimper. A year earmarked for war, disagreement and disasters of all kinds. But it will also be a big, bold year. Nothing will be done on a small, timid scale. Everything, good and bad, can and will be carried to extremes. Fortunes can be made and lost. If you take a chance, gamble for high stakes, but understand that the odds are stacked against you.

People will do drastic and dramatic things on the spur of the moment. It is not surprising that Watergate and the drama of Nixon's resignation culminated in the hotheaded year of the Tiger. Tempers will flare all around and it will be a trying time for diplomacy. Like the Tiger, we will tend to charge without thinking and end up regretting our rashness.

Friendships, joint ventures and deals requiring mutual trust and cooperation made at this time are brittle and will be easily broken. However, the forceful and vigorous Tiger year can also be used to inject new life and vitality into lost causes, sinking ventures and drab or failing industries. It will likewise be a time for massive change, for the introduction of new and bold, especially highly controversial, ideas.

The fiery heat of the Tiger's year will no doubt touch everyone's life. In spite of its negative aspects, we must realize that it could have a cleansing effect. Just as intense heat is necessary to extract precious metals from their ores, so the Tiger year can bring out the best in us.

Just one brief word of advice for this unpredictable year. "Hang on to your sense of humor and let things sizzle out!"

THE TIGER PERSONALITY

In the East, the Tiger symbolizes power, passion and daring. A rebellious, colorful and unpredictable character, he commands awe and respect from all quarters. This fearless and fiery fighter is revered as the sign that wards off the three main disasters of a household: fire, thieves and ghosts.

The Tiger is a fortunate person to have around, provided you are prepared for all the activity that comes along with his dynamic personality. The impulsiveness and vivacity of the Tiger person are contagious. His vigor and love of life are stimulating. He will arouse every sort of emotion in people, except indifference. In short, the captivating Tiger loves being the center of attention.

Restless and reckless by nature, the Tiger is usually impatiently geared for action. However, because of his suspicious nature, he is prone to waver or make hasty decisions. He finds it hard to trust others or to quell his emotions. He must speak his mind when upset. But just as he is quick-tempered, he is equally sincere, affectionate and generous. What's more, he has a marvelous sense of humor.

Every tiger has the humanitarian touch in him. He loves babies, animals, jazz or anything that can catch his imagination and attention for the span of the moment. When he gets involved, his involvements are total. Everything, even breathing, will have to take second place to the object of his adulation. He is never halfhearted about his endeavors, and one can trust the Tiger to give 100 percent of himself or even more if he had it in him to do so.

The more sensual types usually have a fling at the bohemian life in their youth. Some never grow out of it. Adventurous models seeking romance in Paris, budding painters displaying their wares on street corners, amateur bands on the road, one-night-stand pop singers or ambitious actors working on shoestring budgets are all more likely to be Tiger children than flower children. This may be because, aside from being an optimist, the Tiger is just not materialistic or security conscious.

He must have one phase in his life in which he acts out his impulses—play all the fantastic roles he has cut out for himself. A chance to thumb his nose at what he disapproves of. A time to lash out at society and scoff at binding traditions. The Tiger must express himself, find his identity and shape his personality, and if rebellion or open defiance of accepted modes will offer him the opportunity, then that's the road he will take. Could one love him any less for these imperfections, if they can be labeled as such? No, nine times out of ten we find ourselves rooting for him. We may shake our heads at his audacity and gasp at his insane acts of daring, but just the same we never forget to say a silent prayer for him and feel we have experienced a warm personal triumph when we see him succeed.

When the Tiger is dejected he will need cartloads of sincere, undiluted sympathy. Don't rationalize about who is right and who is wrong. Logic does not appeal so much to him. That's beside the point. Don't be stingy about comforting him. He would do twice as much for you if the situation were reversed. He will love to hear your words of wisdom and will hang on to every kind word of advice. But this doesn't mean that he will take it. There is a difference, you know. It never pays to be arbitrary with this fellow.

Better just hold his hand and wait till he talks himself dry, bounces all his feelings off of you and collects all the pieces of his shattered ego. Then, he will kiss you, hug you and let you go off feeling like you have just put Humpty Dumpty back together again.

After he packs you off, well, in all probability he will go out and do exactly what he was planning to do in the first place.

No matter how down and out the Tiger is, no matter to what depths of despair and depression he plunges, don't believe for one moment that he will ever say die! There will always be a tiny spark left somewhere in that unquenchable spirit of his to rekindle the fire and start him living and loving all over again.

A bit too intense to rely on in times of stress, the Tiger is still renowned for his ability to sway the crowd. At his best, he is warm, sensitive and sympathetic. At his worse, he is obstinate, unreasonable and selfish.

The lady Tiger is the most charming and radiant of hostesses. She can combine home and social life with aplomb. Solicitous, vibrant and absolutely disarming, she is a sweet little kitten only because this act gets her good reviews. But don't taunt her, she keeps her claws sharpened just in case she has need of them.

Fashion-conscious, articulate and liberated, the Tigress likes to pamper herself and can spend hours experimenting with new hair styles, makeup and costumes. She is the type who is constantly lamenting that she has nothing to wear. Actually she is at home just as much in blue jeans as with haute couture. Give a ball and she will turn out to stun them every time. She is great with the children, too. She tells lovely stories, mimics and makes fun of herself, flashes her brilliant smile and, most of all, endears them to her forever by bending all the rules in their favor. When she is around, they can have sweets before dinner, double helpings of ice cream and stay up late for their favorite TV program. Strange to say, her children are no more spoiled than others. They learn their lessons well. Perhaps this is because, after she shows she loves them, she makes sure to enforce the law. She makes them mind their manners, and if they perform well, she is extremely generous with rewards. There will be picnics galore, trips to the zoo and the national parks, or boating and fishing expeditions. Now, how can anyone resist that?

Like the Dragon and Rooster, the Tiger native has a super ego. Money, power and fame will mean nothing if his ego is hurt. Thwarted, the Tiger could turn out to be the meanest and pettiest bully you ever came across. He will go to any length to get revenge, even to bringing down the house with him. Little slights will enrage him, but he may let big issues pass without a fuss. Just remember, he hates being ignored!

Paradoxically, his two main shortcomings in life will be his rashness on one hand and indecision on the other. If he can learn to take the middle of the road, the Tiger will be a roaring success.

At heart, the Tiger is a romantic. He is playful yet passionate and sentimental all at the same time, and it will be quite an experience being in love with or married to one. He or she is also inclined to be overpossessive and quarrelsome when jealous.

The first stage of the Tiger's life will probably be the best. In these formulative years, he could be taught to keep a tight rein on the explosive emotions which could be the ruin of him. In his youth and prime, the Tiger will be absorbed in the pursuit of success and the fulfillment of his dreams. His old age could be calm if he could learn to give up the front seat and just relax. However, this will be difficult as he will be plagued by bittersweet regrets about the things he did and did not do.

On the whole, the Tiger's life will be volatile. It will be filled to the brim with laughter, tears, pain, joy, despair and every conceivable emotion in the book. If there is one thing one should never do it is to feel sorry for him. He won't need it, either: he can only love life if he is allowed to live it to the hilt in whatever manner he chooses. The Tiger is the ultimate optimist who will always bounce back for fresh challenges.

The Tiger could make a good life with the Boar. The honest and good-natured Boar, or Pig as he is often called, will complement the Tiger's rash moods and lend him stability and security. The Tiger will also do extremely well with the realistic and practical Dog. The loyal

Dog will stick by the Tiger and is capable not only of restraining the Tiger but of reasoning with him as well.

The colorful but nevertheless down-to-earth Horse will also make a prime partner for the Tiger. They will share the same zest for life and love of activity. But the quick and nimble Horse will sense danger before the headstrong Tiger does, and the Tiger will benefit immensely from the Horse's fine reflexes and good sense.

Persons born in the year of the Rat, Sheep, Rooster or another Tiger will have no difficulty getting on with the Tiger. The one thing the Tiger should never do is challenge the authority of one born in the year of the Ox. This is one serious and uncompromising fellow who will take no nonsense from the Tiger. In a confrontation, the Ox could gore the Tiger to death.

Likewise, the union between a Snake and Tiger is ill-advised. The only thing these two have in common will be their suspicious nature. But the Snake is quiet, cool and deadly with his misgivings, while the Tiger is loud and accusing. They will not find harmony.

Last, but not least, the Monkey will be the most elusive foe of the Tiger. This quick-witted imp never tires of teasing the Tiger, who ends up losing his infamous temper and making a fool of himself. The matchless guile of the Monkey will prove too much for the Tiger and in his dealings with the Monkey, the Tiger could suffer.

THE TIGER CHILD

A Tiger child could be a bundle of joy and a holy terror at the same time. A little live wire who dashes about sparkling with activity, he will throw himself into the thick of things. Even a very quiet one will know exactly where the action is and make a bee line for it.

He is a charming, bright and self-confident chatterbox, and there will be no holding him back. His insatiable curiosity and inquisitiveness will lead him to pounce at anything that moves, and he will get into all sorts of predicaments. Hyperactive and high strung, he likes romping, screaming and rough play.

Like the Dragon, he may also bully those less aggressive into submission. But people will also be naturally drawn to him by his warm, affectionate and gregarious character.

The Tiger child will express his feelings outright. You will have to put up with his strong opinions on how things should be run and he will air his views without hesitation. He doesn't like anyone to keep secrets from him and he himself is poor at keeping them.

Since he does not bottle up his emotions, you will know immediately when something is troubling him. Just be sure he is given enough outlets to release his pent-up energy.

If the Tiger's assertiveness is unchecked, he could dominate his parents completely and turn into a dreadful brat. He should be taught to hold his temperamental character in check early, as well as to listen to reason and understand the values of compromise. But the little rebel won't just take your word for it. He won't be himself if he does not keep testing the boundaries and limits set for him. It will be no mean task making him toe the line. But the earlier he realizes who is boss, the better for him and everyone else around.

However, if he is given the proper stimuli of discipline, coupled with love, warmth and loads of understanding, no other child will respond as spontaneously as the lovable little Tiger. Life may not always run smoothly with him around, but then it would be all too empty without him. Having a Tiger child will be a reward in itself.

THE FIVE TYPES OF TIGERS

METAL TIGER—1890, 1950, 2010

This is definitely not a reticent type of Tiger. The Metal Tiger is bound to be active, aggressive and passionate. He may or may not be artistic but he will certainly see to it that he projects a glamorous image and personality that will not go unnoticed. Self-centered and ostentatious, he is a competitive and untiring worker when motivated in the right way.

He will approach his problems in a direct or even a radical way and is never in doubt about what he wants to accomplish. The problem is that he wants too much and too soon. He tends to be overoptimistic about expected results.

When Metal is combined with his native lunar sign, it could produce a Tiger who can be sudden, unorthodox and drastic in his actions. He is a person who is constant only to himself and his desires, even if he has to step on a few toes along the way. This particular Tiger is easily stirred by both good and bad influences and will tend to act independently, as he hates having his freedom curtailed.

WATER TIGER—1902, 1962, 2022

This type is an open-minded Tiger who is always inclined toward new ideas and experiences. He also has a gift for seeing things objectively, because the Water element combined with his lunar sign gives him a calmer nature. He is humane and an excellent judge of the truth, as he can relate to the way others feel. He is intuitive and has a well-developed faculty for communicating with people. He does excellent PR work.

This more realistic type of Tiger has his finger on the pulse of the people and knows the things he deals with. He makes few errors in his assessments. His mental abilities are above par, but like all Tigers, he sometimes wastes precious time procrastinating. Still, he is rated as less temperamental than the other Tigers, as he can control his emotional urges and concentrate on his endeavors.

WOOD TIGER—1914, 1974, 2034

This is a tolerant type of Tiger who evaluates situations in a practical and impartial light. He is democratic in his views and understands the importance of enlisting others' cooperation in order to advance more rapidly. He will attract a lot of friends and supporters, as he can mingle with people from all walks of life.

The Wood element gives him a more even and affable disposition, and his charming, innovative personality is very conducive to group efforts. He is sought after in polite society, and has the knack of bringing incongruous people together. But mostly his loyalty is to himself. No one is indispensable to him. If you quit the club, well, he will wish you good luck and waste no time replacing you.

The Wood Tiger is also inclined to be the least penetrating of the Tigers. He may prefer to scan the surface of things and maintain only the semblance of order. Actually, he lacks depth and permanent control. Adept at delegating chores and skillful at commanding and manipulating people into performing for him, he will take on a minimum amount of responsibility. As his lunar sign is not blessed with any great ability for self-discipline, he should not embark on more than he can handle. But it will be hard for him to admit his limitations, and Tigers of all colors do not take readily to criticism, no matter how constructive or kindly given.

FIRE TIGER—1866, 1926, 1986

This type of Tiger finds it difficult to contain his enthusiasm and boundless energy. He is always ready for action and for going from one place to another. Transient by nature, he is most concerned with the present. He is independent and unconventional, and his moves are hard to predict. The only thing one can be sure of is that when he acts, he will be dramatic and influential. Fire makes him even more expressive than he already is. This Tiger never fails to impress anyone he is after or to transmit his electric vitality to any project he decides to undertake.

He seeks constantly to convert his nervous energy and inspirations into forceful action. At times, he is downright theatrical. Generous to the hilt, he will also display more leadership qualities than Tigers of the other elements. To him, everything he does is worthwhile and imperative, so don't try to tell him otherwise. He is a thoroughly optimistic soul and has no use for doomsday prophets.

Brilliantly commanding, imposing and open, the Fire Tiger is sensual and finds it hard ever to be impersonal about anything in his or her life.

EARTH TIGER—1878, 1938, 1998

This type of Tiger will possess a quieter and more responsible personality. He will look for feasibility in what he does; he will not jump to hasty conclusions and upholds equality and justice. Concerned about others and given to uncovering the truth himself, he is mature and sensible in outlook.

This Tiger will be steadier than other Tigers as the Earth element gives him a longer attention span; this enables him to work diligently and objectively on important matters without getting restless. Although he may not be as brilliant and decisive as other Tigers, he is generally clear-headed and reasonable. He sees issues in their true light and rarely allows his emotions to cloud his vision.

He is also the type of Tiger most apt to form relationships on the basis of usefulness rather than personal or sexual attraction He is an intellectual and more of a worrier than a daredevil. He applies his knowledge and capabilities to areas with which he is familiar and which will reap the largest harvest.

Sometimes he can become too proud, insensitive and callous, especially when he is so wrapped up with his own concerns that he cannot identify with anything outside the scope of his objectives.

The Earth Tiger is the least likely to go for the bohemian life, no matter what he may like others to believe. First, he will make it to the top. Then, when he has proven to society and the world that he has the ability and the genius, he may act in a radical, scandalous or unconventional way, just to be different or to be noticed, as all Tigers love to be. Nonetheless, he will always be serious about his work, as his native element makes him desirous of status and recognition through stability and labor.

THE TIGER AND HIS ASCENDANTS

Born During the Hours of the Rat — 11 P.M. to 1 A.M.

A hothead with a loving nature. Could pick a fight just to have the pleasure of making up with you later. Not bad if the Rat in him holds the purse strings.

Born During the Hours of the Ox — 1 A.M. to 3 A.M.

Strong-willed and temperamental combination. Hopefully, the Ox might give him self-discipline, so he will not fly off the handle so quickly. May possess a calmer personality as a result.

Born During the Hours of the Tiger — 3 A.M. to 5 A.M.

All teeth and claws here. Absolutely vivacious and given to numerous contrasting moods. You want someone exciting? Here he is!

Born During the Hours of the Rabbit — 5 A.M. to 7 A.M.

Serene, but his fire is definitely not quenched. The Rabbit may curb his impetuosity and impatience. As a result he makes better decisions and could stay out of trouble.

Born During the Hours of the Dragon — 7 A.M. to 9 A.M.

Will try harder and aim higher because the Dragon here reinforces his ego. Could be an excellent leader if he stops being so suspicious.

Born During the Hours of the Snake — 9 A.M. to 11 A.M.

Perhaps the Snake here could teach the Tiger to keep his big mouth shut. The Tiger profits if he follows the Snake's vibes and does not lose his temper in negotiations.

Born During the Hours of the Horse — 11 A.M. to 1 P.M.

The Horse may make the Tiger a bit more practical and encourage him to take only calculated risks. But this combination is composed of two fancy-free signs which lack any real sense of responsibility.

Born During the Hours of the Sheep — 1 P.M. to 3 P.M.

Quiet and observant but still insanely jealous and possessive. Lovely if the Sheep could tone down the Tiger's aggressiveness and develop his artistic side.

Born During the Hours of the Monkey — 3 P.M. to 5 P.M.

Brawn meets brains. Let's just hope everything will be in the right proportions. If it is, there's no telling how far this fellow will go.

Born During the Hours of the Rooster — 5 P.M. to 7 P.M.

Fascinating personality. The troublemaker meets the troubleshooter here. He won't let you get away with anything and he will insist on being heard—as if you were ever given any choice.

Born During the Hours of the Dog — 7 P.M. to 9 P.M.

Reasonable and more cooperative Tiger, resulting from the Dog's inherent common sense. His bullying tactics will be discouraged by the Dog's strict sense of fair play, but his tongue will be sharper than a razor.

Born During the Hours of the Boar — 9 P.M. to 11 P.M.

Impulsive and naive. Happy and contented—so long as he gets what he wants. Could still turn vindictive under pressure, but you will find him going out of his way to please his family and friends.

HOW THE TIGER FARES IN DIFFERENT YEARS

Year of RAT

Not a very lucky year for the Tiger. Business is difficult and he could find that money is scarce or withheld from him. He will only be rewarded if he exercises prudence and patience. He must avoid impulsive acts and be conservative in his outlook.

Year of OX

A mixed year. Quarrels and misunderstandings result from stubbornness. The Tiger may feel frustrated because he is hindered from getting his way by someone in authority. It would be advisable for the Tiger to curb his rebelliousness at this time. His troubles will work themselves out before the year is over, if he can hold his temper that long.

73

COMPATIBILITY TABLE FOR THE TIGER

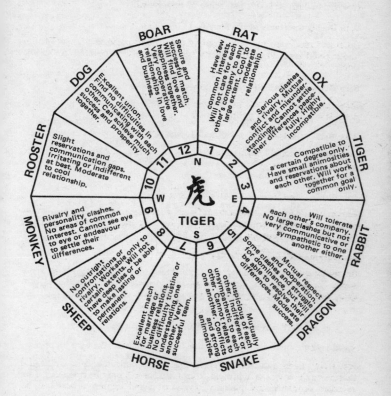

BOAR — Secure and successful match. Will find love and happiness together. Very cooperative relationships in love and business.

RAT — Have few common interests. Will not care for each other's company to any large extent. Cool to moderate relationship.

OX — Serious clashes and rivalry. Mutual conflict and misunderstandings. Cannot settle their differences peacefully. Highly incompatible.

TIGER — Compatible to a certain degree only. Have small animosities and reservations about each other. Will work together for a common goal only.

RABBIT — Will tolerate each other's company. No large clashes but not very communicative or sympathetic to one another either.

DRAGON — Mutual respect and cooperation. Some clashes and struggle for dominance but will be able to resolve their differences. Moderate success.

SNAKE — Mutually suspicious of each other. Indifferent to each other. Unsympathetic to one another. Conflicts and strong animosities.

HORSE — Excellent match for marriage or business relations. No difficulties or understanding. Very trusting or understanding one another. Very successful team.

SHEEP — No outright confrontations or rivalry. Workable only to a certain extents. Will not have deep ties or be able to make lasting or permanent relations.

MONKEY — Rivalry and personality clashes. No areas of common interest. Cannot see eye to eye or endeavour to settle their differences.

ROOSTER — Slight reservations and communication gaps. Irritating or indifferent at best. Moderate to cool relationship.

DOG — Excellent union. Find no difficulties in communicating with each other. Can achieve much success and prosperity together.

虎 TIGER — N E S W — 12 1 2 3 4 5 6 7 8 9 10 11

Year of TIGER

A moderately good year. The Tiger is lucky in the sense that others will come to his aid when he needs help most. Still, he should not take risks as things may turn against him. He will suffer no major illness or upheavals but may be forced to spend money or be unable to save.

Year of RABBIT

A happier year for the Tiger. Some good news is forthcoming and his love and business affairs look rosy again. There are still obstacles in his path but he will surmount them with little difficulty. All in all, he will be quite content with his achievements.

Year of DRAGON

Not much in store for the Tiger this year. He will find it hard to raise money or he may be influenced by others to make unwise investments. Some unhappiness foreseen, such as separation from a loved one or a break in partnership. He finds it difficult to adjust to changes even when they are for his own good.

Year of SNAKE

A fair year for the Tiger. No large losses or gains foreseen and his life could be tranquil if he is cautious enough not to get caught up in the affairs of others. His progress will be steady and his illnesses minor. Most of his disappointments will come from persons of the opposite sex.

Year of HORSE

A very good and happy year. Things will go smoothly for the Tiger. Promotions and recognition are in store. It will be an easy time to make money, and the Tiger will even be able to save money or receive additional income. There will be celebrations as good news is received at home.

Year of SHEEP

A good year although the problems the Tiger encounters take up a lot of his time. Negotiations, bickering at home and tension at work keep him from relaxing, and he should take a vacation even if he cannot afford it. He could also lose some personal belongings but should otherwise count himself lucky, as there will be no serious disasters.

Year of MONKEY

A trying year for the Tiger. Irritations and setbacks test his patience and powers of endurance. He should not voice his objections too loudly and avoid confrontations which could lead to lawsuits. He will entertain or travel more than usual and be forced to compromise.

Year of ROOSTER

A moderate year. The Tiger must not be overanxious. The seemingly large problems that beset him this year can be solved and help will come at the last moment from unexpected places or newfound friends.

Year of DOG

A year in which the Tiger is protected from serious danger. However, he will have to work hard for his success and will feel tired or lonely from having to toe the line. Still, luck favors him and he will be able to steer his plan through as influential people support him.

Year of BOAR

The Tiger will have to curb his free-spending ways this year as the prosperity that comes in the beginning of the year will not last for long. He must be on guard against high-risk investments and new associates.

FAMOUS PERSONS BORN IN THE YEAR OF THE TIGER

Metal
Charles de Gaulle
Ho Chi Minh
Beethoven
Dwight D. Eisenhower
Groucho Marx
Princess Anne
Stevie Wonder

Water
Simon Bolívar
Will Geer

Wood
Alec Guinness
Pierre Balmain

Fire
Queen Elizabeth II
Giscard D'Estaing
Hugh Hefner
St. Francis Xavier
Marilyn Monroe

Earth
Emily Brontë
Isadora Duncan
Diana Rigg
Rudolf Nureyev

Chapter 4
The Rabbit

I am in tune with the
Pulse of the universe.
In my quiet and solitude
I hear the melodies of the soul.
I float above commonplace
Dissent and decay.
I subdue by my ability to conform.
I color my word
In delicate pastel hues.
I epitomize harmony and inner peace.

I AM THE RABBIT.

THE RABBIT SIGN

Chinese name for the Rabbit: TÛ
Ranking order: Fourth
Hours ruled by the Rabbit: 5 A.M. to 7 A.M.
Direction of its sign: Directly East
Season and principal month: Spring—March
Corresponds to the Western sign: Pisces
Fixed element: Wood
Stem: Negative

THE LUNAR YEARS OF THE RABBIT IN THE WESTERN CALENDAR

Starting Dates	Ending Dates	Element
January 29, 1903	February 15, 1904	Water
February 14, 1915	February 2, 1916	Wood
February 2, 1927	January 22, 1928	Fire
February 19, 1939	February 7, 1940	Earth
February 6, 1951	January 26, 1952	Metal
January 25, 1963	February 12, 1964	Water
February 11, 1975	January 30, 1976	Wood
January 29, 1987	February 16, 1988	Fire

If you were born on the day before the start of the lunar year of the Rabbit, e.g., January 28, 1903, you belong to the animal sign before the Rabbit—which is the Tiger.

If you were born on the day after the lunar year of the Rabbit, e.g., February 16, 1904, then you belong to the sign following that of the Rabbit—the Dragon.

THE YEAR OF THE RABBIT

A placid year, very much welcomed and needed after the ferocious year of the Tiger. We should go off to some quiet spot to lick our wounds and get some rest after all the battles of the previous year.

Good taste and refinement will shine on everything and people will acknowledge that persuasion is better than force. A congenial time in which diplomacy, international relations and politics will be given a front seat again. We will act with discretion and make reasonable concessions without too much difficulty.

A time to watch out that we do not become too indulgent. The influence of the Rabbit tends to spoil those who like too much comfort and thus impair their effectiveness and sense of duty.

Law and order will be lax; rules and regulations will not be rigidly enforced. No one seems very inclined to bother with these unpleasant realities. They are busy enjoying themselves, entertaining others or simply taking it easy. The scene is quiet and calm, even deteriorating to the point of somnolence. We will all have a tendency to put off disagreeable tasks as long as possible.

Money can be made without too much labor. Our life style will be languid and leisurely as we allow ourselves the luxuries we have always craved for. A temperate year with unhurried pace. For once, it may seem possible for us to be carefree and happy without too many annoyances.

THE RABBIT PERSONALITY

A person born in the year of the Rabbit possesses one of the most fortunate of the twelve animal signs. The Rabbit, or Hare as he is referred to in Chinese mythology, is the emblem of longevity and is said to derive his essence from the Moon.

When a Westerner gazes at the Moon, he may joke that it is a ball of cheese or tell a child the story of the Man in the Moon. When a Chinese looks at the Moon, he sees the Moon Hare standing near a rock under a Cassia tree and holding the Elixir of Immortality in his hands.

During the Chinese mid-Autumn festival when the Moon is supposed to be at its loveliest, Chinese children still carry lighted paper lanterns made in the image of a Rabbit and climb the hills to observe the Moon and admire the Moon Hare.

The Rabbit symbolizes graciousness, good manners, sound counsel, kindness and sensitivity to beauty. His soft speech and graceful and nimble ways embody all the desirable traits of a successful diplomat or seasoned politician.

Likewise, a person born under this sign will lead a tranquil life, enjoying peace, quiet and a congenial environment. He is reserved and artistic and possesses good judgment. His thoroughness will also make him a good scholar. He will shine in the fields of law, politics and government.

But he is also inclined to be moody; at such times he appears detached from his environment or indifferent to people.

The Rabbit is extremely lucky in business and monetary transactions. Astute at striking bargains, he can always pop up with a suitable proposal or alternative to benefit himself. His sharp business acumen, coupled with his knack for negotiation, will ensure him a fast rise in any career.

Although the Rabbit may assume an outer air of indifference to the opinions of others, he actually withers under criticism. His "rather switch than fight" technique can be deceiving and he can be diabolically cunning when he puts his mind to it. So while the Rabbit person is tender and obliging to his loved ones, he can be superficial and even ruthless in his dealings with outsiders. Suave and self-indulgent, he enjoys his creature comforts and likes to put his own wishes first. It irks him terribly to be inconvenienced for he is a considerate, modest and thoughtful person and he would like others to be the same. He sincerely believes it costs people nothing to be nice to each other and he will always make an effort to be civil, even to his worst enemy. He abhors brawling and any sort of overt animosity.

For all his quiet and misleadingly docile nature, a Rabbit person possesses a strong will and an almost narcissistic self-assurance. He pursues his objectives with methodical precision but always in an unobtrusive manner. If there is anything he isn't going to be accused of, it is that he is an obvious or thick-skinned person. He won't make waves. The special trait that makes the Rabbit person a formidable negotiator is his inscrutability. It is difficult ever to assess his thoughts correctly.

The Rabbit usually has impeccable manners. He seldom uses harsh words and will never resort to foul language or vulgarisms to bring home a point. There is little need to anyway, as he has his own techniques. The Rabbit could hide under this cloak of decency to undermine his opponents. His credentials are usually flawless or at least in good order. He will wine and dine you in the best places and cater to your every whim when he is after something. Then, when you have eaten your fill and are puffing away contentedly at that expensive cigar, he will pull out the contract for you to sign. Before you know it, he has cut you off at the knees. He was so deft, you didn't even feel any pain. It was all over with the stroke of a pen. My sympathies are with you, friend. You are just another victim of the incomparable Hare. Now do you understand why Bugs Bunny always gets his carrots in all those cartoon strips?

The Rabbit may appear a bit slow or overly deliberate at times, but this is due to his inborn sense of caution and discretion. One can be sure he is going to read the fine print before signing any document. Because of his ability to assess people and situations, the Rabbit can afford to be conceited—which, by the way, he is.

The demure Ms. Rabbit is very considerate and understanding with her friends: a great gal to work with, shop with or just tell stories with. She is delightfully warm and witty and her company is always relaxing. She has a lot of energy for the things she likes to do and can tirelessly track down antique shops or plan a friend's wedding to the last detail. But when she feels she has had enough of all that rigmarole, well, you can expect her to drop whatever she is doing, prop up her dainty feet and go all limp. That is the philosophical part of the Rabbit. Do you know why she can keep so serene with all that frantic action going on? The secret is to know when your batteries need recharging, and no one has better knowledge or timing on this than the Rabbit.

While everyone is killing himself in a mad rush to get somewhere, the Rabbit knows that the world will still be here tomorrow. So, what's the big hurry? Why don't you sit down, too? She will probably make you a nice cup of tea and help you forget all about that crazy rat race outside.

In any situation, you can always rely on the Rabbit to be in control of herself. She will notice the license number of the getaway car or remember that the driver was wearing camel-colored trousers or elevator shoes. And while you are at the police station filing that report, she will calmly recall all the details and help you answer all those irritating questions.

All in all, the Rabbit is one who really knows how to live. What's more, he or she is more than willing to let live. Not a spoilsport or disciplinarian with an ever-watchful eye, the Rabbit knows when to refrain from criticism. He never likes to embarrass anyone in public. He is adept at the art of saving face, both yours and his, and if there is any way he can spare your feelings, he will.

Have no doubt—he makes mental notes of your mistakes or progress. But if things are not serious or beyond redemption, he will goodheartedly let you pass. For this trait, he is well-liked and popular. An advantage of this philosophy is that the Rabbit makes few enemies and thus rarely gets into trouble. People respond by being generous to him and letting him pass, too.

No one has a more sympathetic ear to lend you than the Rabbit (except the Sheep) should you need one. But while he is an excellent soother and compassionate listener, he will only take the role of a passive advisor. He is, above all, an intellectual, a realist and a pacifist. Do not expect him to go out with all colors flying and do battle for you. That would be asking too much of him. Let's face it, the Rabbit will never elect to trudge up Mount Calvary with you, no matter what great buddies you two claim to be. He'll lend you the money for the lawyer or bail you out of jail if he can afford it, but that's about all. And if you are getting to be too much of a nuisance, you can count on his making a quick but graceful exit from your life.

The comely and refined Miss Rabbit will not be adverse to marrying a good old-fashioned millionaire instead of a handsome but penniless swain. The former will be able to provide her with the advantages and luxuries she demands as necessities. Her man must be powerful enough to protect and support her in style, and sensitive enough to politely disappear when she is in a sullen mood and wishes to remain undisturbed.

When given the choice, the Rabbit will vote for the easy and good life every time. He or she will wear loose comfortable clothing of superb cut and fabric. Cashmere sweaters, pure silk blouses and durable linens and tweeds. A mink or chinchilla carelessly thrown over the shoulder in a calculated air of nonchalance could also identify the elegant Rabbit native. Flashy, geometric or shocking designs offend the Rabbit's sense of conformity and balance.

While gracious to friends and coworkers, the Rabbit person may be somewhat distant from his own family or simply bored by domestic routine and duties. He or she hates too close associations; he will shake off an encroachment on his privacy or clinging parasitic friends with no regret. He can be bureaucratic and hedgy over difficult issues. As he is one who hates binding commitments or overinvolvement, he can also be an expert at passing the buck.

Mr. Rabbit is singularly debonair. He moves with grace, charm and gentlemanliness, in spite of the fact that while he was singing your praises, he was also drinking all your best wine. Yes, the Rabbit gravitates toward the cream of society and gentlemanly leisure. On second thought, the cream of high society could well be made up of poised and genial Hares.

At his best, the Rabbit is admired for his suaveness and intelligence and sought after for his sensible advice. At his worst, he is too imaginative, oversensitive or just acidly indifferent. He avoids coming into contact with human suffering or misery, as though it were some highly contagious disease.

The Rabbit is not at all easy to trap. He can also become very repressive in his predilection for secrecy or privacy. When the Rabbit person feels threatened, his subtle brooding or concealed antagonism could be expressed by the use of subversive tactics. Joseph Stalin and Fidel Castro and South Africa's Johannes Vorster are Rabbits. It is also worth noting that Thailand's King Bhumibol, admired and well-loved by his subjects for his exemplary life and devotion to music, art and domestic harmony, was born in the year of the Rabbit. So were King Olav V of Norway, Queen Victoria, Albert Einstein, David Rockefeller and David Frost.

For all his positive qualities, a native of this sign will still value himself above all else. When pushed too far, he will discard anything or anyone who dares upset the calm of his existence. His beliefs are known to be flexible and he has the knack of playing both sides for insurance. Security could be an obsession to the weaker types of this specimen; you rarely find a Rabbit in areas of high risk.

This love of ease coupled with his distaste for conflict may give the Rabbit a reputation for being weak, opportunistic and self-indulgent. Unlike the Dragon, Dog, Tiger, or Rooster, who all enjoy a hearty fight now and then, and may even thrive on it, the Rabbit has no relish for combat. He was not born to be a warrior. He is more effective working behind the scenes. Do not be concerned about the Rabbit's well-being. He is agile and sagacious and armed with the good sense to keep out of harm's way. Unlike other signs, who may pursue lofty ideals, the

Rabbit's main objective in life is simply self-preservation.

The Rabbit year is said to bring peace or at least a respite from conflict or war. Likewise, its native will do everything in his power to restore harmony or he will leave the scene.

The Rabbit person makes a good entertainer and is a wonderful host. Pleasant and warm company, he has a good word to say of everyone. But don't let that fool you. He knows more than he will say and you can easily recognize him by his finesse. He will be the best of friends so long as you take care not to ask too much of him.

The well-groomed Rabbit is most compatible with those born in the Sheep year. They will share the same good taste and love of material comforts. Equally well suited will be a relationship with the Dog person or the honest, unimposing Boar native. The Rat, Dragon, Monkey, Ox, Snake and Rabbit will make good secondary matches for him. But he will not be able to tolerate the vanity or criticism of the Rooster, is unimpressed by the dramatics of the Tiger and unappreciative of the quick-tempered and mercurial ways of the Horse.

To sum it up, the Hare simply leaps over obstacles in his path and recovers from calamities with remarkable resilience. No matter how he is tossed, he lands on his feet. He may not be close to his family but will make every effort to provide them with the best of everything. His soft, vulnerable-looking exterior is protected by an armor of cautiousness and sagacity. In life, the Rabbit will avoid being drawn into conflict at any cost, unless, of course, it affects him directly, at which time he will take the appropriate measures to protect his interests.

There is no great inner struggle in the Rabbit's heart between the forces of good and evil. He believes in his own ability to survive, relies on his own judgment and is at peace with himself. His is the sign most apt to find happiness and contentment.

THE RABBIT CHILD

A child born in the Rabbit's year will have a sweet disposition. Even-tempered and obedient, he will be sensitive to the moods of his parents and act accordingly. He may or may not be talkative, but he won't be rowdy or offensive. He can sit quietly and concentrate on one toy or game at a time.

Usually he is a light sleeper and may fret a lot when he is sick. He will be easy to discipline and should have little trouble fitting in at school. He learns his lessons well and with ease. But although he has better than average manners, this does not mean he will not be argumentative in his own soft-spoken way. He can grasp both sides of a question quickly and debate his point with intelligence.

At times, it will be difficult to decipher his thoughts or deeds. Smooth at masking his feelings, the Rabbit will only say what he knows will please you and thus maneuver you to his way of thinking without your even noticing it.

He will be able to fend for himself and protect his possessions. Remarkably observant, he can calculate his chances for getting his way. Instead of directly resisting rules, the subtle Rabbit will carefully devise ways around them. In short, this polite little angel is going to bargain for a better deal every time.

He can take reproach with a defiant or philosophical sort of indifference. Shrugging off his setbacks, the Rabbit will patiently start again from square one. Helpful at home, conforming in school and well-tuned to his environment, this child will know his way around people and problems. Rest assured he will be well-liked and accepted in all circles.

THE FIVE TYPES OF RABBITS

METAL RABBIT—1891, 1951, 2011

This type of Rabbit could be sturdier physically and mentally than Rabbits belonging to other elements. He will not be as compromising either. He has unshakable faith in his own powers of observation and deduction and more often than not he is convinced he has the right answer and solutions to his problems. He can assume responsibility admirably well and will display a good deal of initiative in his work.

Metal matched with his animal sign will make him more preoccupied with his desires, goals and creative urges. He will be more cunning, but his ambitiousness will be carefully concealed with cool logic and intelligence.

A connoisseur par excellance, he will know how to live and will savor the good things life has to offer in a refined way. While he may be indifferent to the opinions of others, he is emotionally and physically moved by good art, music and other forms of beauty. His basic self-assurance and discerning eye will make him an excellent judge of any kind of creative art forms; he may become a collector of great distinction, if he has the means, because of his impeccable taste. Whatever career he chooses he will make his mark early as he is naturally a thorough and devoted worker.

But like all true romantic spirits, this type of Rabbit could be inclined to dark moods, and works well only when he is sufficiently inspired. Ardent in love and with great depth and foresight, still he will allow only a handful of people into the inner sanctum of his life because of his many hidden inhibitions.

WATER RABBIT—1903, 1963, 2023

This is a meditative type of Rabbit with a fragile and emotional nature. He cannot bear harassment or any other unpleasantness, such as dissent and bickering. Perhaps this is due to the fact that he is too empathic and can pick up the thoughts and feelings of others with uncanny accuracy.

He will possess an excellent memory and may have the kind of mental power that, without his knowing it, transmits his ideas to others. Consequently, he attracts the people he wants, and he may be surprised by the many supporters who rally to his defense when he least expects it.

However, he is a subjective soul and his perspective gets distorted by the emotional barriers he sets up. He is not very decisive and in many cases could easily fall in with the dictates of others.

His delicate sensitivity makes him dwell too much on the past and hence he is often reminiscing on long past injuries and indulging in self-pity. In his negative moods, he suspects other's motives, is uncommunicative and overimaginative. In his positive state, he could call upon all the cosmic powers to come to his aid. He is never without friends and influence if he does not carry his neutrality to extremes.

WOOD RABBIT—1915, 1975, 2035

When Wood is exalted in this lunar sign already governed by Wood, it could produce a generous and especially understanding Rabbit who will be too charitable at times for his own good. No doubt he has real and solid ambitions, but often he is intimidated by authority and may choose to ignore mistakes made in his presence in order to maintain the status quo. As a result, others are tempted to take advantage of his sympathetic and permissive attitude.

However, this type of Rabbit usually works out well. He thrives in large corporations or other institutions where he can slowly and diplomatically climb the ladder of success, one rung at a time. Group effort and togetherness appeal to him and give him the kind of security and reassurance he needs. But because of his innate desire to feel part of the group, he may become a bit too bureaucratic and hedge when he has to make a decision that might offend people or set a precedent for a controversial case. In his refusal to meddle or take sides, he may end up hurting everyone, including himself. He should be more discriminating and decisive and take the necessary steps to insulate himself against those who prey on his generous nature. As he is one who is able to bend gracefully without ever breaking, this Rabbit will have no trouble fitting in anywhere he chooses.

FIRE RABBIT—1927, 1987, 2047

Definitely a demonstrative, fun loving and affectionate type of Rabbit. He has more strength of character than the other Rabbits. In spite of Fire making him more temperamental, he is still able to mask his emotions with charm and diplomacy.

His personality is easy and natural. People respond positively to his ideas because he expresses them so well.

Fire may make him prone to emotion and outspoken in expressing his wants. He is more capable of leadership than other Rabbits and his rule is tempered with discretion and moderation. Despite his outgoing and progressive ways, he will never approve of outright confrontation with his enemies and will prefer to use subtle plots or deal with go-betweens as natives of his sign are so adept at doing.

This type of Rabbit will have a high level of intuition and even psychic ability. He is intensely aware of changes in his surroundings and easily moved to anger, hurt or disappointment. He could also become terribly neurotic when negative. He requires approval, whole-hearted support and inspiration in order to sparkle.

EARTH RABBIT—1879, 1939, 1999

A serious and steadfast type of Rabbit, he has definite patterns of thought and is capable of well-calculated moves. He deliberates before giving in to his emotional inclinations. His balanced and rational personality wins him favor in the eyes of his superiors, as does his realistic approach to his goals.

The Earth element makes him more constant and less indulgent, although his constancy will be of a passive sort. His introverted nature causes him to turn inward when beset with problems and he must be in accord with his inner self before he acts. He never hesitates to appropriate whatever resources are available and will use them wisely.

He is a materialistic sort of person, and his well-being is his prime concern, making him indifferent to the needs of others when they are not in accordance with his plans. Still, he possesses the humility to acknowledge his shortcomings and will strive to overcome them if he can.

THE RABBIT AND HIS ASCENDANTS

Born During the Hours of the Rat — 11 P.M. to 1 A.M.

Astute, affectionate and well-informed. The Rat livens up the Rabbit's retiring ways and makes him less indifferent.

Born During the Hours of the Ox — 1 A.M. to 3 A.M.

The Ox's influence makes this Rabbit act with more authority than he normally possesses. Could be very successful with the Ox's strength and self-control.

Born During the Hours of the Tiger — 3 A.M. to 5 A.M.

A fast-talking, fast-thinking Rabbit. The Tiger in him urges him to be more aggressive while the Rabbit side maintains control.

Born During the Hours of the Rabbit — 5 A.M. to 7 A.M.

Philosopher extraordinaire! Wonderful sage who never takes any action because he never takes sides. Only one thing is for sure—he can take good care of himself.

Born During the Hours of the Dragon — 7 A.M. to 9 A.M.

Ambitious and tough Rabbit. He still won't like to dirty his hands and in all probability he won't have to. He can command others to follow his well-devised and commendable plans.

Born During the Hours of the Snake — 9 A.M. to 11 A.M.

Moody and reflective, but self-sufficient and not likely to ever solicit advice. Extremely sensitive to his surroundings and strictly guided by his intuitions.

Born During the Hours of the Horse — 11 A.M. to 1 P.M.

A cheerful Rabbit with more of the Horse's self-confidence. Could be an excellent combination as both signs have winning instincts.

Born During the Hours of the Sheep — 1 P.M. to 3 P.M.

The Sheep in him cajoles the Rabbit toward more sympathy and generosity. The result is a more tolerant and loving personality, but he may also be tempted to spend beyond his means.

Born During the Hours of the Monkey — 3 P.M. to 5 P.M.

A laughing, mischievous Rabbit. Here the Rabbit's intuitive diplomacy and cool front will make a perfect cover for the Monkey's pranks. Get ready for a neat rip-off!

Born During the Hours of the Rooster — 5 P.M. to 7 P.M.

The Rabbit learns to speak his mind with the Rooster behind him. With his basic sensitivity and sound judgment, he may be worth hearing.

Born During the Hours of the Dog — 7 P.M. to 9 P.M.

The Rabbit is made more friendly and outspoken by the Dog in him. He may even be actually concerned about the welfare of others and less lethargic when it comes to committing himself.

Born During the Hours of the Boar — 9 P.M. to 11 P.M.

The Boar could add texture to the Rabbit's refined tastes. The Boar's influence could diminish the Hare's telltale love of self and make him disposed to offering his help.

HOW THE RABBIT FARES IN DIFFERENT YEARS

Year of RAT

A good, calm year for the Rabbit. No surprises, no big problems, but not as fruitful as he wishes either. Progress will be steady as no serious opposition is foreseen in his work or home areas. A time to make plans for the future or buy property.

Year of OX

The Rabbit faces a rough and rigorous year. Disappointments, aimless traveling or working without seeing the desired results. He could have health problems caused mainly by too much anxiety. Departure or separation from a loved one. Not a time for the Rabbit to contemplate changes in his environment. Plans take longer to develop than he expects.

COMPATIBILITY TABLE FOR THE RABBIT

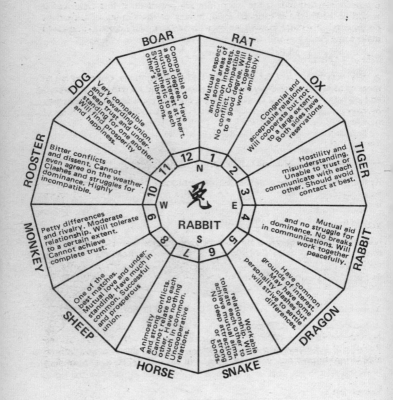

RABBIT

BOAR — Compatible to. Have a good degree of mutual interest in each other's vibrations. Sympathetic to each other's vibrations.

RAT — Mutual respect and some areas of common interests. No conflict. Will work together amicably. Compatible to a good degree.

OX — Congenial and acceptable relations. Will cooperate but not to a large extent. Both sides have reservations.

TIGER — Hostility and misunderstanding. Unable to trust or communicate with each other. Should avoid contact at best.

RABBIT — Mutual aid and no struggle for dominance. No breaks in communications. Will work together peacefully.

DRAGON — Have common grounds or interest. May have some personality clashes but will strive to settle differences.

SNAKE — Workable relationship. Will tolerate each other. No deep or strong bonds. Achieve mutual aims.

HORSE — Animosity and strong conflicts. Cannot relate to each other. Have nothing much in common. Uncooperative relations.

SHEEP — One of the best matches. Mutual love and understanding. Have much in common. Successful and prosperous union.

MONKEY — Petty differences and rivalry. Moderate relationship. Will tolerate to a certain extent. Cannot achieve complete trust.

ROOSTER — Bitter conflicts and dissent. Cannot even agree on the weather. Clashes and struggles for dominance. Highly incompatible.

DOG — Very compatible and rewarding union. Deep trust and understanding for one another. Will find prosperity and happiness.

Year of TIGER

A year in which the Rabbit must be extra careful and diplomatic, as he has the tendency to get drawn into conflicts. Lawsuits or disputes arising from unreasonable demands made upon him are prevalent at this time and it would be best if he is cautious about money or the signing of important documents. Otherwise, he will get by without too much hardship and could make some gains toward the end of the year.

Year of RABBIT

A very auspicious year for the Rabbit native. Promotions, career advancement or financial success can be foreseen for him and he will reap unexpected benefits or recover lost funds. His plans are easily executed and there may be happy tidings at home or celebrations at the arrival or homecoming of new or old members of the family.

Year of DRAGON

The Rabbit can expect a moderately happy but busy time at home and in his career this year. Things may be mixed or mediocre money-wise, but the Rabbit will still find it easy to be congenial and contented as his overall gains will exceed his losses. He may make powerful new friends who will prove useful.

Year of SNAKE

Not much tangible progress for the Rabbit during this year. He may have to travel or be faced with difficulties from several directions. A change of residence or career is also indicated as he tries to consolidate or better his current position. He could also find less time to spend with his family or be faced with many unplanned expenses.

Year of HORSE

A good year in store for the Rabbit, as his luck will come from meeting helpful people who will be happy to use their influence for his benefit. The Rabbit will not experience any big upheaval or illness this year and thus be able to recoup previous losses. He may have much traveling or entertaining to do.

Year of SHEEP

An excellent year for the Rabbit. Many wonderful achievements can be accomplished and his plans progress smoothly. A prosperous year for him but he must pay strict attention to details or he may have trouble later on about a settlement. No large problems at home or work.

Year of MONKEY

A fair year for the Rabbit provided he is not too optimistic. Financial deals or contracts may meet with unexpected snags or fail to materialize due to the betrayal of a trusted ally. His family life remains calm but he could experience several minor illnesses that impede his progress.

Year of ROOSTER

A difficult year for the Rabbit, as he finds money dwindling away and meets setbacks that cause extra expense. A time for him to merge with others and let them carry him through. He should be conservative this year and not act independently. Problems and obstacles at home and at work will be overcome, but not before they cause him a lot of frustrations.

Year of DOG

A smooth year foreseen for the Rabbit. He will make some gains and straighten out past problems. He finds time for recreation and will have no family troubles. Career-wise, he may be criticized by superiors or hampered in some way by other associates.

Year of BOAR

A mixed time for the Rabbit. Things look brighter than they actually are and he must be very realistic and avoid making promises or handing out guarantees. Unlikely difficulties have a tendency of cropping up this year so he must not be overconfident and must take every precaution to protect his interests.

FAMOUS PERSONS BORN IN THE YEAR OF THE RABBIT

Metal
Henry Miller
Jomo Kenyatta

Water
King Olav V of Norway
Benjamin Spock
Franz de Voghel

Wood
Orson Welles
David Rockefeller
Ingrid Bergman
Johannes Vorster

Fire
Fidel Castro
Harry Belafonte
George C. Scott
King Bhumibol
Peter Falk

Earth
Albert Einstein
Joseph Stalin
Queen Victoria
David Frost
Ali McGraw

Chapter 5
The Dragon

I am an unquenchable fire,
The center of all energy,
The stout heroic heart.
I am truth and light,
I hold power and glory in my sway.
My presence
Disperses dark clouds.
I have been chosen
To tame the Fates.

I AM THE DRAGON.

THE DRAGON SIGN

Chinese name for the Dragon: LONG
Ranking order: Fifth
Hours ruled by the Dragon: 7 A.M. to 9 A.M.
Direction of its sign: East-Southeast
Season and principal month: Spring—April
Corresponds to the Western sign: Aries
Fixed element: Wood
Stem: Positive

THE LUNAR YEARS OF THE DRAGON IN THE WESTERN CALENDAR

Starting Dates	Ending Dates	Element
February 16, 1904	February 3, 1905	Wood
February 3, 1916	January 22, 1917	Fire
January 23, 1928	February 9, 1929	Earth
February 8, 1940	January 26, 1941	Metal
January 27, 1952	February 13, 1953	Water
February 13, 1964	February 1, 1965	Wood
January 31, 1976	February 17, 1977	Fire
February 17, 1988	February 5, 1989	Earth

If you were born on the day before the lunar year of the Dragon, e.g., February 15, 1904, you belong to the animal sign before the Dragon—which is the Rabbit.

If you were born on the day after the lunar year of the Dragon, e.g., February 4, 1905, then you belong to the sign following that of the Dragon—the Snake.

THE YEAR OF THE DRAGON

A magnificent comeback after the recuperative year of the Rabbit. We will throw caution to the four winds and roll up our sleeves for all sorts of grandiose, exhilarating, colossal, overambitious and daring projects. The indomitable spirit of the Dragon will inflate everything to larger than life size. Somehow we will find ourselves bubbling with excess energy. It will be wise not to overestimate ourselves or our potentials in this combustible year. Things appear better than they actually are.

On the brighter side, business will be good and money can be generated or obtained easily. It is the time to ask your bank for a loan. Big spending and lavish plans are the rule of the day. The mighty Dragon sneers at the prudent and penny-pinching. He gambles for all or nothing. He will stimulate us to think and act big, even overstepping the bounds of caution.

Orientals consider this to be an auspicious year to get married, have children or start a new business, as the benevolent Dragon brings good fortune and happiness.

However, this is also a time to temper our enthusiasm and look twice before taking a plunge. For although the lucky Dragon showers his blessings indiscriminately on all, he disappears when the time comes for making retributions for our errors. Successes as well as failures will thus be magnified. The Fire Dragon (January 31, 1976 to February 17, 1977) is especially feared, as he wreaks more havoc than the Dragons of the other elements.

In the Dragon's year, fortunes as well as disaster will come in massive waves. This is a year marked by a lot of surprises and violent acts of nature. Tempers will flare the world over and everyone will be staging some real or imaginary revolt against constrictions. The electric atmosphere created by the mighty Dragon will affect us, one and all.

THE DRAGON PERSONALITY

The mighty and magnificent Dragon of mythical folklore never ceases to enchant or stir the imagination. So it must be said that some of its magical qualities, illusory or not, are contained in those born under his sign.

The Dragon person is magnanimous and full of vitality and

strength. To him, life is a blaze of colors and he is constantly on the go. Egotistical, eccentric, dogmatic, whimsical or terribly demanding and unreasonable, he is still never without a band of admirers. Proud, aristocratic and very direct, the Dragon-born establishes his ideals early in life and demands the same high standards and perfection from others that he has for himself.

In China, the Dragon symbolizes the Emperor or the male. It represents power; those born in the Dragon year are said to wear the horns of destiny. A Dragon child will tend to take up important burdens and responsibilities even if he happens to be the youngest in the family. Often, older Dragon children can bring up their younger siblings with more authority than the parents.

The Dragon is a veritable storehouse of energy. His impetuosity, eagerness and almost religious zeal can blaze like the fabled fire the Dragon emits from its mouth. He has the potential for accomplishing great things, which is fortunate as the Dragon likes to perform on a grand scale. However, unless he contains his premature enthusiasm, he may burn himself out and end up in a puff of smoke. He is the most liable to become fanatical over an issue. Whatever the Dragon does, good or bad, he will never fail to make the headlines. The Chinese call him the guardian of wealth and power. Certainly a prosperous sign to belong to. But then again, the Dragon is the sign most prone to megalomania.

The powerful Dragon is difficult to contest, at times even impossible. He tends to intimidate those who dare challenge him. An angry, spurned Dragon could be like the big bad wolf at your door. He'll huff and he'll puff until he blows your house down.

But the Dragon is likely to be filial in spite of his strong temper and dogmatic ways. Whatever differences he or she may have with the family will be forgotten or set aside when they call for aid. The Dragon can put aside domestic resentments and come to the rescue promptly and with largesse. However, his family can also count on a severe lecture from him once the crisis is over. The Dragon seldom minces words. He cites his views like Imperial Edicts. Although he may rave about the virtues of free speech and democracy—don't buy it. He feels himself to be above the law and doesn't always practice what he preaches.

Sometimes being civil, affectionate and honey-tongued can be a terrible strain on the Dragon. He would much rather be rough, rude and utterly inconsiderate when provoked. But don't try to give him back the same medicine. Somehow, it just won't work, unless you happen to be another Dragon and decide to do battle. Then we can all sit around and watch the magnificent fireworks that will make the 4th of July look like candles on a birthday cake.

In spite of his volcano of emotions, the Dragon cannot be said to be sentimental, sensitive or very romantic. He takes love and adulation for granted: they are his just due. But while he may be stubborn, irrational and overbearing when irked, the Dragon can forgive you the moment he gets over his outburst. And since things are supposed to work both ways, he expects your forgiveness for his errors, too. He may even neglect to apologize at times, which may seem callous, but then the Dragon really has no time to explain himself or be bothered by grudges or trifles; he just wants to get on with his work.

While the Dragon may be strong and decisive, he is not cunning or guileful. He shuns easy adaptability and tricky negotiations. Were the contest to be decided on strength alone, the Dragon would conquer hands down; but he is often overconfident, brash and deluded by his wonderful visions—thus neglecting to pay attention to possible upsets or underhanded plots that could overthrow him. Instead of sniffing around for brewing schemes, he prefers to plunge into battle, often refusing to retreat even in the face of overwhelming odds. Too proud, he disdains to call for assistance; too sure, he rarely keeps anything in reserve. Too intent on going forward, he forgets to protect his rear and flanks. Too upright, he refuses to lie. Further, he is unable to interpret clever insinuations and generally fails to spot the evil and subversive intent of his enemies.

To the Dragon person, having a purpose or special mission in his life is vital. It's just not healthy for him to lie around with nothing to do. He must always have a cause to fight for; a goal to reach; a right to wrong. Otherwise, how do you expect him to keep that inner fire burning? Without his pet projects, rallies and other impossible schemes, the Dragon is like a locomotive without fuel. He fizzles out and becomes dull and listless.

The Dragon has the same affinity for success as the Snake, but because he expresses his views more openly and his failures are more likely to involve some form of physical exertion, he is usually spared deep psychological problems. Being a doer, he will take to one-man crusades, lead demonstrations, write letters to the newspapers or collect a million signatures on a petition. This method of belching fire and brimstone effectively rids him of any inner neurosis that could result otherwise.

The Dragon lady is the Grand Dame of the cycle. She will be a suffragette, a believer of equal rights for women. Double standards and discrimination will arouse her wildest passions. What a man can do, she can probably do better. Don't ever underestimate her. She is going to beat you at your own game—or die trying. She'll never stand idly by and accept her fate. She is the stuff empires are built on, the matriarch of old. Cross her and the sky will fall.

To tell the truth, the Dragon female is strictly a no-nonsense person. She will show this by the way she dresses. Practical and functional clothes appeal to her most. No frills, flimsy laces, buttons and bows, but a minimum of complications. Clothes that go on and off easily and provide her with maximum movement will be her top choice. She hates restrictions and limitations. Actually, she may even secretly prefer a uniform if she has military or institutional inclinations. This way, starched, crisp and superbly efficient, she can pop off to work every day without the bother of having to decide what to wear.

The Dragon girl seldom, if ever, overdecorates herself. Her brilliance is in her mind and this will shine forth, without any trimmings. Self-esteem rates very high with all Dragons, so the Dragon female will be no exception. She doesn't expect to be treated like divinity though she does have her airs. She just wants your respect and she will do everything in her power to get it.

The lady Dragon is totally emancipated, so strongarm tactics will get you nowhere. You might as well resign yourself—she will have the last word.

Despite his faults being as numerous as his virtues, the luster of the Dragon shines on everyone. He is not petty, nor is he begrudging with favors. He may grumble a lot, but he cannot resist helping the needy or coming to the rescue when you are in trouble. This may not be because he feels real compassion or genuine concern; more often than not, the Dragon helps because he has a profound sense of duty to all.

The Dragon will somehow always have a notable contribution to make. You can count on his support, for he will not let you down if he can help it. The Dragon will exhaust all his resources before he admits failure. An extrovert and lover of nature, this person will be an active sportsman, a travel bug and an excellent talker. He has the makings of a supersalesman and he and his band of loyal followers will always be promoting something.

The weather conditions at the time of a Dragon's birth will affect his life a great deal. A child born during a storm will lead a tempestuous and hazardous life beset by danger or spectacular experiences. One born on a day when the sea (his ancestral home) and the heavens are calm will have a protected existence and a more amiable nature.

The Dragon native will either marry young or prefer to remain single. He can be happy leading a solitary life, as his work and career will keep him occupied. He will seldom lack friends or admirers to keep him company.

The Dragon is not a spendthrift, but he is not a miser, either. He is generous with money but never too concerned about his bank balance unless he happens to have a strong combination with money-making signs.

The Dragon person is superpositive. Nothing will keep him down for long, and even when he has a bad case of the doldrums, he will snap out of it faster than anyone else. His buoyancy defies rhyme or reason.

For a sign that never accepts defeat, the Dragon provides his own worst opposition. He will dash headlong into a disastrous situation when he is convinced he is right. Pompous and self-destructive, you say? No, not really. It is just that this person must follow his plans through—irregardless of the consequences. After all, he was put on earth to raise standards to superlative heights and the more you try to change his course of action or steer him away from trouble, the more headstrong he becomes. He lives up to his reputation for taking the lead even when it becomes most unpleasant.

Whatever else, the Dragon will be an open person—you can read him like a book. It is difficult for him to pretend emotions he does not feel. He rarely even bothers to try. He is not secretive either, and cannot keep a confidence for too long. Even when he swears not to breathe a word of it, you can be sure he will blurt it out when he gets angry and the sparks begin to fly. You say he promised to keep it a secret? What secret? How can you bother him with such a trivial thing at a time like this?

His feelings are genuine and always straight from his heart. When he declares he loves you, you can be absolutely sure he is sincere.

Should he belong to the rougher variety of Dragons, he could be too abrasive. His direct, brusque manners and callousness could well antagonize people. But generally speaking, he will inspire action. He should personally attend to things he wants done immediately instead of writing or dealing over the phone. His presence and magnetism will swing people over to his way of thinking. He motivates everyone he comes into contact with. He himself needs no motivation, as he is more than capable of generating his own momentum.

It will never be hard to place your confidence in the truthful Dragon. He seldom wavers, cowers or shifts responsibility. He possesses little or no self-doubt. With his natural pioneering spirit, his attempts will be stupendous successes or unbelievable exercises in futility. He must drive right to the very edge of the precipice and take a look for himself. Just hold your breath, keep your fingers crossed and pray that he has good brakes.

I guess Frank Sinatra, who is a Dragon, and his song "My Way" concisely sum up how the Dragon ticks.

Of all the animal signs, the Dragon will be attracted most to the irresistible Monkey. The Monkey will similarly be drawn to the Dragon's majesty and they will make an unbeatable team. A Dragon-Rat union will be an equally winning combination as the Rat is crafty where the Dragon is strong. They could do great things together. The Dragon will likewise make a good match with the cool and venerable Snake, whose wisdom could check the Dragon's excessiveness.

Tiger, Rooster, Horse, Sheep, Rabbit and Boar will all seek the Dragon out for his beauty and his strength. Two Dragons will get along pretty well but the Dragon's relationship with the Ox may be a bit strained by the Ox's similar authoritativeness. Of all the animal signs, perhaps only the Dog will make a miserable partner for the Dragon. The Dragon will come under the close scrutiny of the Dog and the Dog will be too cynical to fall under his spell.

Above all, it is worth remembering that although the Dragon is dazzling, he is not deep. Only when he can harness his legendary powers can he perform miracles. He needs people to believe in him!

THE DRAGON CHILD

The high-spirited Dragon child is an innovator. Forceful, fearless and vibrant—nothing will daunt his idealistic outlook on life. He will formulate his own principles early in life and will need or ask for very little help. He is respectful of his elders and will be able to obey commands precisely.

This intense child needs to anchor his passions to something or someone he considers worthy of his devotion. He will have countless idols—his teachers, his parents or anyone he regards highly. He is bright, aggressive and independent. Tough and resilient, he can take teasing or shoving around because he is willing and ready to fight for his rights. Outspoken and ambitious, he should be given responsibilities in order to keep him occupied and make him feel useful. However, he should not be allowed to bully less assertive children. His domineering ways must be checked at an early age.

The Dragon child must be made to feel his worth. He would prefer that you needed him instead of just loved him. His efforts are always sincere and should be praised, as he will work very hard to please you and gain your respect. Never bruise his ego by laughing at him, even if he goes about performing a simple chore as if it were some intricate ritual. The Dragon's self-esteem is immeasurable. His dreams of greatness are all real and tangible to him. In life, his emotions will touch soaring heights and unfathomable depths. If he fails at anything, he has to be reassured that the sun will shine again the next day. He judges himself very harshly. Once he realizes his mistake, there will be no need for you to reproach or punish him, as he will be the first to chastise himself and make amends.

If your child is a Dragon, he will want or maybe even demand that you rely on him and he will do his best never to disappoint you. This proud and self-reliant youngster will be strong and faithful to his ideals always. He was born to lead and excel.

THE FIVE TYPES OF DRAGONS

METAL DRAGON—1880, 1940, 2000

This type could well be the most strong-willed of the Dragons. Honesty and integrity are paramount virtues to him and although he may be bright, open and expressive, he is also unbending and critical.

Action-oriented and combative, he will seek out and motivate those on his own level of intelligence or social standing. He has little patience with the lazy and the foolish. Unpliable Metal combined with his natural lunar sign, Wood, will also enable him to intimidate weaker beings into submitting to his will. Otherwise, he is the magnificent warrior at his best.

He is tremendously intense and will stake his life on his convictions. It is futile to try to convince him that certain things just cannot be done. This type of Dragon will try to exorcise whatever evil he sees in life and could be fanatical regarding his convictions and moral beliefs.

When he is negative, he will have exaggerated views of his own importance. He is a bit short on diplomacy and has the habit of going it alone if others disagree with him or refuse to accept his leadership.

The strong Metal Dragon will rush in where angels fear to tread. He will succeed because he will give himself no other recourse. He burns his bridges behind him so that he cannot turn back once he attacks.

WATER DRAGON—1892, 1952, 2012

A less imperious type of Dragon who favors optimum growth and expansion. He can put aside his ego for the good of all and is less selfish and opinionated. An inhibited but progressive person, he tries hard not to be as conspicuous as other power-hungry Dragons. Neither is he going to be labeled as the conciliatory one. He can assume a wait-and-see attitude and his wits are as formidable as his strength of will.

The Water Dragon lives by the to-thine-own-self-be-true philosophy and will not seek revenge on those who choose to go the opposite way. Democratic and liberal-minded, he can accept defeat or rejection without bitterness.

Water is calming and beneficial to this lunar sign and he will know how to act wisely and do what is essential for his progress. He is quick and reliable and is capable of marketing his ideas with untiring devotion. He is likely to be successful as a negotiator, as he knows when, where and how to apply force.

His main drawback is that he may be like an overoptimistic builder who forgets to reinforce the foundation. By trying to hold on to too much he may lose everything. He must learn to make difficult choices and to relinquish whatever is unfeasible or unnecessary. This way, he will be able to devote his energies to fewer but more rewarding endeavors.

WOOD DRAGON—1904, 1964, 2024

A creative and magnanimous type of Dragon capable of developing bright, new revolutionary concepts. Wood combined with his sign makes him good at formulating and implementing his ideas and working cooperatively with others, even if he may be a bit condescending on occasion.

Gifted with an exploratory nature, the Wood Dragon loves to look into cause and effect theories; his every action will be guided by sound logic. However, he also has a tendency to overinvestigate subjects or to submit people to endless debate when he is faced with opposition.

Nonetheless, here is a generous Dragon who is amenable to taking the middle road; who tries to offend as few people as possible; who subtly conceals his domineering ways. The Wood element produces a less fierce and unreasonable variety of Dragon who will compromise when he sees it is to his advantage. Still, as a Dragon, he will ultimately have to relate everything to his oversize ego and will condescend to change only when he is sure of the benefits to himself.

Not as vindictive or self-centered as Dragons of the other elements, he will still be outspoken, proud and fearless when challenged.

FIRE DRAGON—1916, 1976, 2036

The most righteous, outgoing and competitive of all dragons, the Fire Dragon will expect a lot from everyone. But while he may be demanding and aggressive, he is also blessed with enormous energy and has a lot to offer in return. The trouble is that he may go around with an air of superiority plus authority and make people fear or shy away from him. His leadership qualities are often marred by his desire to be treated like the Messiah. Fire matched with his forceful lunar sign will give him overzealous and dictatorial inclinations. He pushes too hard even where there is little resistance.

In reality, he is an open and humane person given to impartiality and uncovering the truth at all costs. His criticisms are objective and he has the power to arouse the masses with his vibrant personality. A natural empire builder, he will look toward the supreme order of things, with himself at the helm, of course.

Because the Fire Dragon is often enveloped by insatiable personal ambition, he is short-tempered, inconsiderate and unable to put up with anything less than perfection. He also overgeneralizes or jumps to conclusions, frequently lumping people into categories without allowing for or even perceiving their individual differences.

Nonetheless, here is a performer of the highest degree who could easily be a source of inspiration to his fellowman and a personality who will catch the public eye—when he learns to master his negative traits and communicate more humbly with others.

EARTH DRAGON—1868, 1928, 1988

This sociable, executive-type Dragon will have a compulsive drive to control his environment and the people who surround him. As a Dragon, he is bound to be autocratic and it would be folly to expect less. However, he will be fair and appreciative of other people's opinions, even if he doesn't agree with them. Earth makes him realistic, stable and, oftentimes, even a bit impersonal.

Although not as severe as the other Dragons, he will still have the basic urge to subjugate others. But he will approach problems with reason and his leadership is less dictatorial. He works incessantly to develop his talents and exploit his resources.

The Earth Dragon's self-control does not mean that he is lacking in initiative. It's just that the Earth element influences him to be unhurried and his aspirations are more liable to be solid and uncluttered.

Straight as a rod, this aristocratic Dragon is quiet, strong and brave. Given to reflection and organization, his outbursts of temper will be few, nor will he demean himself by arguing with those beneath him when he is angered. However, he will retaliate quickly once his dignity is offended.

THE DRAGON AND HIS ASCENDANTS

Born During the Hours of the Rat — 11 P.M. to 1 A.M.

His typical Dragon generosity may be mixed with Rat frugality. The Rat's affectionate nature also makes it difficult for him to be absolutely objective and decisive.

Born During the Hours of the Ox — 1 A.M. to 3 A.M.

Slow-moving Dragon who likes to be sure of what he is doing. Nonetheless, he is still breathing fire and could employ the Buffalo's heavy-handed ways in dealing with those that cross him.

Born During the Hours of the Tiger — 3 A.M. to 5 A.M.

Could get hysterical when plans go awry. He has the Tiger's wild impulses and is motivated by emotional reasons. On the other hand, he could be a compulsive worker, too.

Born During the Hours of the Rabbit — 5 A.M. to 7 A.M.

Strength and diplomacy combined. A quiet Dragon given to reflection and sound thinking. Very strong and subtle.

Born During the Hours of the Dragon — 7 A.M. to 9 A.M.

The high priest or priestess type. Exacts unquestioning devotion and obedience. Will probably have to establish a cult of his own if he wants to have a large following.

Born During the Hours of the Snake — 9 A.M. to 11 A.M.

A Dragon who plots every move and executes plans with precision. Slightly sinister and overambitious, but the Snake's charm masks this intensity.

Born During the Hours of the Horse — 11 A.M. to 1 P.M.

A gregarious wit who may like to gamble with high stakes. No party is complete without him. But the Horse's preoccupation with his own selfish desires may overshadow the Dragon's sense of duty.

Born During the Hours of the Sheep — 1 P.M. to 3 P.M.

Modest and understanding, this Dragon is one who can really get things done to perfection without having to resort to brute force.

Born During the Hours of the Monkey — 3 P.M. to 5 P.M.

A superstar in his own right. A good combination of strength and guile. He jokes and clowns around but don't be fooled—he is made of steel and you'll never get past him.

Born During the Hours of the Rooster — 5 P.M. to 7 P.M.

A fearless and imaginative Dragon with immeasurable pride and some of the Rooster's folly. Never a dull moment!

Born During the Hours of the Dog — 7 P.M. to 9 P.M.

A down-to-earth Dragon with practical ideas. The Dog in him makes him assess situations in a more detached way and lends him good humor and stability. May also have a nasty bite when he is angry.

Born During the Hours of the Boar — 9 P.M. to 11 P.M.

Deeply devoted and warm-hearted Dragon. Wonderful to have as a friend as he will go all out to support you. The Boar's influence may even give this Dragon a touch of humility.

HOW THE DRAGON FARES IN DIFFERENT YEARS

Year of RAT

A lively year ahead for romance and pursuing business interests. Money will flow in but one bad deal could make a dent in the Dragon's resources. He will find it easy to relax and his overall performance will be good. No big problems confront him at home or at work.

Year of OX

A fortunate year for the Dragon. Although progress is moderate, he should consider himself lucky as the numerous disputes and troubles that go on around him will not affect him directly. A protected time in which he will not be involved in many difficulties and his family life will be free of interference.

Year of TIGER

A worrying and taxing time. The Dragon's plans are blocked by others and he finds it difficult to achieve desired results without much argument. He has to choose between bitter camps of opposing views and finds it hard to please his associates. Home is disturbed by sad news or the departure of some member.

Year of RABBIT

Calm returns to the Dragon's life in the year of the Rabbit. Fair progress can be expected as the winds of fortune blow on his sails again. His home life is more settled, although he could experience minor health problems. A stable time as no financial upsets or bad news await him.

Year of DRAGON

A very good year for the Dragon native. Numerous benefits in store and he could gain recognition or make fantastic progress in his work. Success comes easily to all his undertakings as this busy and exciting year keeps the Dragon very occupied and alert.

107

COMPATIBILITY TABLE FOR THE DRAGON

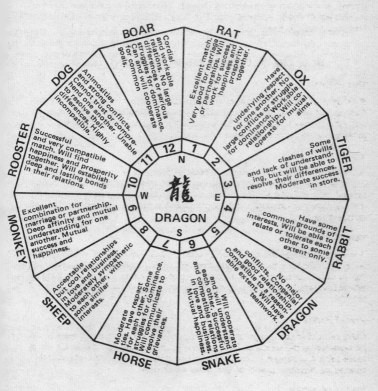

Year of SNAKE

A lucky year for the Dragon's business endeavors. His plans still go smoothly although he meets minor opposition. He may have some personal or romantic problems as home life and love life are neglected by him.

Year of HORSE

A year mixed with uncertainty and unpleasant surprises for the Dragon. Some news could upset or change his life temporarily, although problems in general tend to work themselves out if he is not too headstrong or aggressive. He will find this year an uneasy time as real and imaginary worries beset him.

Year of SHEEP

The Dragon can only expect moderate performance during the Sheep's year for his financial ventures and career advancement. Some health problems, but his family life is quiet. No upheavals or unwelcome changes in his environment.

Year of MONKEY

A mixed year for the Dragon. Progress can be foreseen in his career and financial undertakings but he must not be deceived by favorable preliminary results or else he could get caught in legal tangles. Broken friendships or romantic quarrels can result if he is too determined to have everything done his way. A time for compromises and heeding the advice of others.

Year of ROOSTER

A happy and eventful year for the Dragon: good news, promotions and the return of money given up for lost. His family life is smooth and he is able to recoup losses or make new influential friends.

Year of DOG

A difficult year for the Dragon, as unexpected problems arise from nowhere and plans go awry. A time in which he must try his best to avoid confrontation with his enemies or those who do not agree with his views. He could relieve tension by changing his environment or dealing through trusted associates.

Year of BOAR

A good year as things go back to normal for the Dragon and luck shines through the dark clouds that hovered over him during the Dog's reign. He could still have mixed results at work or financially but there are few major problems. He will have to travel or entertain a lot but no troubles are foreseen in his family life.

FAMOUS PERSONS BORN IN THE YEAR OF THE DRAGON

Metal
King Constantine
Queen Margarethe II
John Lennon
Ringo Starr
Valerie Harper

Water
Francisco Franco
Haile Selassie
Mae West
Jimmy Connors
St. Joan of Arc

Wood
Salvador Dali

Fire
Frank Sinatra
Betty Grable
Edward Heath
Yehudi Menuhin
Harold Wilson
Anthony Quinn
Kirk Douglas

Earth
Ché Guevara
Walter Mondale
Shirley Temple Black

Chapter 6
The Snake

Mine is the wisdom of the ages.
I hold the key to the mysteries of life.
Casting my seeds on fertile ground
I nurture them with constancy and purpose.
My sights are fixed.
My gaze unchanging.
Unyielding, inexorable and deep
I advance with steady, unslackened gait,
The solid earth beneath me.

I AM THE SNAKE.

THE SNAKE SIGN

Chinese name for the Snake: SHÉ
Ranking order: Sixth
Hours ruled by the Snake: 9 A.M. to 11 A.M.
Direction of its sign: South-Southeast
Season and principal month: Spring—May
Corresponds to the Western sign: Taurus
Fixed element: Fire
Stem: Negative

THE LUNAR YEARS OF THE SNAKE IN THE WESTERN CALENDAR

Starting Dates	Ending Dates	Element
February 4, 1905	January 24, 1906	Wood
January 23, 1917	February 10, 1918	Fire
February 10, 1929	January 29, 1930	Earth
January 27, 1941	February 14, 1942	Metal
February 14, 1953	February 2, 1954	Water
February 2, 1965	January 20, 1966	Wood
February 18, 1977	February 6, 1978	Fire
February 6, 1989	January 26, 1990	Earth

If you were born on the day before the start of the lunar year of the Snake, e.g., February 3, 1905, you belong to the animal sign before the Snake—which is the Dragon.

If you were born on the day after the lunar year of the Snake, e.g., January 25, 1906, then you belong to the sign following that of the Snake—the Horse.

THE YEAR OF THE SNAKE

A year for reflection, planning and searching answers. A good time for shrewd dealings, political affairs and coups d'état. People will be more likely to scheme and ponder over matters before acting on them. An auspicious year for commerce and industry. Solutions and compromises can be arrived at, but not without some mutual distrust at first. The Snake likes to resolve his differences one way or another. If he fails and things cannot be peacefully settled, then he will declare war.

Looking back into history, we find that the year of the Snake has never been tranquil. Perhaps this is because it is the strongest negative force in the cycle and it follows the Dragon year, which is the strongest positive one. Many disasters which had their beginning in the year of the Dragon tend to culminate in the year of the Snake. These two signs are very closely related and the calamities of the Snake years often resulted from excesses committed during the Dragon's reign.

This will be a lively time for romance, courtship and scandals of all sorts. A good year to pursue the arts. Fashion will become more elegant and fluid; music and the theater will blossom; and people will strive for a more sophisticated life. Notable contributions will also be made by science and technology.

The venerable wisdom of the Snake will be evident in many facets of our life, particularly in those requiring decisions. Although everything may look refreshingly quiet on the surface, the year of the Snake is always unpredictable. The Snake's cool and collected front hides the deep and mysterious ways of his nature. It should be noted that once the Snake uncoils to strike, he moves like lightning and nothing can stop him. Similarly, changes that occur during the Snake's year can be as sudden and devastating.

Tread lightly and be more cautious this year. Gambling and speculation is strictly taboo. The consequences will be overwhelming. The Snake is not merciful.

Whatever else happens, the Snake will give us faith in our convictions and coerce us to act and to act forcefully during his reign. This is not a year for fence-sitters.

THE SNAKE PERSONALITY

Philosopher, theologian, political wizard, wily financier—the Snake person is the deepest thinker and enigma of the Chinese cycle. He is endowed with an inborn wisdom of his very own; a mystic in his own right. Graceful and soft-spoken, he loves good books, food, music, the theater; he will gravitate toward all the finer things in life. The most beautiful women and powerful men tend to be born under this sign. So if you are one of the Snake people, you are in good company.

A person of this sign generally relies on his own judgment and does not communicate well with others. He can be deeply religious or psychic, or on the other hand, totally hedonistic. Either way, he trusts his own vibrations rather than outside advice. More often than not— he will be right!

Like the Dragon, the Snake is a Karmic sign. His life ends in triumph or tragedy as his past actions dictate. And although he will deny it, he is very superstitious behind his sophisticated front. People born under other signs may defer payment to the next life (if one so chooses to believe), but the Snake seems destined to pay his dues before he leaves. Perhaps this is also of his own choosing, as a person born under this sign is unusually intense and will seek to settle scores, consciously or unconsciously, in everything he does.

A native of the Snake year is not likely to be bothered by money problems. He is fortunate to have what he needs. Should funds be low, he is extremely well-equipped to remedy the situation. However, a Snake person should not gamble; he will come out poorer in the end. In the event that he does suffer sizable losses, it probably will not happen a second time; the Snake learns fast. He can recoup with amazing speed and as a rule is prudent and shrewd in business.

A Snake who experiences poverty or extreme deprivation in his youth may never get over it. He could then be fanatical about accumulating wealth and turn into a covetous and miserly man.

By nature, the Snake person is a sceptical being, but unlike the Tiger, he tends to keep his suspicions to himself. He treasures his privacy and will have many a dark secret locked up within him.

Elegant in speech, dress and manners, the Snake person does not like indulging in useless small talk or frivolities. He can be quite generous with money, but is known to be ruthless when he wants to attain an important objective. He has no qualms about eliminating anyone who stands in his way.

Some Snakes may have a slow or lazy way of speaking but this does not reflect in any way their speed of deduction or action. It's just that they like to ponder things, to assess and formulate their views properly. Generally speaking, Snakes tend to be very careful about what they say.

It is never safe to draw a line and predict that this is how far the Snake will go. His computer-like brain never stops plotting and he can be viciously unrelenting. Remember, he is one of the most tenacious signs of the Chinese zodiac.

In his relationships with others, he is possessive, and very demanding. And yet at the same time, he views his associates with a certain distrust. He will never forgive anyone who breaks a promise. He is also prone to being neurotic, even paranoid, where his pet fears and suspicions are concerned.

When the Snake's anger is roused, his hatred can be limitless. His antagonism is silent and deep-rooted. An icy hostility will express his displeasure instead of a volley of hot words. The more lethal types will like to crush their enemies totally. There is no foretelling the Snake's movements. His mind is calculation itself and he has the staying power to wait until the time is ripe for his revenge. For those luckless souls who incur his wrath, self-exile to Siberia may not seem like such a bad prospect.

The Snake lady is the original femme fatale. Her cool, serene and classic beauty will mesmerize people. She is confident and collected and although she oftentimes lolls around, giving the impression of indolence and love of ease, she is far from slothful. Her brain is never at rest.

Despite being finely tuned and high strung by nature, Snake people of both sexes are characterized by beautiful complexions. The Snake-born is usually not ridden with pimples or blemishes even when he or she does not give particular care to their skin. It seems that tension tends to affect the Snake's digestive and nervous systems more than his epidermis. Underneath their flawless good looks, a good many of these natives succumb easily to stomach ulcers or nervous breakdowns from containing all that stress internally.

Ms. Snake will opt for well-cut clothes, fluid and classical in design. She loves jewelry and chooses her accessories with care. If she can afford it, she will buy the real thing: diamonds, pearls, emeralds and rubies of the best quality. Besides being beautiful baubles, jewels are an excellent form of investment. No cheap gold plating or imitations for her, please. She is definitely not a peasant and she would rather go without if she cannot have the real thing. You won't find her decked out in worthless junk.

Her standard for a mate will be similarly high. She admires power and the influence money can bring. When she cannot wield it herself, then the next best thing is to marry it. At any rate, no matter how rich or powerful her man is, she will be his biggest asset once they are married. And should he not have made the grade yet, but has the potential, then the Snake wife will move heaven and earth to make him successful. She will dress the part, play the perfect hostess, while shrewdly pointing out every opportunity to him along the way. With such guidance, dedication and support, there won't be anywhere for him to go but up.

The philosophical Snake woman is never too concerned about the equality of the sexes. You don't find her agonizing over women's rights. Why should she compete when she can so easily entice men to do her bidding? (While allowing them to think it was their idea.) Her legion of male admirers will fall over each other carrying her suitcases, opening doors, lighting her cigarettes, etc.

So you can't blame her if she seems a bit puzzled by all the fuss made over equal rights for men and women. She has always had the secret notion that girls were born superior, although she has never been so stupid as to spill the beans to those unsuspecting squires that court her so lavishly. Why spoil a perfectly workable arrangement? She will humor the guys so long as they give in to her wishes.

Contrary to common belief, Ms. Snake is not always a raving beauty. If you take her feature by feature, you will find she has some flaws, too. Her nose may be too large or her eyes set too close. No, with her it's the total effect that counts. She has her own formula and when she puts it all together—its magic!

See the girl in the striking black number with the diamond brooch pinned strategically on her bosom? Nine out of ten times, she will be a Snake. This lady loves expensive perfume, too, another subtle but effective ploy that is part of the game. But she knows how to use such dynamite sparingly. Just a touch of it here and there. Enough to give her that clinging aura that makes her so alluring and irresistible.

All Snakes have a sense of humor. Of course, they may have different brands. Some prefer to be dry, others sardonic, scintillating, or even diabolical at times. Nonetheless, it's there. The best time to observe this is when he or she is under duress. In a crisis, the Snake can still crack a joke to lighten the atmosphere. Even when he is weighed down by enormous troubles, the Snake-born will not lose that twinkle.

Orientals sometimes regard the Snake as a supernatural creature with a touch of the sinister. This is because he lives for such a long time and renews himself by shedding his skin for a new one each time he outgrows it. This particular trait symbolizes his ability to be reborn and to emerge from conflict with restored vigor.

By now, you must gather that it will be no mean task dealing with the Snake. What makes it even more tricky is the fact that under all that serenity he is always on guard. His outward calm never betrays his true feelings. He knows and plans his moves well in advance. He has willpower and will maintain his position to the bitter end. He can be very evasive and elusive when he chooses and just when you think you have got a grip on him—he wriggles free. Needless to say, he makes the perfect politician. He can negotiate anything under the sun when he puts his mind to it.

The Chinese believe that a Snake born in the Spring and Summer will be among the most deadly of the lot. Winter Snakes are quiet and docile, as this is the time they hibernate. A Snake born during a hot day will be happier and more contented than one born during bad weather.

Snake people are passionate lovers; they are also reputed to have roving eyes. Actually, this is a false reputation which they have acquired because they are always sensual about anything they undertake. He or she may exhibit the same fervent ardor in chasing a much-coveted business deal as in winning the affections of his or her latest heart throb.

Snake people usually lead dangerous lives full of excitement and intrigue, especially those Snakes who have an insatiable lust for power and the limelight.

The best partners for the Snake will be the dependable Ox, the dauntless Rooster or the illustrious Dragon. He could do well teaming up with the Rat, Rabbit, Sheep and Dog, too.

But the Snake should steer clear of the defiant Tiger, who may not appreciate his discerning ways. The impulsive and equally demanding Horse will make only a mediocre match, while the clever Monkey may challenge the Snake with his own brand of cunning. Two snakes could cohabitate peacefully. The Boar and the Snake will not find much in common; the snake is sleek and sophisticated, the boar too honest and mundane. They have entirely opposite compositions.

In times of confusion and trouble, the Snake person is a pillar of strength because he maintains his presence of mind. The Snake can deal with bad news and misfortune with great aplomb. He has a profound sense of responsibility and an unsinkable constancy of purpose. It will be this constancy of purpose coupled with his natural hypnotic charisma that could carry him to the highest realms of power.

THE SNAKE CHILD

The Snake child is a complex personality. Quiet, alert and intelligent, he will have a serious nature and is inclined to be particular. Being the worrying type, he will take on a pensive outlook on life. He is studious and hard working in school and likely to be the teacher's pet. Do not spoil him; the Snake child will be all too aware of his charms. He can be sulky, vindictive and temperamental when not given his way.

Although secretive and brooding by nature, this child will be able to discipline himself. He makes up his mind easily about what he wants and will be very practical in setting his goals. You won't find him reaching for something he knows is unattainable. Persistent, realistic and unrelenting, he will stick to a task until he masters it.

Besides his natural aptitude for learning and a high I.Q., this child has the ability to keep his own counsel. He will not interfere with others and would prefer others to mind their own business, too. Careful and attentive, he knows how to keep himself out of trouble. He may not be very outgoing but he makes long and lasting friendships.

A capable and meticulous planner, this child excels as a leader, as he will use his powers wisely and fairly. Other children will look up to him and support him. However, he could have ulterior motives for some of his actions. He is so intent on being first that he may not care what he has to do in order to be No. 1.

His many talents and natural abilities will make him vastly sought after but he will also be the object of jealousy and vicious lies. He must learn to live with criticism and to bear the risks of being among the elite.

His reticent character makes him hide his pain; he is likely to hold grudges for a long time. He is often misunderstood because he refuses or fails to explain himself properly. His lines of communication with others are sometimes poorly connected.

Whatever happens, the Snake child will always strike out for himself. In life, he will know precisely how to use people and situations to his best advantage. There will be no holding him back; he is destined for fame and fortune.

THE FIVE TYPES OF SNAKES

METAL SNAKE—1881, 1941, 2001

This type of Snake will be gifted with a calculating, intelligent mind and forceful willpower. Armed with discriminating tastes and a keen eye for locating opportunity, this Snake person can be a scheming loner. He likes to move quickly and quietly. He will establish himself in a solid position before you have a chance to stop him.

Metal combined with his native sign will make him crave luxury and easy living. Thus, he will devote himself to the pursuit of wealth and power. His vision is clear and farsighted and he will aspire to the best of everything.

The Metal Snake is also by far the most secretive, evasive and overconfident. Consequently, he often suspects others of hidden motives—sometimes to the point of paranoia.

In spite of his ability to wield power and influence, this Snake will have an envious streak in him and will try constantly to outdo the opposition, either by fair means or foul. He finds it hard to ever accept defeat or failure.

Possessive, domineering and, at times, strangely uncommunicative, he will mark out his path early in life and stick to it with dedication. He can be generous and cooperative with others, but always in a guarded sort of way.

WATER SNAKE—1893, 1953, 2013

Just as water seeps through practically any barrier, so will a Snake born in its year wield encompassing influence through his profound insight.

This unassailable Snake is gifted with strong charisma and an inquisitive nature. Shrewd, business-minded and materialistic, the

Water Snake possesses great mental abilities and powers of concentration. He can block out distraction, and brush aside unimportant issues for effective overall planning. He never loses sight of his goals or gets out of touch with reality.

Artistic and well-read, the intellectual Water Snake is also practical. He is adept at managing people as well as finances. While he may assume an unperturbed appearance, in actuality this particular Snake person has a long memory and harbors lifetime grudges. He could have the patience of Job combined with the bite of a King Cobra.

WOOD SNAKE—1905, 1965, 2025

An earnest Snake with kindly wisdom and a prophetic understanding of what is going to prevail in the course of events, especially in history.

He has a need for complete intellectual freedom, but in his affections he will be constant and enduring. He seeks emotional stability as well as financial security. This type of Snake will express himself well and could be an eloquent speaker.

The Wood element in conjunction with his fixed element of positive Fire will make him very interesting. He will shine like a beacon light, attracting instead of pursuing the objects and people he desires.

He will have expensive habits and could be vain about his personal appearance. Because he craves admiration and public approval, he will do his utmost to achieve lasting and large-scale success.

The Wood Snake is well-informed but he gathers knowledge not for its own sake but to put such information to everyday use. Good judgment, discretion and a sharp sense of values will make him a superb investor and appreciator of the fine things in life. Here is an amenable Snake who will be very close to art, music, the theater and the beauty of the Earth.

FIRE SNAKE—1857, 1917, 1977

An intense and masterful snake. Active in mind and body, he performs energetically. Fire added to the already imposing Snake personality can give him great public appeal and charisma. He exudes confidence and the ability to lead. People will vote for this type of person if he chooses to go into politics.

Although he may hold open forums to solicit or assess the views of the majority, the Fire Snake is terribly suspicious by nature and has total faith only in himself. He is too quick to censure and to condemn. Sometimes he insulates himself with a closed circle of friends and advisors, thereby isolating himself without knowing it. His strong, almost maniacal desire for fame, money and power will make him insist on concrete results. Persevering and uncompromising, he sets his sights on the highest goals and once he gets to the top, he will cling to power indefinitely.

The Fire Snake is the most sensual, fervent and jealous kind of Snake. He will display excessive love or hate and be very preoccupied with himself.

EARTH SNAKE—1869, 1929, 1989

The warm and spontaneous variety of Snake who will form slow but correct opinions of people. More principled, persistent and reliable, the Earth Snake will be able to communicate with the public and function effectively in group activities.

Armed with a peripheral vision and basic Snake ambition, he can take control and bridge gaps during times of confusion and panic. He or she will not be easy to intimidate and may refuse to be influenced by the crowd. This snake reserves the right to pass his own judgment.

By and large, this will be the most graceful and enchanting of all the Snakes. Cool, collected and immensely charming, he will be loyal to friends and have an army of supporters.

Conservative and frugal with money, the hard-working and systematic Earth Snake will succeed in banking, insurance and real estate investments and can reconcile his needs with his resources. Here is a Snake who knows his limits and who will be careful not to overextend himself.

THE SNAKE AND HIS ASCENDANTS

Born During the Hours of the Rat—11 P.M. to 1 A.M.

An affable, sweet-talking Snake that could turn out to be a real hustler. He is sentimental about everything and that includes his money.

Born During the Hours of the Ox—1 A.M. to 3 A.M.

Stubbornness hidden by elusiveness and charm. Twice as formidable to deal with if he has the Ox's stamina and willpower.

Born During the Hours of the Tiger — 3 A.M. to 5 A.M.

A sizzling Snake with a warm and versatile personality. Both signs being suspicious, it will be best for you to ignore his way-out accusations.

Born During the Hour of the Rabbit — 5 A.M. to 7 A.M.

A mellow, smooth-talking Snake, but his bite is just as poisonous. Never makes a bad deal in business.

Born During the Hours of the Dragon — 7 A.M. to 9 A.M.

A Snake with a touch of socialism and philanthropy. With wisdom and power combined, he may instigate real and lasting reforms. His commitment is always total—be it for good or bad.

Born During the Hours of the Snake — 9 A.M. to 11 A.M.

Possessive, enigmatic and very, very deep. You will never figure this one out, so don't bother trying. The only thing you can count on is that when he gets a grip on what he is after, he will never let go.

Born During the Hours of the Horse — 11 A.M. to 1 P.M.

A happy, humorous Snake who will see the brighter side of life. As both signs here are strongly amorous, they could produce a playboy or playgirl of the highest order.

Born During the Hours of the Sheep — 1 P.M. to 3 P.M.

From these two feminine signs may emerge an artistic Snake with impeccable flair. What's more, he knows how to support his expensive tastes. His cunning motives will also be disguised by the Sheep's sweet nature.

Born During the Hours of the Monkey — 3 P.M. to 5 P.M.

A sinewy genius. Incredibly hard to resist. Wisdom, glamor and wit blended to perfection. Never plays a game he cannot win.

Born During the Hours of the Rooster — 5 P.M. to 7 P.M.

The community bandleader type with serious designs on absolute power beneath his gaily decorated front. Very persistent and knowledgeable.

Born During the Hours of the Dog — 7 P.M. to 9 P.M.

A loyal Snake hopefully with more of the Dog's strong convictions and morals. Likely to be highly intellectual as both signs are thinkers.

Born During the Hours of the Boar — 9 P.M. to 11 P.M.

Wine, women and song—here is a Snake who really knows how to live it up,

123

COMPATIBILITY TABLE FOR THE SNAKE

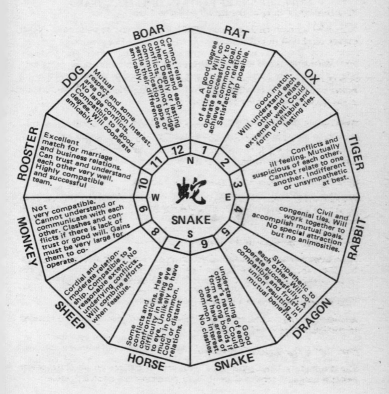

but still shrewd enough never to get duped in his dealings. The Boar's innate goodwill could give him more credibility.

HOW THE SNAKE FARES IN DIFFERENT YEARS

Year of RAT

A year of activity for the Snake. New outlooks and opportunities present themselves. The Snake will make some advancement in career. This will also be a year for dramatic events, both good and bad. His financial gains will balance out his losses and his problems will be solved by goodwill. A time in which he should neither lend nor borrow money.

Year of OX

A moderate year. The Snake can expect people to challenge his decisions this year and some obstacles or financial miscalculations are bound to occur in spite of his inborn cautiousness and intuition. A time to take things in stride and not complicate matters by being obstinate.

Year of TIGER

A year of small but numerous irritations. The Snake may be easily drawn into conflicts not of his own making and will find it hard to please those who surround him at home or at work. He must keep his sense of humor and not indulge in senseless acts of revenge. This way he will receive the help he seeks and avoid major upheavals.

Year of RABBIT

A fairly happy year for the Snake although many commitments keep him very busy. A year of not being able to spend enough time with those he likes because of fulfilling other promises. Money comes and goes easily.

Year of DRAGON

A difficult year in store for the Snake. No sizable gains can be expected in business or career. He must beware of malicious gossip and jealous associates. The worst of his troubles will be over by summer and the cold weather should bring some welcome news. A year to avoid extravagances and hold on to his money.

Year of SNAKE

A fair year for the Snake although he may feel that his achievements are not up to expectations. It is a year for him to bide his time and not make sudden changes. Patience and a cool head are essential if he is to keep himself out of trouble. Business misunderstanding, romantic problems or a slight injury to the body are foreseen. His gains are modest but he is going to be more concerned with securing his position or retaining control.

Year of HORSE

An energetic time for the Snake native. He must refrain from being emotional and hasty if he wants all his hopes to be fulfilled. Unsettled *1990* problems and worries affect his health. All in all, he will succeed admirably this year. His troubles are temporary.

Year of SHEEP

A protected year for the Snake. No great gains but neither are there any sizable losses to be expected. Life could be calm and leisurely if he takes advantage of this time to cultivate influential friends who will benefit him greatly later on. Some sad news or minor inconveniences at home.

Year of MONKEY

A good year as the Snake will find help when he needs it most. He may still be involuntarily drawn into disputes but things will burn themselves out if he does not add fuel to the fire. Still, these adverse conditions may cause undue anxiety. A year to remain conservative or neutral.

Year of ROOSTER

A very auspicious year. The Snake's achievements can be fantastic as he will receive the recognition or promotion he deserves. He will be rewarded for his patience and past perseverance. Profits or some big increase in income can also be expected. Home life is pleasant as the Snake reaps the fruits of his labors.

Year of DOG

Good opportunities present themselves to the Snake. An excellent time to launch new ideas although he may have minor health problems or be the victim of a small robbery. A fine time for the Snake to travel or entertain.

Year of BOAR

A hectic and mixed year. The Snake will have to exert maximum energy for minimum gains. He may suffer financial mishaps caused by poor judgment, a problem with the law or separation from someone close to him. A time to look before he leaps.

FAMOUS PERSONS BORN IN THE YEAR OF THE SNAKE

Metal
Picasso
Carole King
Ann-Margret

Wood
Howard Hughes
Greta Garbo
Seni Pramoj

Earth
Abraham Lincoln
Edgar Allan Poe
King Hassan of Morocco
Jacqueline Onassis
Princess Grace

Water
Brahms
Mao Tse-tung
J. Paul Getty
Mary Pickford

Fire
Schubert
Henry Ford II
Gamal Abdel Nasser
Ferdinand Marcos
John F. Kennedy
Indira Gandhi

Chapter 7
The Horse

I am the Kaleidoscope of the mind.
I impart light, color and perpetual motion.
I think, I see, I am moved by electric fluidity.
Constant only in my inconstancy
I am unshackled by mundane holds,
Unchecked by sturdy, binding goals.
I run unimpeded through virgin paths.
My spirit unconquered—
My soul forever free.

I AM THE HORSE.

THE HORSE SIGN

Chinese name for the Horse: MA
Ranking order: Seventh
Hours ruled by the Horse: 11 A.M. to 1 P.M.
Direction of its sign: Directly South
Season and principal month: Summer—June
Corresponds to the Western sign: Gemini
Fixed element: Fire
Stem: Positive

THE LUNAR YEARS OF THE HORSE IN THE WESTERN CALENDAR

Starting Dates	Ending Dates	Element
January 25, 1906	February 12, 1907	Fire
February 11, 1918	January 31, 1919	Earth
January 30, 1930	February 16, 1931	Metal
February 15, 1942	February 4, 1943	Water
February 3, 1954	January 23, 1955	Wood
January 21, 1966	February 8, 1967	Fire
February 7, 1978	January 27, 1979	Earth
January 27, 1990	February 14, 1991	Metal

If you were born on the day before the start of the lunar year of the Horse, e.g., January 24, 1906, you belong to the animal sign before the Horse—which is the Snake.

If you were born on the day after the lunar year of the Horse, e.g., February 13, 1907, then you belong to the sign following that of the Horse—the Sheep.

THE YEAR OF THE HORSE

A lively and high-spirited year for all. Life will be hectic and punctuated with adventures. People will find themselves reckless, romantic and carefree. A definite time for advancement. We will find it quite agreeable to keep in step with the delightful Horse.

This will be a time when decisions and projects will be incorporated at high speed and with efficiency. Action will be the key word. Everything is on the go and we should take care not to drive ourselves too hard. It will be a rewarding but exhausting year.

Exhilarating yet frustrating at times, this year's pace will tax our reserve energies and leave us feeling depleted. It is a good time for letting off steam and doing all the whimsical things you ever dreamed about. Listen to your senses. The wind may be changing constantly, but once you have picked up the scent, follow your intuitions.

Planning and procrastinating will be shoved aside. The impulsive influence of the Horse, coupled with his self-confidence, will dictate our actions and emotions. Industry, production and the world's economy will be on an upswing. Tempers, too, may be a bit frayed in areas of diplomacy and politics. But good humor will prevail.

Brace yourselves, the volatile Horse will quicken our pulses and bring tension and stress into our everyday lives. The Horse's tempo is fast, his disposition sanguine but erratic. But in spite of everything, we will retain his common sense approach toward money matters. An excellent time to strike out on your own. There will be freedom of movement this year. Be brave, bold and shocking!

THE HORSE PERSONALITY

A person born in this year is said to be cheerful, popular and quick-witted. He has raw sex appeal rather than straight good looks. Earthy and warmly appealing, he is very perceptive and talkative. His changeable nature may lead him to be hot-tempered, rash and headstrong at times. The unpredictable Horse will fall in love easily and fall out of love just as easily.

In most cases the Horse will leave home early. If not, his independent spirit will goad him to start working or to take up some career at an early age. An adventurer at heart, still he is noted for his keen mind and ability to manage money. Self-reliant, vivacious, energetic, impetuous and even brash, the Horse is a showy dresser, partial to bright colors and striking designs to the point of being gaudy on occasion.

The Horse loves exercise, both mental and physical. You can spot him by his rapid but graceful body movements, his animated reflexes and fast away of speaking. He responds quickly and can make snap decisions. His mind works at remarkable speed and whatever he may lack in stability and perseverance, he will certainly make up for by being open-minded and flexible. Basically, he is a nonconformist.

The native of this sign is often called the playboy or playgirl of the cycle. He loves fanfare and being where the action is. Definitely a fun person, he loves to pay compliments as well as receive them. He is just as skillful in business as in love. The quick and nimble Horse appraises situations astutely and is able to manipulate both people and events.

On the negative side, the Horse person is impulsive and stubborn. He has an explosive temper, though he quickly forgets his outbursts. Others, however, do not find them amusing and may not recover as fast. Often this trait will cause him to lose respect and credibility. He tends to rush people and is unhappy when they do not perform as quickly or efficiently as he does. He demands a great deal but is prepared to surrender little, particularly when it comes to his all-important freedom. He can be childish and petty in satisfying his whims and caprices. Often he is forgetful, absentminded and given to jumping to conclusions.

The Horse-born will want things done his way. Self-centered by nature, he likes his home and environment to revolve about him. With his remarkable powers of persuasion, he will set out to sway people to his way of thinking. Snapping his fingers and clicking his heels, this trailblazer can talk you into anything once he begins to dish out that charm. He sells himself as Mr. Personality Plus.

To be able to really understand a Horse, you have to know one thing. He or she firmly believes in "Life, Liberty and the Pursuit of Happiness"—chiefly his own! And if you happen to subscribe to these same things yourself, well, he won't stand in your way. He is not possessive, suspicious or jealous. The Horse only becomes aggressive when he fails to get his way after trying every angle.

His selfishness rarely extends into the monetary or material side of things. It would be more accurate to say that he is selfish with his time, his affection, his concern for others, his willingness to modify his ways in order to suit the group. He doesn't set out to be deliberately inconsiderate or contrary. He just cannot wait for other mortals to catch up to him, to match either his mental speed or hectic physical activity. For this reason, while he may be an outstanding performer, he is a poor teacher.

The Horse's inconsistency stems from his varying moods. He senses nuances that may go unnoticed by everyone else and he modifies his assessments accordingly. In other words, he goes by the feel of things. Don't ask him to explain his hunches and uncanny deductions. He can't. His is the amazing ability to improvise while the game is in progress. Frequently, he will be playing several games at the same time and be more than able to hold his own. Once he makes his swift decision, he does not hesitate on his course of action. You find him either dashing about doing 101 things or flat on his back from sheer exhaustion. More often than most signs, the Horse finds it difficult to unwind and may suffer from insomnia.

He keeps odd hours. A Horse is unable to stick to schedules not of his own making and has a lack of respect for standard procedures. When an idea strikes him, he will work around the clock without eating or sleeping. Then, when things are lax in the office, he is not above taking the day off to play hookey. He needs a stimulating job to display his competence.

He thinks up great promotional ideas, devises dynamic new approaches, solves tricky problems. So, if you have a Horse working for you, give him variety and plenty of rope, send him on missions impossible. His many valuable assets will come to the fore when he is given a free hand. But for goodness sakes, keep him busy. His performance will suffer when a job is undemanding.

When you are talking to a Horse, emulate him. Come to the point quickly, otherwise you will lose whatever fragile hold you may have on his attention. Whether the answer is Yes or No, give it to him directly, without disguise; he is quite able to revise his plans when they meet with opposition or to figure out a different way. Stringing him along will just bring out the worst in him. He will not take offense at frankness and will appreciate your being blunt if it means that you don't want to waste his time.

It would be unfair to ask a Horse to restrain himself unduly, to bottle up his feelings. He has to express himself. If he is forced to hold back his emotions, he may openly revolt—or break out in a rash if he is the silent type. Suspense and strait-jacket procedures will kill him.

The Horse can be a fickle soul. If he cannot be with the one he loves, then why not love the one he is with? Anyhow, there will be little harm in his flirtations: long, drawn-out entanglements do not appeal to him. The Horse knows which side his bread is buttered on. He won't get caught in a one-sided contract unless it happens to be on his side. He has a multitude of friends and makes more and more each day. But he learns never to rely too heavily on any of them.

The Horse could come prancing into your dull existence like a bright summer's day and make an invisible exit the minute you take your eyes off him. Then, just when you will have given up hope of ever hearing from him again, he could come waltzing back and pick up where he left off just as if he had never left.

Quick to warm up and reach top speed, a person born under the Horse sign is equally quick to lose interest. Neither can he sustain a long siege. He certainly won't break down your door like a Dragon. He will leave his card and call another day when you are likely to be more receptive. When the winds of change blow, the Horse will alter his course.

While he may not have long staying powers, you can never be sure when a Horse will resume negotiations on a long-shelved project. His mind is like a jigsaw puzzle; if and when he finds a piece that will fit, he uses it.

Like his best friend, the Tiger, the Horse will sow some pretty wild oats in his heyday. But reminding him of his blunders will be useless. If there is anything this person dislikes, it's to dwell on his mistakes. With a cheerful but contrite "mea culpa," the Horse will shrug and chalk it up to experience. You can't expect him to win them all! Next time, he promises to step more carefully.

The lady Horse is full of spunk. She is tart and saucy; pert and pretty; nimble on her toes and intelligent. She could be a chatterbox without reprieve, a tennis champion or a Grand Prix driver.

She can do her nails, write a letter, watch TV, talk on the phone and mind the children, all at the same time. Her ideas for relaxing can be taxing. She works off her energy with play that could seem like hard labor to the rest of us. Did anyone mention climbing Mt. Everest? Give her two minutes to pack—she will join the expedition.

The Horse lady loves to get things done. She would be in ten places at the same time if she could. Sometimes, one could swear that she is competing with herself. There isn't anyone else around who can do so much so fast.

Horse girls may look as soft as whipped cream and will usually smell as fresh as lavender, but underneath it all, they have razor-sharp minds that match their agile bodies. She may be the kindly brown-mare type or the firebrand who tosses her hair defiantly against handling, but she'll never lose that talent for assessment. She makes friends easily and will take her romantic involvements lightly. Home is a practical, easy and well-located station where she can refuel and take stock of her situation. But you won't find her parked in one place permanently.

She will love crispness, greenness and outdoor sights and sounds. She refreshes herself in a thousand ways. The ocean's roar, the rustle of the trees, the magic of the woods, the majesty of the mountains, will all call to her sense of adventure. When she takes off, she isn't being unfaithful or unreliable. It's just her nature to respond to such exciting stimuli. If you love her and want to keep her, don't fence her in.

Horses of both sexes will accumulate wealth but not security. They don't care that much for security so they won't be missing all that much. They have an inclination to oversell, to stretch the truth, to ad lib with little white lies, all of which in their eyes are not faults but by-products of their creative imagination. They are not timid about taking the lead, and will run themselves out, so to speak, before stopping to listen to advice.

Orientals believe that whatever unbridled passions the Horse possesses, they will be multiplied many times over when he or she is born in the year of the Fire Horse, which comes once in every sixty-year cycle. The last Fire Horse year was in 1966 and it will not come again until the year 2026. In days of old (when liberated and overly assertive women were frowned upon as troublemakers and difficult to marry off) it was considered most unlucky to have a daughter born in this year.

Legend has it that the Fire Horse will consume everything in his path and wreak havoc wherever he goes. Many a lady Fire Horse, so they say, has ruined the life of a good man simply because of her passionate nature.

The male Fire Horse is not always considered as bad; he may even be fortunate as he can bring distinction on himself and be credited with famous as well as infamous deeds. The Horse, of course, like the Dragon and the Tiger, is identified as a strong masculine sign.

However, the fame and fortune of the Fire Horse, as well as Horses of other elements, seldom benefit their immediate family, especially as they usually leave home early. Leonid Brezhnev, King Faisal of Saudi Arabia and Otto Preminger (all born 1906) are but some examples of modern-day Fire Horses. Aristotle Onassis gave his year of birth as 1905, but some historians put it in 1906, as he is said to have made himself a year older when he left home in order to get a job. Looking into his biography and phenomenal life style, I am willing to wager that he was indeed a Fire Horse instead of a Snake.

The animated and affable Horse is said to be very susceptible to the perils of love. He could easily lose everything if he falls head over heels in love. Consequently, he may have many affairs that end unhappily or even several marriages and divorces.

A Horse born in the summer will lead a better life than a winter Horse. His best stage in life will come during his middle age when he is mature enough to grudgingly accept the shackles of responsibility.

The best partners for the Horse will be the Tiger, Dog and Sheep. The next best matches will be with Dragons, Snakes, Monkeys, Rabbits, Boars, Roosters or another Horse.

The Horse will not fall for the Rat, who will not like the Horse's shifting ways either. He could also come into direct conflict in his dealings with the rigid Ox people. The Ox will demand consistency and the Horse cannot and will not comply.

THE HORSE CHILD

A child born in the Horse year will be animated, boisterous and mercurial. He or she will have a passionate love of life and a buoyant personality. He likes to do things quickly and will be able to learn new things easily. (Many horse youngsters are also born left-handed.) This child will tend to be disobedient, stubborn and willful when held back, but he is not the whining, crybaby type. This sprighty little fellow will love the outdoors and should be allowed plenty of exercise and independence—otherwise he will just take it.

Although he may roam the neighborhood and indulge in all sorts of rough games, he will always find his way home at meal time. He will be plagued by a restless and searching spirit and needs to be constantly occupied.

He will walk and talk early and will resent parents who restrict him too much. He is affectionate and demonstrative but won't like too much cuddling. Constrict him with rules, regulations and demanding schedules and he will bolt. A happy-go-lucky daredevil, he does things on the spur of the moment.

It would be well to discipline the Horse child as he should learn to control his volatile temper and impulsive ways. Self-centered as he is, the realistic Horse will conform and adapt himself once he sees that there is no other way out.

No doubt this adventurous little person will get himself into countless predicaments, but he won't be needing you to bail him out. He is quite capable of getting himself out of danger. Although he does not deliberately look for trouble, he does not scare easily and will like to fight his own battles.

All in all, the colorful and lively personality of the Horse will perk up any household.

THE FIVE TYPES OF HORSES

METAL HORSE—1870, 1930, 1990

A popular but peripatetic and unruly type of Horse. Demonstrative, impetuous and bold, he will be a most engaging personality. He is highly amorous and very appealing to the opposite sex.

Gifted with a prolific mind and fine intuition, he can be extremely productive when he is positive. It will be difficult trying to keep up with him as he seems to be everywhere at the same time.

Blessed with strong recuperative powers, the Metal Horse is never out of action for long. He is constantly seeking excitement and climbing to breathtaking heights.

Metal will make this Horse more stubborn and self-centered than other types of Horses. He may be a proverbial bubbling stream filled with brilliant ideas but he is not a consistent administrator. If his work gives him no satisfaction, no fun, no rewarding stimulation, he will become irresolute and irresponsible. He cannot exist on a diet of daily routine. Nor can he function with someone glancing over his shoulder.

He thirsts constantly for new experiences and challenges. When he is negative, he will have an irrational need for liberty and be unable to establish deep personal involvements for fear they may curtail his freedom or make demands on his time.

WATER HORSE—1882, 1942, 2002

A cheerful, dapper Horse with excellent business acumen, but inordinately concerned with his own well-being, status and comfort. He is very adaptable to change and can make extensive adjustments without batting an eyelash.

This nomadic type of Horse could be more restless than the others. A travel bug and sports enthusiast, he won't let any grass grow under his feet.

He could also have the habit of changing his mind frequently and may take up an entirely different course of action without bothering to give any explanation. His mind and movements are guided by sporadic bursts of nervous but inspired action.

He will have a delicious sense of humor and can be very amusing when he wants to be. A smart and colorful dresser, he can discourse on any subject with anyone.

When he is negative, he is pretentious and inconsistent and can exhibit a deplorable lack of consideration for others. The Water Horse must develop long-range planning and dedication.

WOOD HORSE—1894, 1954, 2014

Friendly, cooperative and less impatient, this type of Horse could be the most reasonable of the lot. But he will still resist being dominated. The Wood element enables him to discipline his mind better and he will be capable of clear and systematic thinking. The Wood Horse will have a happy disposition and be very active in social affairs. Amusing and a good conversationalist, he is not overly egoistical and will not constantly vie for the headlines.

But, as he is progressive, modern and unsentimental, he will throw out the old and welcome in the new. Changes and new inventions capture his imagination and he will not shrink from trying the unconventional.

He will like to explore many other fields but will try hard to fulfill his reponsibilities first. The strong, high-spirited and sanguine Wood Horse does not have a lazy bone in his body, but he would do well to learn to be more cautious and discerning.

FIRE HORSE—1906, 1966, 2026

A flamboyant and itinerant Horse with a superb intellect and great personal magnetism. He tries to bring about the changes he desires through force and sheer willpower.

This is a double Fire sign (Fire also being the Horse's fixed element), and it will produce a native who is highly excitable and hotblooded.

The Fire Horse is easily distracted and is too inconsistent to stick to repetitive tasks. He has flair, wit and charm but his continuous stream of bright ideas makes him extremely volatile. His personality is many-faceted and he requires a great deal of spice and variety in his life. He is happiest leading a double or triple life or having several professions to his credit.

He will love to travel, anticipates action and change and works most efficiently when put in charge. He rarely accepts supervision from others, even his superiors.

The Fire Horse is a thrill-seeker. He can sort out and deal with all kinds of people and situations within a minute's notice. He is skillful at resolving sticky affairs but is not above being argumentative.

This type of Horse will have the gifts of ingenuity and resourcefulness but not perseverance.

EARTH HORSE—1918, 1978, 2038

A happy, congenial Horse; more precise and slow moving. He is apt to be more logical but less decisive. He likes to consider all sides of a question before acting.

With Earth as his element, he will be less abrupt. He can settle down and learn to toe the line when necessary. He offers less resistance to authority. Still, he is a finely tuned animal with an ability to sniff out feasible investments. He can bring shaky business back to life and give impetus to lagging industries.

Although he is the look-before-you-leap type, he is, nonetheless, very capricious about little things and will not make up his mind easily. He may hedge on one occasion and then take on more than he can handle on another.

THE HORSE AND HIS ASCENDANTS

Born During the Hours of the Rat — 11 P.M. to 1 A.M.

A merry-making, more companionable Horse with the affectionate Rat in him. Both signs are good at acquiring and handling money.

Born During the Hours of the Ox — 1 A.M. to 3 A.M.

A serious, perhaps even consistent Horse after the Ox gets through toning down his restlessness. Could stick to one thing at a time and will not fall madly in love so easily.

Born During the Hours of the Tiger — 3 A.M. to 5 A.M.

A good combination of daring and skill. The Tiger has the daring, the Horse the ability to steer out of trouble. Now, if only the doubting Tiger will follow the Horse's uncanny hunches.

Born During the Hours of the Rabbit — 5 A.M. to 7 A.M.

A horse with a touch of moderation in his actions. His rich and sometimes vulgar tastes will be reduced by the Hare's discerning preferences.

Born During the Hours of the Dragon— 7 A.M. to 9 A.M.

A race Horse who can't help winning or stop running for that matter. Too powerful for inexperienced hands to handle. He also has the tendency to overreact!

Born During the Hours of the Snake — 9 A.M. to 11 A.M.

Let's hope the Snake can distill some of his wisdom into this Horse. The result will be that he may move slower but is more assured of success with the Snake's guidance.

Born During the Hours of the Horse — 11 A.M. to 1 P.M.

A thoroughbred who really knows his business. He may have a very restless and fidgety nature, but he moves with amazing grace. But he is also conceited and insufferably capricious.

Born During the Hours of the Sheep — 1 P.M. to 3 P.M.

A Horse that is less boisterous, with some of the Sheep's harmonious and compassionate ways. Still flirtatious and fun-loving.

Born During the Hours of the Monkey — 3 P.M. to 5 P.M.

A strong alliance of agility and wits. Both signs are egoistic and swift. He will always strike out for himself. A glib talker you will find hard to pin down.

Born During the Hours of the Rooster — 5 P.M. to 7 P.M.

A competent and perceptive Horse with an ultrasunny disposition. With the Rooster's dauntless outlook on life, he will never feel the need to worry.

Born During the Hours of the Dog — 7 P.M. to 9 P.M.

A more faithful and honest Horse. But both signs here are practical, agile and mentally sharp; this may make him condescending, impatient and easily agitated.

Born During the Hours of the Boar — 9 P.M. to 11 P.M.

A more steadfast and cooperative Horse with some of the Boar's sincerity. He may be less shifty but, at times, he is also too complacent.

HOW THE HORSE FARES IN DIFFERENT YEARS

Year of RAT

A difficult year for the Horse. Problems and unhappy romantic involvements. He must steer clear of confrontation, especially with the law. Some monetary troubles in the family. A time for the Horse to be cautious and persevering. Should not lend or borrow money.

Year of OX

Life will be smoother for the Horse in the year of the Ox. He will still have to work hard to achieve his goals but he will be given the power to control his own situation. Few untoward incidents and some monetary gains are in store for him. Problems tend to come from children or subordinates.

Year of TIGER

A moderately happy year for the Horse. No health problems but a lot of entertainment and additional expenses foreseen. Advancement in his studies or on the technical side of his profession can be expected. Disputes or broken friendships could result from his losing his temper this year.

Year of RABBIT

A lucky year for the Horse, especially in his investments. His life will be smooth but very involved. He can expect happy news or new members in the family. A protected year in which he can venture anywhere and encounter few problems.

COMPATIBILITY TABLE FOR THE HORSE

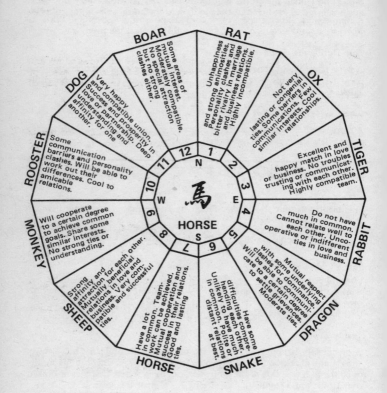

BOAR — Some areas of mutual interest. Moderately compatible. Moderate attraction but no strong clashes either.

RAT — Unhappiness and strong animosities. Personality clashes, bitter rivalry and business relations. Highly incompatible.

OX — Not very lasting or congenial ties. Some barriers in communications. Few similar interests. Cool relationships.

TIGER — Excellent and happy match in love or business. No troubles trusting or communicating with each other. Highly compatible team.

RABBIT — Do not have much in common. Cannot relate well to each other. Unco-operative or indifferent ties in love and business.

DRAGON — Mutual respect with some underlying clashes for dominance. Will be able to relate to a certain degree to settle grievances. Moderate ties.

SNAKE — Have some difficulties comprehending each other, tending to have much in common. Unlikely to have a polite or distant. relations at best.

HORSE — Have a lot in common. Team-work can be achieved. Mutual cooperation and success in their relations. Good and lasting ties.

SHEEP — Strong affinity and attraction for each other. Mutually beneficial relations in love and business. Very compatible and successful ties.

MONKEY — Will cooperate to a certain degree to achieve common goals. Share some similar interests. No strong ties or understanding.

ROOSTER — Some communication barriers and personality clashes. Will be able to work out their differences. Cool to amicable relations.

DOG — Very happy and compatible union in success and prosperity in love or partnership. Deep understanding and affinity for one another.

HORSE

馬

N
E
S
W

12 1 2 3 4 5 6 7 8 9 10 11

Year of DRAGON

A mixed year. Many unsteady and unsettled affairs try the Horse's patience and worries weigh upon his mind, causing health problems. He must not expect the worst. The storm will blow itself out and there may not be as much damage as predicted. A time to look to the bright side of life, cultivate friends and placate enemies.

Year of SNAKE

A busy, involved year that brings taxing demands on the Horse's time and energy. Difficulties come from partners or friends and delays are caused by unseen obstacles. He will find support in his family but cannot expect a great deal of achievement in spite of all his efforts.

Year of HORSE

A good and prosperous year for the Horse. Recognition or promotion brings him satisfaction and happiness. Plans are realized without much effort and he will be lucky playing his hunches. A year in which the Horse is also susceptible to contagious disease, so he must not visit sick people or expose himself unnecessarily. He must not break friendships or partnerships this year.

Year of SHEEP

A moderate year for the Horse. Changes in residence or a long trip are indicated. The good balances out the bad this year and no serious problems or worries affect him.

Year of MONKEY

A lucky year for the Horse, as sudden gains or unlikely benefits are foreseen. He will be able to find whatever he is searching for, but he must also be careful about freak accidents that are likely to occur. There may be sad news in the family, but the troubles of others will not affect him personally.

Year of ROOSTER

A fair year. Good tidings at home but slight disturbances in career. The problems he encounters will not be large ones but they may slow down his progress and he will tend to get upset too easily.

Year of DOG

A good year for the Horse academically. He could pass exams with honors or be given a job he has sought after. Important people will notice him. A lawsuit in the family or the departure of a loved one is indicated. No health problems or financial setbacks are foreseen.

Year of BOAR

Not-so-favorable year as some of the Horse's success is destroyed by outside interference and illness delays plans and progress. Investments and projects develop snags and he must deal with many complications. His troubles should start to fade with the onset of winter.

FAMOUS PERSONS BORN IN THE YEAR OF THE HORSE

Metal
Neil Armstrong
Lord Snowdon

Water
F. D. Roosevelt
Ulysses S. Grant
Barbra Striesand
Paul McCartney
Raquel Welsh

Fire
Rembrandt
Leonid Brezhnev
Roberto Rosselini
King Faisal
Otto Preminger
Agnes Moorehead

Wood
Duke of Windsor
Nikita Khrushchev
Chris Evert
Patty Hearst

Earth
Theodore Roosevelt
Kurt Waldheim
Pearl Bailey
Aleksandr Solzhenitsyn
Helmut Schmidt
Leonard Bernstein
Billy Graham
Anwar Sadat

Chapter 8
The Sheep

I am nature's special child.
I trust and am rewarded by trust.
Fortune smiles upon my countenance.
All things blossom
In the gentleness of my love.
I strive to find beauty in all I behold.
I am fair of face
And full of grace.

I AM THE SHEEP.

THE SHEEP SIGN

Chinese name for the Sheep: YÁNG
Ranking order: Eighth
Hours ruled by the Sheep: 1 P.M. to 3 P.M.
Direction of its sign: South-Southwest
Season and principal month: Summer—July
Corresponds to the Western sign: Cancer
Fixed element: Fire
Stem: Negative

THE LUNAR YEARS OF THE SHEEP IN THE WESTERN CALENDAR

Starting Dates	Ending Dates	Element
February 13, 1907	February 1, 1908	Fire
February 1, 1919	February 19, 1920	Earth
February 17, 1931	February 5, 1932	Metal
February 5, 1943	January 24, 1944	Water
January 24, 1955	February 11, 1956	Wood
February 9, 1967	January 29, 1968	Fire
January 28, 1979	February 15, 1980	Earth
February 15, 1991	February 3, 1992	Metal

If you were born on the day before the start of the lunar year of the Sheep, e.g., February 12, 1907, you belong to the animal sign before the Sheep—which is the Horse.

If you were born on the day after the lunar year of the Sheep, e.g., February 2, 1908, then you belong to the sign following that of the Sheep—the Monkey.

THE YEAR OF THE SHEEP

This is a smooth year following that of the energetic Horse. A year to relax and make peace with oneself as well as with others. Things progress slowly and we find ourselves more sentimental and emotional. The Sheep's influence will draw us closer to home and our families. We find ourselves caring more about those close to us and being more liberal with our time and money.

Patron of the arts, the Sheep will bring out all the creativeness in our natures. We will be productive and imaginative in artistic and aesthetic ventures. The pessimistic vibrations cast by him will also make us oversensitive and fretful of little problems. In our undertakings, we may become easily discouraged or hypercritical when things are not to our liking.

On the world scene, things will be tranquil and subdued. Take time off to cater to your whims and fancies. Make new friends and travel; invest in art and antiques. But keep a tight hand on your purse string, too, as there could be repercussions caused by overspending.

Hopefully, the Sheep's love of harmony and keen sense for coexisting with his enemies will preserve this year from many upheavals. The moderates and doves will be heard and heeded. Wars, international conflicts and mutual animosities usually end in the year of the Sheep.

The serenity of the Sheep's peaceful ways will slow things down a bit for the more intensely active signs, but after all, this is not a year for whirlwind activities—it is one for introspection.

THE SHEEP PERSONALITY

This is the most feminine sign of the Chinese zodiac. A person of the Sheep year is called the good Samaritan of the cycle. He is righteous, sincere and easily taken in by sob stories. He is likely to be mild-mannered, even shy. At his best, he is artistic, fashionable and a creative worker. At his worst, he tends to be easily overcome by his emotions, pessimistic and withdrawn.

The Sheep is known for his gentle and compassionate ways. He can forgive easily and be understanding about others' faults. He dislikes strict schedules and cannot take too much discipline or criticism. Fond of children and animals, he is close to nature and a general homebody. The Sheep is apt to mother or even smother the objects of his affections. He is possessed by varying moods and finds it impossible to work under pressure. He also finds it difficult to be objective.

The subdued outer appearance of the Sheep belies his inner determination. When threatened, he can respond passionately and firmly even though he detests fighting. Caught in an argument, he would rather sulk than come right out and tell you what he is upset about. His stony silence and pouting will probably achieve more than angry words and he will eventually have his way. As a child, most often he will be spoiled by one or both of his parents.

The Chinese believe that good fortune smiles on the Sheep because of his pure nature and kind heart. He is generous with his time as well as his money. When you have nowhere to go and no money, you can be sure the Sheep will not turn you away. He will always have the three most important things in life: food, shelter and clothing. Wherever he goes, he is bound to meet people who can and will assist him. A person of this sign will make it a point to marry well and will be cherished not only by his mate, but his in-laws as well.

It is said that a Sheep person born in the winter will have a hard life because in this season there is an absence of grass and it is the time Sheep are generally slaughtered for food. However, even in the roughest circumstances, the Sheep will still possess his three basic necessities and people will care deeply for him. His is the eighth sign, and to the Chinese the number 8 symbolizes prosperity and comfort.

He has fantastic luck; people often leave him money in their wills and even the poorest of these natives will be able to inherit something of value from their parents or relations. Admirers present the Sheep with expensive presents and rich and powerful patrons take him under their wing. Famous personalities will adopt him and take him as their protégé. Somehow the fortunate sheep will always have things made easier for him. His every fall will be cushioned by those who look out for his interests.

Yes, the Sheep can be ingratiating when it comes to currying favors. Consequently, like the Rabbit, he will obtain his wishes without force or violence. He will have great passive endurance and will wear you down with pleas and entreaties. You will never know his mettle until you try to break him. He isn't that warm and woolly after all. Basically a survivor, the Sheep will know how to placate or evade his enemies. Failing that, he'll run home crying and get his big brother to beat you to a pulp.

The Sheep's oblique approach can be positively infuriating to natives of more direct lunar signs. Admittedly, his roundabout ways can be quite tiresome, but that is the way he is. The lower type of Sheep can be so theatrical at times that he can drive you up the wall. Don't expect him to come right out and say exactly what is troubling him. There is no fun for him in being so blunt and brazen. You must be prepared to pry it out of him bit by bit. Entice him with rewards. Promise that you won't be angry. Humor him. Give him a wide margin and lots of sympathetic nods. He has little sense of time, so you will probably have to rearrange your other appointments, too. Finally, if all else fails, go ahead and bully him, bang the table (he will be impressed), stomp around the room, act like an ogre, but never stop showing that you love and care about him. Then he will come up with the secret hurts he has been nursing for weeks and the two of you will be able to clear the air.

At times, it will be advantageous for the kindly Sheep to have bossy, strong associates. Managers who will both discipline him and put his talents to use. Tough secretaries and even tougher chaperones who will turn down all those unreasonable demands made on his good nature. In short, people to insulate him from being hassled, from playing host to human parasites.

The Sheep never really cuts his umbilical cord. He will always come home to mother and his favorite apple pie. He never forgets birthdays, anniversaries and special occasions. And he will make it a point to celebrate these days ostentatiously (especially when he is not footing the bill). But he is equally sensitive about his own special dates, too. Woe to you if you forgot his birthday or neglected to pay him a visit or send him a get-well card (at the very least) that week he was in the hospital. As far as he is concerned, you practically broke his poor heart in two and he will probably be scarred by this for the rest of his life.

The Sheep is basically a worrier. He tends to be pessimistic about events and is prone to predict the worst. Of course, he expects you to vehemently dispel his dark thoughts and he will make sure that there is always someone around to cheer him up. It's useless to cry alone. He'd rather have an audience, please. Misfortunes touch him deeply and he does not get over hardships easily. Lest others forget, he will also take to recounting his miseries ad infinitum. Another one of his shortcomings is that he has difficulty in denying himself anything. He always overspends and should avoid handling his own finances. An extreme type of Sheep may spread cash around as if he were personally obliged to circulate the currency for the Treasury Department.

The Sheep damsel is inclined to like dainty things and will vote for all the frills and trimmings that come along with them. She is decidedly coquettish and may spend hours on her toilette. She rarely arrives on time for anything, and acts as fragile as bone china. She'll move like a princess and may have a fresh rose on her desk every morning, to remind her (and you) that she enjoys being a girl. The Sheep lady will be spanking clean; she is most concerned with personal hygiene, even though her house may be a mess and she doesn't know where anything is. The more aloof types will be preoccupied by sanitary standards. Her children will be scrubbed clean and always look presentable. She has flawless taste in choosing clothes and likes smart accessories.

She will be good at costuming, window dressing, doing stage sets. Disorganized and scatter-brained as she may appear, everything will fall perfectly into place at the last minute, and she will confound all her critics.

The Sheep girl will openly show her favoritism and will consort day in and day out with those she dubs her special people, her confidants. If she doesn't love you, well, don't complain. At least she will just ignore you without trying to reform you or come after you with a cudgel like a Dragon or an Ox lady. Hers is the voice of gentle persuasion. She'll twist your arm, but in the most engaging manner. For her, half the fun will be the "getting there," the flirting, the cajoling. Her "Yes" could always mean "No" and her "No" could mean "Maybe." If you are a knight in shining armor and you want to win this fair maiden, it will always be worth the challenge to find out.

All Sheep people, from nine to ninety, are diehard romantics. Soft music, moonlight and intimate candlelit dinners never fail to work their magic on them.

A person born under this sign will have the beguiling knack of turning his very weakness into strength. He knows how to get what he wants by insinuations and subtle hints. He is master of the soft-sell technique, so don't ever underestimate him or you will be caught off-guard. His sedate, earnest and sometimes whimpering ways have proven effective in wearing down the strongest defenses. He can plead his case so convincingly with unfeigned emotions that sometimes he doesn't even have need for many words.

The Sheep will come up with preposterous requests, bordering on blackmail and highway robbery. And just when you are about to smack him down with a loud, resounding "No," you notice that chaste and innocent look on his face, that tear hanging from the corner of his eye, the slight quivering of his lips, and suddenly you feel like some horrible monster taking a lamb to the slaughter. Needless to say, you reluctantly give your consent to his ludicrous demands, still not clear on why or how such a harmless-looking, vulnerable creature could do you in. Case closed.

Certainly not one to make decisions, the Sheep would rather follow and complain when things do not turn out right. Yet, people will sincerely love him as he is so good-natured and is kind enough to share whatever he has. He or she will be very close to the family and will overindulge them.

As the Sheep person will never like to deliberately displease those he loves, he may float about doing nothing in order to avoid conflict and be criticized in the end for failing to take a firm stand on issues. He is difficult to deal with as he is supersensitive, and given to excessive self-pity and even tears.

Appreciation of his talents will make the Sheep blossom spectacularly. He craves love, attention and approval—in that order. He should go into any creative field where he excels, and be given a free hand to do what pleases him most. Where beauty is concerned, don't worry, the Sheep will not disappoint you. He has very discriminating taste and discerning preferences. Then again, it is only fair to warn you that he also tends to spend a lot and may not be very practical.

Unless he was born at the time of day governed by a strong sign such as a Dragon, Snake or Tiger, he should not take on jobs with too much responsibility or decision-making. Being passive by nature, he shuns confrontation and law enforcement.

On the whole, it can be said that the Sheep will not have to work hard for a living. Good things come to him naturally, which is perfect, as he loves luxury and ease. Like his best friend, the Rabbit, he has the soul of a connoisseur. Anything ugly or lowly depresses him. He is so sensitive to beauty and balance that his moods are largely governed by his surroundings. He functions best in bright, airy and tastefully appointed rooms.

In his life he will need strong and loyal people to lean on. The outgoing and optimistic characteristics of the Horse, Boar and Tiger will complement his personality. He will also find perfect harmony with the Rabbit. Monkey, Dragon, Rooster, Snake or another Sheep will do very nicely together, too.

The Rat will dislike the Sheep's spendthrift ways and lack of self-denial. The Sheep will not find sympathy or happiness with the stern people of the Ox year or the practical Dog persons, who will have no patience to listen to the Sheep's petty woes.

THE SHEEP CHILD

The gentle Sheep child will be a treasure to his parents. He will love being cuddled, fussed over, petted and thoroughly spoiled. A sensitive artist and lover of beauty, he will appreciate music, poetry, sweet-smelling soap for his bath and all sorts of delicate trimmings that stimulate his fine senses. Ultradependent, he won't like to do anything for himself—if he can help it. Warm, soft, vulnerable and submissive, he likes being catered to.

Like little Linus in the Peanuts comic strip, he is most likely to cling to his old woolen blanket or, in case of a girl, her worn-out rag doll. He hates being teased and if strongly criticized or embarrassed in school, he may not want to return for many days. He will seek out more dominant youngsters to take him under their wings. When he is feeling down, he will need loads and loads of sympathy to pep him up. His fertile imagination and morbid fears can actually make him ill. He can be easily influenced or adversely affected and will positively drown you with his sorrows when he is in a melancholy mood.

When ridiculed or rejected, he can withdraw into a magical world of his own and it will be difficult to lure him out. Food and comfort represent love and security to him. The Sheep will be in no hurry to leave home if he is loved and well cared for. When he does decide to set up housekeeping on his own, you can be sure he will do it with exquisite taste. He loves getting dressed up and has a flair for arranging things. Fickle-minded, inconsistent and trivial at times, he makes up for it by being extremely creative, modest and patient. He is very compassionate about the sorrows of others; when he is fond of someone, his love and generosity know no bounds. It will be rewarding to care for him as he will repay your affections a hundred-fold. It will be impossible to be cross with him for long. He may have his flaws, but he is still a jewel of the highest quality.

Don't be afraid of leading him by the hand or helping him make decisions. He will never get enough reassurance and, as a matter of fact, he may seek his parents' advice or approval on everything he does.

Don't try to wipe the fairy dust off his eyes; or change him, mend him or rearrange him into sterner stuff. It will be useless, as the Sheep will always see life and the world through rose-colored glasses.

THE FIVE TYPES OF SHEEP

METAL SHEEP—1871, 1931, 1991

The Metal Sheep will have great faith in himself and know the value of his talents. He can camouflage his high degree of sensitivity by putting up a brave front, although actually he has a very vulnerable ego and is easily offended by offhand remarks.

Metal reinforces his flowing artistic tastes and he will be inspired to search continuously for beauty in all forms. His home could be a masterpiece of interior decoration, as he is most concerned about harmony and balance in his daily life. Leaving a familiar environment can be traumatic for him; he will find it hard to adjust to change.

This type of Sheep will also aspire to security in both his domestic and financial life. His services won't come cheap, although he is not averse to handing out free meal tickets now and then.

His social activities will be limited to those people he cherishes or those who could be of use to his career. The uninitiated will have to wait for him to warm up to their advances.

Beneath his calm and helpful exterior, the Metal Sheep has unstable emotions that he finds hard to control. As a result, he can be possessive, jealous and overprotective of his loved ones. He should allow people about him more freedom. Expecting everyone to be at his beck and call will only cause resentment, as well as resistance to the invaluable contributions he could make.

WATER SHEEP—1883, 1943, 2003

This type of Sheep will be extremely appealing to others. There may be dozens of people around who will want to mother him, and if he is in need of help—he can summon an army.

Popular but not really knowledgeable, meek but innately opportunistic, the Water Sheep will seek out people he can rely on. When Water is joined with his basic sign, it encourages him to travel the route of the least resistance. He is impressionable and will always go along with the wishes of the majority or those who have strong influence on him. But while he may readily absorb the ideas of others, he will still cling to what he is accustomed to. He fears changes in his life style and will not be too crazy about exploring the unknown.

Although he has a diversified personality and can mix well with almost anyone, he also has a martyrdom complex and will feel rejected and persecuted whenever he is not allowed to have his way.

WOOD SHEEP—1895, 1955, 2015

A thoughtful, good-humored Sheep, with leisurely ways, but mindful of other people's wishes. He is sentimental and strives to please; with Wood as his element he will be prevented from being too flippant. His nature will be steadier and more generous and he will have high moral principles.

This loving sheep will have complete trust in those he believes in. He will put his life in their hands with the faith of a child. Even while he knows his intrinsic worth, this Sheep allows others to take advantage of him. He capitulates too readily when harassed and makes unwise sacrifices for the sake of keeping the peace.

The Wood Sheep has the tendency to mother others and can be most devoted to those he cares about. He will be overwhelmed by the circumstances of those less fortunate than himself and may have a collection of human as well as animal strays to feed.

His good deeds and compassion will not go unrewarded. Because he won't mind supporting others, money will always come to him when he is in need. He will receive financial help or inherit money from unlikely sources.

FIRE SHEEP—1907, 1967, 2027

The Fire Sheep is sure-footed; he is more courageous about following his intuitions and he will take the initiative in his work.

His creativity lies in his ability to dramatize rather than invent. He can highlight strong points and play down weaknesses. Even experimenting with vivid colors, he can still produce restful and pleasant compositions.

He would like to own a stately home if possible, because he is indulgent where his personal comforts are concerned and he likes to entertain lavishly. Consequently, he is likely to overextend himself financially and mismanage his own affairs.

Fire makes him very energetic and aggressive. He is outspoken when offended. He will exhibit an enticing personal grace but his emotionalism could, at times, defy logic.

When the Fire Sheep is negative, he is given to wistful thinking without realizing the benefits of his present situation. He reaches for the proverbial pie in the sky and will be sullen and spiteful when discouraged by reality.

EARTH SHEEP—1859, 1919, 1979

This type of Sheep is optimistic and more self-reliant. Inspite of his strong attachments to the domestic scene and devoted loyalty to family members, he will still try to maintain a certain degree of independence.

Earth as his element makes him conservative and careful. He won't like to waste money but he won't be counting the pennies either. But being a sheep, he will still find it difficult to deny himself. What may appear as luxuries to other people will be bare necessities to him.

However, just as he plays hard, the Earth Sheep will work hard. He can take his responsibilities seriously and will go out of his way to help his friends. It is unlikely that he will ever turn his back on someone in trouble.

Although he may be more adept at concealing his emotions, this particular Sheep is also prone to being neurotic and ultradefensive when criticized.

THE SHEEP AND HIS ASCENDANTS

Born During the Hours of the Rat — 11 P.M. to 1 A.M.

An opportunistic and crafty Sheep. Both signs here are emotional and self-indulgent. But the rat's presence could make him more dependable and less inclined to fall apart during a crisis.

Born During the Hours of the Ox – 1 A.M. to 3 A.M.

A Sheep who radiates charm mixed with the Buffalo's rugged authority. Punctual, conservative and more set in his ways.

Born During the Hours of the Tiger – 3 A.M. to 5 A.M.

Feline impetuosity accentuated by the Sheep's exquisite but whimsical ways. Creative, innovative and great on the stage, but his temperamental side makes him volatile and undependable.

Born During the Hours of the Rabbit – 5 A.M. to 7 A.M.

A clever but unobtrusive Sheep who is not as charitable as he pretends to be. Cannot be counted on to commit himself readily to anything which involves a great deal of work or sacrifice. Shuns too much involvement.

Born During the Hours of the Dragon – 7 A.M. to 9 A.M.

A Sheep with great determination. The Dragon in him imparts the much needed courage and conviction for him to carry out his ideas and plans. But the Sheep here still has a strong need for adulation and appreciation.

Born During the Hours of the Snake – 9 A.M. to 11 A.M.

A Sheep with great potential and a fine, uncluttered mind. The Snake makes him self-assured and competent. He can make up his own mind and keep his emotions to himself.

Born During the Hours of the Horse – 11 A.M. to 1 P.M.

A Sheep who may really like to swing. Very expressive, expensive and fanciful. The popular Horse in him will be in hot pursuit of money while the dominant Sheep side will certainly know how to dole it out.

Born During the Hours of the Sheep – 1 P.M. to 3 P.M.

Very ardent and responsive, but also somewhat of the clinging vine variety. Would prefer to rely on others to serve him or do his dirty work. May have many notable talents to offer, but basically he is a worrier, frets a lot and is indecisive.

Born During the Hours of the Monkey – 3 P.M. to 5 P.M.

The Monkey could make the Sheep more inclined to taking action and give him self-assurance in the bargain. He could also have the Monkey's delightful way of looking at the sunnier side of things.

COMPATIBILITY TABLE FOR THE SHEEP

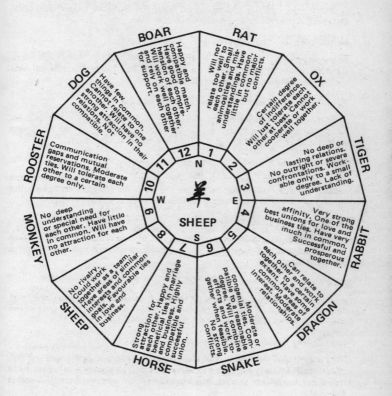

BOAR — Happy and compatible match. Have good comprehension of each other. Will work and rely on each other for support.

RAT — Will not relate too well to each other. Small animosities and misunderstandings. Have little in common, but no major conflicts.

OX — Certain degree of indifference. Will just tolerate each other at best. Cannot cooperate or work well together.

TIGER — No deep or lasting relations. No outright or severe confrontations. Workable only to a small degree. Lack of understanding.

RABBIT — Very strong affinity. One of the best unions for love and business ties. Have very much in common. Successful and prosperous together.

DRAGON — Can relate to each other and work together to certain extent. Have some common areas of interest. Moderate relationships.

SNAKE — Moderate or reasonable ties. Compatible to a reasonable degree. Will combine efforts and work together when feasible. No strong conflicts.

HORSE — Strong attraction for each other. Happy and beneficial ties in marriage and business. Highly compatible and successful union.

SHEEP — No rivalry. Could work together as a team. Have areas of similar interests and common goals. Favourable ties in love and business.

MONKEY — No deep understanding or special need for each other. Have little in common. Will have no attraction for each other.

ROOSTER — Communication gaps and mutual reservations. Moderate ties. Will tolerate each other to a certain degree only.

DOG — Have few things in common. Cannot relate to one another. Will have no strong attraction in their relations. Not compatible.

SHEEP

N 12 1
11 2
10 3
W E
9 4
8 5
7 6
S

Born During the Hours of the Rooster — 5 P.M. to 7 P.M.

Fermenting with ideas that may never materialize. The Sheep is too dependent and the Rooster in him contributes nonsensical solutions. No doubt, he will be brainy and have many positive qualities, but someone else will have to tap his resources and organize his life for him.

Born During the Hours of the Dog — 7 P.M. to 9 P.M.

A Sheep that is more rational and sensible. The Dog gives him more strength of character and helps him to face reality. Will not be easily given to tears or self-pity.

Born During the Hours of the Boar — 9 P.M. to 11 P.M.

A Sheep who will always lend you a shoulder to cry on. But you better have your shoulder ready as he expects the same privilege if you are to be his friend. Hopefully, the sturdy Boar will make him more able to bear his trials and endure hardships without cracking up.

HOW THE SHEEP FARES IN DIFFERENT YEARS

Year of RAT

A very good year for the Sheep. Gifts and gains from unlikely sources such as gambling, lottery, etc. Business opportunities indicated. Home life may be placid but romance and social successes foreseen. No illness or sizable problems.

Year of OX

A difficult year for the Sheep, as quarrels, misunderstanding and demands of family and friends keep him occupied. Financial trouble will result from extravagance and overspending. A hard time to find money. He could expect only moderate gains.

Year of TIGER

A year of mixed blessings. The Sheep native can retain power but will have to strive hard to keep in step with the opposition. Family life is calm, but trouble with relatives is predicted. His work area will be busy but he has the opportunity to meet new and beneficial contacts.

Year of RABBIT

A fair year as the Sheep chalks up some gains at work and in his finances. He could also suffer an upheaval at home or some repercussion for past neglect. Health problems are caused by accidental injuries. But he will emerge from all his troubles with more gains than losses.

Year of DRAGON

Hectic but sober year. The Sheep's gains will be marginal and although there may be numerous disputes he is fortunate not to face any major calamity. The Sheep will find it hard to accumulate money at this time, but he should ride out the storm admirably if he does not gamble or make drastic changes in his life.

Year of SNAKE

A good year as the Sheep regains power, position and popularity. New and influential people help him and he will travel or receive some additional income. Bad tidings may delay his progress temporarily but his goals will be accomplished in the end.

Year of the HORSE

Smooth and tranquil year. The Sheep faces no large problems at home or work. He can get control behind the scenes and overcome obstacles in his path. A slight illness or infection indicated, but in general he will prosper this year. Some problem that has troubled him in the past will turn out to be a blessing in disguise.

Year of SHEEP

A not-so-favorable year for the Sheep native. The year may start out bright and he could make a lot of plans or receive many invitations. Then problems and complications will pop up and his gains may be greatly diminished. A time in which he must trim his expectations and be practical.

Year of MONKEY

A good year for the Sheep. Recognition or promotion at work gives him a sense of fulfillment and he will enjoy a busy but rewarding year. Opposition is negligible and health problems minor.

Year of ROOSTER

An entertaining but rather expensive year. The Sheep spends more than he earns and may be faced with irritating disputes or conflict at home. A year in which he should not try to please everyone and watch his finances very carefully.

Year of DOG

A distressing year for the Sheep as he has to deal with unhappy changes, debts, romantic problems or family troubles. Not a good time for him to travel or make investments or long-term commitments. He must retain an optimistic but very conservative outlook.

Year of BOAR

A fair year for the Sheep as he recovers from his past troubles. His position is still shaky and he is unable to relax as he suspects friends or associates of deceiving him. Home life could be neglected by him. He will have access to funds previously withheld from him.

FAMOUS PERSONS BORN IN THE YEAR OF THE SHEEP

Metal
Andy Warhol
Barbara Walters
Catherine Deneuve

Water
Muhammad Ali
Douglas Fairbanks
Bobby Fisher
Billie Jean King
John Denver

Wood
Andrew Carnegie
Archbishop Fulton J.
  Sheen
King George IV
Rudolph Valentino
Michelangelo

Fire
Miguel de Cervantes
James Michener
Takeo Miki
Sir Laurence Olivier

Earth
Dino De Laurentiis
Pierre Trudeau
Ian Smith
The Shah of Iran
George Wallace

Chapter 9

The Monkey

I am the seasoned traveler
Of the Labyrinth.
The genuis of alacrity,
Wizard of the impossible.
My brilliance is yet unmatched
In its orginality.
My heart's filled with potent magic
That could cast a hundred spells.
I am put together
For mine own pleasure.

I AM THE MONKEY

THE MONKEY SIGN

Chinese name for the Monkey: HÓU
Ranking order: Ninth
Hours ruled by the Monkey: 3 P.M. to 5 P.M.
Direction of its sign: West-Southwest
Season and principal month: Summer—August
Corresponds to the Western sign: Leo
Fixed element: Metal
Stem: Positive

THE LUNAR YEARS OF THE MONKEY IN THE WESTERN CALENDAR

Starting Dates	Ending Dates	Element
February 2, 1908	January 21, 1909	Earth
February 20, 1920	February 7, 1921	Metal
February 6, 1932	January 25, 1933	Water
January 25, 1944	February 12, 1945	Wood
February 12, 1956	January 30, 1957	Fire
January 30, 1968	February 16, 1969	Earth
February 16, 1980	February 4, 1981	Metal
February 4, 1992	January 22, 1993	Water

If you were born on the day before the start of the lunar year of the Monkey, e.g., February 1, 1908, you belong to the animal sign before the Monkey—which is the Sheep.

If you were born on the day after the lunar year of the Monkey, e.g., January 22, 1909, then you belong to the sign following that of the Monkey—the Rooster.

THE YEAR OF THE MONKEY

Everything will be workable this year. At least the agile Monkey will not give up before trying every angle. There will be success even in impossible ventures, there will be inventions and improvisations galore. Politics, diplomacy, high finance and business will be engaged in one big poker game with everyone trying to outbluff each other. A rather amusing and exciting time in which everyone will be given the opportunity to try his hand at the game. No direct confrontation here, as the Monkey is one who can laugh off his mistakes and improve his bargaining prowess in the next round.

This is a year that will find us all trying to get a better deal by outsmarting the other man. It is hard to keep track of who is winning, as the right hand has no idea of what the left hand is up to. One thing is for sure, this will be an extremely progressive time. We will all steam ahead, and even if we do not apply ourselves to the utmost, we will be carried forward by the surging tide of the Monkey's natural talent for learning and advancement.

The lucky imp of a Monkey who rules this year will urge us to gamble, speculate and exploit risky but ingenious options. If you are quick on the draw, this year will yield huge dividends. It is definitely not a year for the faint-hearted or slow-witted. The Monkey gives no concessions and asks none in return. If there is a recession, the year of the Monkey will quickly put an end to it. Business will skyrocket under his optimistic and shrewd influence. The Monkey's resourcefulness will amaze and confound everyone.

It is very interesting to note that America was born in the year of the Fire Monkey, 1776. Perhaps this explains her phenomenal growth and fantastic achievements within such a short span of time.

It is said that the Monkey's year will bring many new and unconventional ways of doing things. The motto of this year should be: "Don't take No for an answer!"

THE MONKEY PERSONALITY

Of all the animals in the lunar cycle, the Monkey bears the closest resemblance to the Naked Ape himself, Man. It is therefore no wonder that it should be he who will inherit most of man's intelligence as well as his capacity for deceit.

The Monkey is the sign of the inventor, the improvisor, and the motivator in the Chinese zodiac; a charlatan capable of drawing everyone to him with his inimitable guile and charm. Being the quick-witted genius of the cycle, he is clever, flexible and innovative. The Monkey can solve intricate problems with ease and will be a very fast learner. He can master anything under the sun and usually has the aptitude for being a good linguist. A person born during this year will be successful at whatever he chooses to do. No challenge will be too great for him.

On the negative side, the Monkey person has an inborn superiority complex. He doesn't have enough respect for others. Or rather, from his point of view, he has too much for himself. He can be extremely selfish, egoistic and vain. There is also a jealous streak in him that surfaces every time someone gets a promotion or something that he does not have. He is extremely competitive, but good at concealing his feelings and planning his cunning moves. In his pursuit of money, success or power, the Monkey's prowess is unbeatable.

With his innate versatility, the Monkey-born can be a good actor, writer, diplomat, lawyer, sportsman, stockbroker, teacher, etc. He is an immensely sociable character who can get on the good side of every-one. He has the rare gift of making you like him even after he has tricked you.

In the Monkey's many-sided personality the one quality that isn't missing is confidence, no matter how shy or docile he may look. He will take care to display a good bearing, well-rehearsed politeness and a calm dignity. He has an intense and unshakable belief in himself. But it would be inaccurate to dub the Monkey as a completely selfish person. No, he is more like a child in his delightful preoccupation with himself. He can be totally oblivious of others if they are not directly involved in what he is doing at the moment. He views himself with the same fascination and ecstatic joy that a baby exhibits the first time he learns how to play with his fingers and toes. Observe how the infant reacts when he discovers how to clap his hands. He will squeal with glee and proceed to do the same thing over and over until he masters the act. Totally occupied with his marvelous discovery, he is unaware of anything else.

So you will find the Monkey showing the self-same unabashed joy at his own cleverness and brilliant accomplishments. He won't mas-querade his pride but neither will he be artificial about it. He honestly believes there isn't anyone else around who can top his act.

If you really know the Monkey well, you will always find it hard to begrudge this wonderful joie de vivre. It's what makes him so different from others, so enviable at times.

Even in the Bible one can spot a Monkey. Methinks that Mary Magdalene could well have been a she-Monkey, while the Prodigal Son was definitely a he-Monkey. If you recall, they both got to eat their cake and keep it, too. How unfair that they should get to slide back into everyone's good graces like that. But there you have it. The Monkey's not only lucky and clever, but also unsinkable.

Throwing insults, accusations and reprimands at him will prove ineffective—even frustrating. They will just bounce off him harmlessly. It's simply unthinkable for him to believe all those nasty things you call him. It can't be true. He will find your admonitions baseless, maybe even hysterically funny. He has such an accurate picture of himself, his talents and his well-deserved good fortune, that you must be insanely jealous to make such ridiculous statements.

The Monkey does not lack credibility. His main problem lies in yielding to temptation, because he finds it amazingly easy to devise ways to justify his actions or to solve dilemmas without too much expense. Consequently, he finds it difficult to instill in others a total sense of trust. With such an innately clever personality, others are always tempted to suspect his motives. Often, Monkey people are judged harshly or accused erroneously by others who are below his scope. His popularity ratings could go up and down like a yoyo. Yet, he never seems overly concerned about your present opinion of him, no matter how contrite he appears. Perhaps it's because he knows that he can always get around to changing it.

This does not mean that the Monkey is callous or refuses to accept criticism. Not in the least—when you get to know him, that is. It is just that he realizes ahead of everyone else that nothing is ever permanent or irreparable. Don't sulk, despair or cry "Doomsday." Let him put his gray matter to work and soon things will be right side up again. Remember, to him, records were made to be broken; standards to be upgraded by higher specifications; inventions to be rendered obsolete by more sophisticated designs. He is the impresario, the perpetual improver. Rarely discouraged by his failures or impressed by the success of others, the Monkey strives constantly to do better and often astonishes even himself.

When dealing with a Monkey—be factual. Objectivity is something he lives by. But ultimately, you might as well know, it doesn't matter to him whether or not you approve of his methods. He needs but one sanction—his own.

The Monkey-born can clinch any bargain with flourish. You will find him conscientious about wheedling the little extras that go along with the deal, too. He may not pounce on you like the Tiger or immobilize you with the power gaze of a Dragon; he will just take one teeny-weeny inch at a time, which may seem quite harmless, but do your arithmetic quickly and you will find that twelve inches make a foot and three feet a yard. But by the time you finish your calculations you may be surprised at how far he has crept up on you.

His coups de grace have a lethal whiplash all of their own. But then, after you regain consciousness, you must admit that never before have you been kayoed with more charm and ingenuity.

But don't worry, you will live. And just as soon as you have recovered sufficiently from the first shock, he'll be back with an even nicer package, a brand-new failproof scheme, and sure enough you will fall neatly under his spell again. See what I mean? What has he got—witchcraft, sorcery? Never mind, it's too late now; you are a Monkey addict and you are hooked on him or her.

The Monkey is an intellectual and will possess a fine memory. With his superb intelligence and proficiency, he cannot help but be a winner. His genius is fueled by insatiable curiosity. He must try anything at least once. If he is stumped by a problem, he will nonchalantly go on to invent a solution. What else? Besides being bright and crafty, the Monkey is practical; he counts his dollars and cents. You won't find him wasting time on losing enterprises.

A realist, adroit in self-preservation, the Monkey will not hesitate to take the easiest way out of a trap. When he is cornered, he can be unscrupulous in his means of escape. But the Monkey does have a conscience and when it bothers him too much he will be hit by bouts of charity and may be overwhelmingly generous all of a sudden. Make hay while the sun shines, for these bouts will not last long.

The Monkey girl is Miss Sparkle herself. A natural show woman, she brings excitement and stimulation wherever she goes. Few people will be left unstirred by her liveliness and provocative beauty.

She has a good head for figures and will adapt easily to change. She will work with any group, given enough incentive and sound reasons to do so. A great party-goer, entertaining speaker, gracious hostess and tactful confidant, the lady Monkey must never never be underestimated. She is ultracompetitive, observant and calculating. Ms. Monkey will also be attracted to the stagelight and could be a gifted performer. Cheerful and resourceful, she can take disappointment in stride and will be able to fend by her own initiative from the word "Go." This efficient female will not be needing you to lead her by the hand and point out every step of the way. Independent and self-assured, she knows exactly where she wants to go and may be able to teach you a few handy shortcuts of her own. She may be nosey, but she won't be giving away any of her secrets in exchange for your well-guarded information.

The Monkey girl will be guided by incentives. She won't work for free! Good at choosing her words, she will say the right thing at the right time. She rarely blunders on important matters or makes silly, unfounded remarks. She's as adept at getting her own way as she is an excellent judge of character, and she will never exceed her limits. You won't find her doling out money either. One has to perform if one expects her to pay for something—and perform well, because she can be very critical and snobbish.

The Monkey female is a fashionable but orderly dresser; she is especially vain about her hair. Her grooming and her coiffure will be as excellent and as chic as she can afford. It should also be noted that the Monkey native is most prone to skin ailments or allergies. The Monkey girl will have sensitive skin and break out with a rash if she uses too much cosmetics. Although she seems to pamper herself unstintingly, you won't find her tardy or disorganized. Besides her many activities, she will still find the time and energy to take up several hobbies and to look into every aspect of things that appeal to her. She is one of the most up-to-date women in town.

Every Monkey will be an original; they don't make molds of this character and stamp them out by the dozen. Yet in spite of his many individual flaws, people will rally around him simply because they cannot do without the Monkey's expertise and skills.

He is the top PR man—remarkably original, shrewd with money and, in fact, such a wizard at manipulating everything that industry, politics and trade would be lost without him. The Monkey's guile is famous in Chinese history and his name is synonymous with cleverness. He is certainly a big asset to have on your team. But first make sure that he is 100 percent on your side. There are bound to be some mercenary Monkeys in the tribe.

It is difficult to be angry with him for long because the Monkey person is an expert at making himself likable and indispensable. He will always maneuver himself into a lucrative position. When he loses, the Monkey is no stubborn fool; he knows how to give in when the odds are stacked against him. Master of the art of survival, the Monkey thrives by the "better to run away and live to fight another day" philosophy.

The Monkey is born a strategist. He never moves without a plan, most probably several plans. He'll never turn his back on opportunity (which he will recognize in any disguise) and he'll hitch his wagon to a star, a Cadillac, a jet plane or anything else that moves for that matter. He just loves free rides and will travel first-class whenever possible.

The Monkey makes a good critic. He can pinpoint the specific area where something went wrong and suggest workable remedies. Of course, how he goes about it will depend on what type of Monkey he is. Some lower types can be so smug about their know-how that you would rather die before accepting their help.

But generally speaking, a Monkey is a warm, natural and spontaneous person who is prepared to work hard—especially if he gets a piece of the action. The bigger the piece, the harder he pitches. Pay him with peanuts and he will turn the tables on you, giving you nothing but peanut shells in return. Take a good piece of advice: never try to trick a Monkey. Chances are you won't get away with it. Aside from being an expert at taking revenge, the Monkey-born will usually have a wry sense of humor. You catch him chuckling wickedly more often than laughing heartily.

Since the Monkey gets what he wants without too much effort or struggle, he will not treasure his conquests. He loses interest. He should learn to be more constant and more serious. In his life, he will trust only a handful of people and will not have many real or long friendships because of his complicated and suspicious personality. He dislikes confiding in others.

Nonetheless, the Monkey is very much in demand. The Rat will be enchanted by his ingenuity. They will recognize each other by the dollar signs in their eyes. The Dragon will seek him out for his superior wits. Rabbit, Sheep, Dog, Horse and Ox will all benefit from the Monkey's versatility and value his competence. The Boar and Rooster will likewise have need of the Monkey's genius.

Naturally, the Snake with all his wisdom and similarly doubting mind will never be completely comfortable with the Monkey. The Tiger should avoid getting into the Monkey's path, as he will be the prime target of the Monkey's mischief and pranks. The Monkey cannot but show his prowess when challenged, and upon discovering that the Tiger is a bad loser, he will revel in annoying him.

THE MONKEY CHILD

The Monkey child will be captivating. Bright-eyed and bushy-tailed, he won't keep still for a moment. Mischievous, jovial and very competitive, he will steal his way into your heart. Skillful at flattery and extremely good at playing up to your weaknesses, the incorrigible Monkey will always get what he is after.

Curious, unpredictable and ingenious, this youngster will usually be found fidgeting with some device. Don't be too upset if he breaks his toys. It is simply because he is not attracted by the outer decor; he takes things apart to get inside and see what makes them tick. Intricate or mechanically moving contraptions never fail to amuse or fascinate him. He will be forever tugging at your apron strings and stomping after you with brilliant questions about the universe.

One of these days, when you are about to throw away that unreliable clock that never worked well, your Monkey child will pick it up and fix it with a hairpin. He is never contented with what he has. The grass always look greener to him on the other side. The ambitious and conniving little imp will always have his eye on other people's possessions.

He is constantly goaded to improve himself and he prides himself on his vast accumulation of knowledge and skills. He will be involved in a myriad of activities. Today he will be investigating the theory of photography and tomorrow he may be building himself an amateur radio. The remarkable thing is that the Monkey can spread his attention to several subjects and be able to master them all. He can be snobbish and cocky and will like to tease others with his versatile wit. Optimistic and forever hopeful, he will never concede defeat. He will try and try again until he succeeds.

The Monkey child will have a selfish streak and may refuse to share what he has while skillfully helping himself to other children's toys. Excitable, pretentious and crafty, he will be oblivious of any regulation that restricts him. He should be taught that life is not a one-way street. Even when he does share, he will carefully consider what he can get in return. Even the smallest Monkey is adept at weighing the pros and cons. He will cry foul at the slightest edge others may have over him, but he expects you to close both eyes if the scales tip in his favor.

Then, just when you have reached the saturation point and become totally exasperated with him, the Monkey will turn on his sweet saintly smile, apologize from the bottom of his heart, pour flattery all over your wounds and stand on his head to make you laugh. You will forget all the harsh measures you were going to take against him and be his willing captive all over again.

THE FIVE TYPES OF MONKEYS

METAL MONKEY—1860, 1920, 1980

This is the fighting Monkey. Strong, sophisticated and independent, he will have an irrepressible urge for financial security. Capable of making wise investments, this type of Monkey will prefer to run his own business or else earn money from outside work if he has a regular job. He is consistent and will be able to hold on to his savings if he doesn't speculate in risky ventures.

Metal makes him ardent and demonstrative in his affections. He will have high aspirations and may appear to be status-seeking or overdramatic at times in his behavior.

Characterized by a lively disposition, the passionate Metal Monkey can be warm, positive and very convincing. He will sell you anything conceivable and his designs, if he is creative, will be both aesthetic and useful. The Metal Monkey could be an excellent trend-setter.

When he is negative, the analytical Metal Monkey can be exceedingly self-conscious and proud. His loyalties will be few and linked only to himself.

Hard-working and practical, he shuns assistance from others and will be more than able to take care of his own interests.

WATER MONKEY—1872, 1932, 1992

This is a cooperative but speculative Monkey. The "You scratch my back and I'll scratch yours" sort of person. Yet, in spite of his dignified and worldly appearance, this type of Monkey takes offense easier than other Monkeys. He will have a secretive although kind nature, and can be deft and patient in the pursuit of his objectives.

Water mated with his native sign imparts to him a greater sense of purpose. But he will know not to be too direct or obvious in showing his intentions. He can compromise with grace and will know how to work around barriers rather than waste his time and energy in knocking them down.

The Water Monkey will have flair and originality; he motivates himself as well as others with his pleasant ways, and his ideas meet little resistance because of his ingenious way of introducing them. He will present things in their best possible light. He has a keen understanding of how human relationships function and will use this knowledge to achieve his ends.

When he decides to be negative, the Water Monkey can suffer from lack of direction. He vacillates and becomes in turn erratic, evasive and meddling.

WOOD MONKEY—1884, 1944, 2004

Good communications with others will be essential to this type of Monkey. But he will not like to pry into the affairs of those around him if possible, and prides himself on being able to keep his house and accounts in good order.

Although he is basically honorable and desirous of prestige, this Monkey will be restless and have a strong pioneering spirit. He is aware of everything that is going on around him and is very curious about new inventions or modes of thinking. The Wood element gives him an intuitive mind which will be able to foresee the course of events. He searches constantly for answers and will not take setbacks calmly.

While maintaining his own admirable standards, the Wood Monkey will strive constantly to elevate himself above his present station. He is always looking forward and never quite satisfied with what he has. On the lookout for greener pastures, this type of Monkey will leap at new challenges.

This resourceful person will establish order in whatever work he decides to take up. He is rarely given to exaggeration or speculation. Carefully, carefully, he whittles away the opposition bit by bit.

FIRE MONKEY—1896, 1956, 2016 *

An energetic, gesticulating Monkey, who will show traits of being a natural leader and innovator. He is self-assured and determined, expressive and truthful with his emotions and very interested in the opposite sex.

The Fire element will lend him great vitality, and he will have a tendency to dominate or teach those less aggressive than himself. He will possess a fertile imagination and should not let his ideas run away with him. He is inventive but not always careful.

The Fire Monkey will have a powerful and constant drive to be on the top of his professional field. He is competitive to the extreme and will be capable of great jealousy. His creativity is born of willpower, necessity and initiative, and these will enable him to upstage others and keep one step ahead of the game.

The Fire Monkey is the most forceful of all the Monkeys. He relishes being in full control and can be opinionated, stubborn and argumentative when he is negative. He is lucky in speculative ventures and he can correctly evaluate risks. But in spite of the bold and collected face he presents to the public, this type of Monkey hides morbid suspicions of how others may be deceiving him.

EARTH MONKEY—1908, 1968, 2028

A placid and reliable Monkey who may have a cool and collected nature. He is expansive and given to disinterested acts of charity.

He quietly demands admiration and appreciation for his talents and services, and when this is not forthcoming, he can sulk and become insolent.

He is likely to be an intellectual and will be academically studious or very well read if he cannot pursue a higher education. Generally, he will be honest and straightforward and will achieve distinction through his thoroughness and devotion to duty.

The Earth Monkey will not be too fond of entertaining unless it is a necessity, but he will be genuinely kind and loving to those he cares for. Less concerned about his ego, he can devote himself unselfishly to the good of all. He will value his integrity and can even be overconscientious about operating only within the law.

*America was born in 1776 (year of the Fire Monkey).

THE MONKEY AND HIS ASCENDANTS

Born during the hours of the Rat – 11 P.M. to 1 A.M.

Sparkling personality. Nothing will stop this combination from savoring everything life has to offer and hanging on to his money at the same time. Gets to eat his cake and keep it, too.

Born during the hours of the Ox – 1 A.M. to 3 A.M.

A stodgy Monkey, straitlaced but with better credentials. Less inclined to pull tricks on you. And even when he does, it's hard to tell as he keeps such a straight face!

Born During the Hours of the Tiger – 3 A.M. to 5 A.M.

A forceful and exuberant Monkey. Both signs here are too self-confident and wary of other people. He could land smack in a heap of trouble and still be unwilling to take advice or concede defeat.

Born During the Hours of the Rabbit – 5 A.M. to 7 A.M.

A subtle, less mischievous Monkey with more caution and restraint in him. Could be almost psychic in his assessments and dealings with others.

Born During the Hours of the Dragon – 7 A.M. to 9 A.M.

An overconscientious and doubly ambitious Monkey. With his own phenomenal prowess and the Dragon's high-powered drives, he usually bites off more than he can chew.

Born During the Hours of the Snake – 9 A.M. to 11 A.M.

If the wisdom of the Snake is thrown into this combination, we could have a Houdini in the making. A Monkey with great intellect and penetrative powers. Could have been here and gone before you know it.

Born During the Hours of the Horse – 11 A.M. to 1 P.M.

A not-so-persevering Monkey who will change sides without a moment's notice. A gamesman who usually plays by his own rules.

Born During the Hours of the Sheep – 1 P.M. to 3 P.M.

A dreamy, romantic Monkey with many wiles. Still inclined to be opportunistic and conniving, but has a more agreeable and acquiescent nature.

Born During the Hours of the Monkey – 3 P.M. to 5 P.M.

A sacrosanct imp. This extremely adroit and highly evolved personality will be convivial and supremely optimistic. There isn't anything he cannot get away with.

Born During the Hours of the Rooster – 5 P.M. to 7 P.M.

An unconventional and adventurous Monkey with very high aspirations. With the Monkey's aptitude, perhaps even the Rooster's daydreams could come true.

Born During the Hours of the Dog – 7 P.M. to 9 P.M.

An emotionally detached and rustic Monkey. Most likely to be a cool satirist. Still, he is immensely popular because he never loses his sense of humor or departs from reality.

Born During the Hours of the Boar – 9 P.M. to 11 P.M.

A sporting and less self-conscious Monkey. With the Boar's presence, he is less spurious and easier to deal with. Will strive hard to keep his end of the bargain.

HOW THE MONKEY FARES IN DIFFERENT YEARS

Year of RAT

A lucky and prosperous year for the Monkey. Money comes from unlikely sources and it is an excellent time for him to advance his position or ask for loans. Problems are easily solved and he is feted or sought after by important people. New members are added to his family.

Year of OX

A somewhat moderate year. The Monkey's profits and enjoyment are restricted and the loss of personal belongings is indicated. His family life will remain smooth but he will be forced to travel or suffer from some chronic illness. His progress is not up to his expectations. A time to curtail his overambition.

Year of TIGER

A very unsteady time for the Monkey. He is very vulnerable to the attacks of his enemies and may be forced to flee, travel, work for others or borrow money at high interest. People tend to take advantage of his weak position. He must remain patient and lie low. A year for him to consolidate his resources and refrain from embarking on new ventures.

Year of RABBIT

A good year. The Monkey's prospects are bright again and he will receive help from unlikely people or places. Tranquility is restored at work and home, and business is back to normal although his gains will only be modest. A time for him to seek out new opportunities or make changes in his environment.

COMPATIBILITY TABLE FOR THE MONKEY

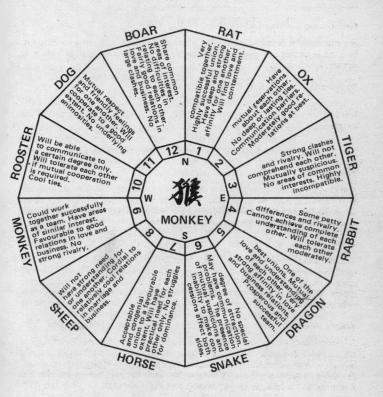

BOAR — Share common areas of interest. No difficulties in relating to each other. Fairly good relations in love and togetherness. No large clashes.

RAT — Very compatible together. Highly successful union. Have deep and strong affinity. Will find love and contentment.

OX — Have mutual reservations about each other. No deep or lasting ties. Communication barriers. Moderately good relations at best.

TIGER — Strong clashes and rivalry. Will not comprehend each other. Mutually suspicious. No areas of common interests. Highly incompatible.

DOG — Mutual respect and friendly feelings for one another. Will cooperate to a good extent. No underlying animosities.

ROOSTER — Will be able to communicate to a certain degree only. Will tolerate each other if mutual cooperation is required. Cool ties.

MONKEY — Could work together successfully as a team. Have areas of similar interest. Favourable to good relations in love and business. No strong rivalry.

SHEEP — Will not have strong need for understanding of one another. Cordial to a relatively cool extent in marriage and relations in business.

HORSE — Acceptable and congenial union to a favourable extent. Will have practical need for each other only. No struggles for dominance.

SNAKE — No special degree of attraction. May have communication problems. The presence of mutual suspicions and inability to make concessions affect both sides.

DRAGON — One of the best unions. Mutual love and understanding of each other. Very strong affinity in love and business relations. Prosperous and successful team.

RABBIT — Some petty differences and rivalry. Cannot achieve complete understanding of each other. Will tolerate each other moderately.

N 12 1 2 3 E 4 5 S 6 7 8 9 W 10 11

猴

MONKEY

Year of DRAGON

Gains this year for the Monkey will be in the form of knowledge or technical know-how. The benefits he receives will not be tangible or immediately realized. Troubles and unsettled differences cloud his mind and he may have to spend his own money or savings to push his plans through. A year to watch and learn. He must not speculate.

Year of SNAKE

A moderately happy year as the Monkey receives assistance from friends or support from his superiors. Good times are in store although there are some disputes at home. A year in which he must hold his tongue and avoid confrontation at all costs.

Year of HORSE

A fair year for the Monkey although he is still faced with worries and frustrations. His difficulties will be able to work themselves out if he does not rock the boat and agrees to lower his expectations a bit. A year to join the opposition when it becomes clear he cannot beat them. He must be conservative and observant to succeed.

Year of SHEEP

An involved and busy year. The Monkey finds it easy to make money but his profits will be reduced by unexpected expenses. He meets new and beneficial associates and will have to entertain or travel more than usual. Some minor health upset or unhappiness at home is indicated. A year to be secretive, as others may try to obtain classified information from him.

Year of MONKEY

An excellent time for the Monkey native. He can start his own business as achievements, happiness and recognition are indicated. He will make fantastic progress. Headaches will come mainly from subordinates, debtors or people who finance his bold undertakings. Health problems stem from overexertion.

Year of ROOSTER

A moderate but stable time for the endeavors of the Monkey person. He will have the extra money he needs and the right contacts to push his plans through, but in turn he will neglect his home life, take on too much forced socializing and find himself exhausted or overextended where commitments are concerned. A year in which he must not underestimate his opponents.

Year of DOG

A difficult year as the Monkey's plans go awry and people break their promises to him. He may suffer losses in his investments and should not lend money to anyone. A year in which he will discover who his real friends are. Disappointments will make him realize where and how he went wrong.

Year of BOAR

An active but trying year. The Monkey will have business disputes, financial or legal troubles or even complications in his illnesses. His problems can be resolved but not without much compromising. He will have to make difficult concessions or take insults from his enemies. A year in which he should not even trust his best friend. Joint ventures will prove unrewarding or even dangerous.

FAMOUS PERSONS BORN IN THE YEAR OF THE MONKEY

Metal
Federico Fellini
Walter Matthau
Milton Berle
Mujibur Rahman

Water
Leonardo da Vinci
Charles Dickens
Queen Sirikit of
   Thailand
Edward Kennedy
Andrew Young

Wood
Harry Truman
Eleanor Roosevelt
Mick Jagger

Fire
Duchess of Windsor

Earth
John Milton
Paul Gauguin
Lyndon B. Johnson
Joan Crawford
Bette Davis
Mary Hemingway
Nelson Rockefeller

Chapter 10

The Rooster

I am on hand
To herald in the day,
And to announce its exit.
I thrive by clockwork and precision.
In my unending quest for perfection
All things will be restored to
    their rightful place.
I am the exacting taskmaster.
The ever-watchful administrator.
I seek perfect order in my world.
I represent unfailing dedication.

I AM THE ROOSTER.

THE ROOSTER SIGN

Chinese name for the Rooster: JĪ
Ranking order: Tenth
Hours ruled by the Rooster: 5 P.M. to 7 P.M.
Direction of its sign: Directly West
Season and principal month: Autumn—September
Corresponds to the Western sign: Virgo
Fixed element: Metal
Stem: Negative

THE LUNAR YEARS OF THE ROOSTER IN THE WESTERN CALENDAR

Starting Dates	Ending Dates	Element
January 22, 1909	February 9, 1910	Earth
February 8, 1921	January 27, 1922	Metal
January 26, 1933	February 13, 1934	Water
February 13, 1945	February 1, 1946	Wood
January 31, 1957	February 17, 1958	Fire
February 17, 1969	February 5, 1970	Earth
February 5, 1981	January 24, 1982	Metal
January 23, 1993	February 9, 1994	Water

If you were born on the day before the start of the lunar year of the Rooster, e.g., January 21, 1909, you belong to the animal sign before the Rooster—which is the Monkey.

If you were born on the day after the lunar year of the Rooster, e.g., February 10, 1910, then you belong to the sign following that of the Rooster—the Dog.

THE YEAR OF THE ROOSTER

The optimism of the Monkey year overlaps the year of the Rooster, but the Rooster tends to be overconfident and is prone to come up with nonsensical plans. While the colorful Rooster brings bright and happy days, he also dissipates energy. Better stick to practical and well-proven paths. Forget about that controversial best seller you were going to write. No get rich quick schemes this year, please!

It may require a great deal of effort this year to resist going off on wild goose chases. Refrain from making speculative ventures. Disappointments and conflicts will result. The Rooster likes to flaunt his authority and a lot of trouble can come from his domineering attitude. But since he also symbolizes the good administrator and conscientious overseer of justice in the barnyard, the peace will still be kept. Everything will be precariously balanced in the Rooster's year, as his dramatic personality can set off all kinds of petty disputes.

This year we may have to expend maximum effort for minimum gain. Try not to fuss too much. Details do need looking into, but don't forget to view the whole picture. Be cautious. Do not aim too high. One is liable to get shot down.

Politics will adhere to hard-line policies. The diplomatic scene will be dominated by philosophical orators who rave a lot about nothing. Governments will be found flexing their muscles at each other, but just for show. There may be no real confrontations. It is just that everyone will be too occupied with himself to hear or care what the other person is saying. The self-conscious influence of the Rooster will cause us to take offense at the smallest slight. We will tend to be terribly ostentatious about the splendid image we think we project. Dissensions and debates on all fronts will signify the Rooster's penchant for argumentative exercises and will not be likely to do permanent damage to anyone when taken in the right context.

This will be a buoyant year in spite of the Rooster's knack for making simple things complicated. One thing is for sure: he seldom comes up empty-handed. This is the year of one very self-sufficient bird that will never go hungry.

Just keep your eyes open and your mouth shut and check facts and figures before making unprecedented moves. We should all get by without too much hardship. Our pockets will not be empty although our nerves may be a bit frayed.

THE ROOSTER PERSONALITY

The Rooster, or Chicken as he is also called, is the Don Quixote of the Chinese cycle. The dauntless hero who must look to the earth to survive, he is the most misunderstood and eccentric of all the signs. Outwardly, he is the epitome of self-assurance and aggression, but at heart he could be conservative and old-fashioned.

The Rooster-born, especially the men, will be attractive, even dashingly handsome. The princely fowl is radiant and proud of his fine feathers and has an impeccable carriage. You don't find any roosters slouching; they strut about with dignity. Even the shyest member of the Rooster family will cut a neat, trim figure and maintain a special bearing wherever he goes.

There are two distinct types of Roosters. The rapid-firing, extremely talkative ones and the deadly solemn observer types with the X-ray vision. Both are equally hard to deal with. The Rooster has many outstanding qualities to crow about. He is sharp, neat, precise, organized, decisive, upright, alert and most direct. He can also be critical to the point of brutality. Don't ever ask him for his frank, candid opinion—you may never recover from his comments. He loves to argue and debate, showing how knowledgeable and smart he is, sometimes with little regard for the feelings of others. But when his feathers are ruffled in return, he is insufferable. He isn't cut out to be a diplomat. Situations requiring tact, delicacy and discretion will cramp his style. His way is to go about trying to convert everyone to his way of thinking with missionary zeal.

An outstanding performer, the Rooster shines when he is the center of attraction. Tremendously imposing as a personality, he could well pursue any career that exposes him to the public eye. Gay, witty and amusing, the magnificent Rooster will never pass up an opportunity to recount his adventures and ennumerate his accomplishments. He is adroit at expressing himself both in speech and in writing. You will have to concede that he is well-versed and prepared for any subject to be discussed. If you intend to challenge him on a controversial issue, be ready to fight long and hard—the Rooster has amazing stamina, does his homework and can wear you out.

When the Rooster is negative, he is egoistic, opinionated and too abrasive for his own good. In his mind, he is 100 percent right. He presides over gatherings to exhibit the excellent opinion he has of himself. However, if you look closely, you will find that he puts on this act more as a way to constantly reassure himself of his own worth rather than to irritate anyone. For all his poise and bravado, the Rooster is not that sure of himself, and is therefore most susceptible to flattery or delusions of grandeur.

All members of the Chicken family can handle money. They are just fascinated by accounting, sorting out finances and generally guarding the cash box. He budgets everything he can get his hands on and that includes his time, your time, the mailman's time, company time, ad infinitum. Even the smallest one will most likely be elected as Treasurer of the Little League. He will handle his pennies wisely, and before you know it he may be running his own mini-bank, giving loans and charging interest from more careless youngsters.

If you have problems with your finances due to a lack of self-control—turn your money over to a Rooster. He'll make you an ironclad budget and slap your wrists every time you touch one cent more than allowed.

While you may live to lament this move, you can be sure he is doing it all for your own good—even if he does seem to be sadistically enjoying it a bit too much and even if it is your money. Don't be so ungrateful! You should thank your lucky stars he condescended to help you at all.

Now all those bits and pieces of paper you scattered around have been neatly filed away by this efficiency expert. Your income is reconciled with your expenditures for the first time in years. You start to see the light of day. And the Internal Revenue wolf has not cast his dark shadow on your doorstep now that the Rooster is here and your creditors no longer haunt you day and night. You would be worse off, you know, if it weren't for this financial savior.

I know, too, at this point you may think you have got more than you bargained for. You will complain bitterly how he won't let you off lightly even for your smallest error. You are now in a state of perfect financial accord, yet totally miserable in this newfound bliss. Your blood pressure shoots up every time you have one of those profound discussions with him. Well, relax. Don't take it so hard.

Try to think back. Remember that day you took him on and how he made that sacred vow to help you out of the woods and stick to you "for better or for worse"? It is just that you get to see the worse part first. Stick around, things are bound to get better. His key word is service and he won't disappoint even your greatest expectations. You may not be able to live with the Rooster, but you will find that neither can you get along without him.

Actually, the Chinese character for the Rooster is "Ji," which simply means Chicken. But since this person will do anything but "chicken out" of a situation, I have respectfully chosen to address him as the Rooster. Besides, the Rooster's personality really enhances and dominates that of the entire chicken family. If there were to be an ad in tomorrow's paper for a "Superman with Fine Fiscal Abilities," you can be sure the Rooster would apply and be qualified for the job, too.

His is the sign of the collector, too. Outstanding accounts bug him terribly. And you know what chickens do with bugs. My, my, you have all these uncollectable debts due you? Just watch the Rooster roll up his sleeves and take on those culprits who owe you money. You cannot find anyone finer to carry out an important directive. He loves difficult assignments. But don't expect him to improvise. He is an explicit person and you have to give him explicit orders. On top of all his virtues, you cannot ask him to be versatile and inventive too. That would be asking too much.

To truly understand a Rooster, you must accept his predilection for controversy. This may be because of the mental exercise it provides him. You must comprehend, difficult as it may sound, that there is nothing personal in his moves. You should have enough sense to keep out of the crossfire when you know his gun is always loaded. And while he does seem knowledgeable and wordly about everything else, it should also be noted that the Rooster can be puritanical about sex or affairs of the heart.

For the Rooster to make smooth, unimpeded progress it would be well if he first realized that people will not be so adverse to accepting his excellent advice—if only he could do better with the packaging. A little sugar coating, perhaps? He doesn't have to be like the old-fashioned doctor who prescribes bitter-tasting concoctions with no regard for our delicate taste buds!

When a Rooster spends lavishly, he must be doing it to appease his oversize ego. He is a sharp dresser and loves to attract attention. Therefore, he occasionally will have the tendency to overdecorate his home, his office or even himself. He is also very impressed with awards of all kinds, medals and honorary titles. Every Rooster will try to win at least one award, have one professional title to his credit or get a minimum of one medal per war. With money, he will only be generous with his immediate family or in order to win love and admiration from his followers. Otherwise, the only thing you can be assured of getting from him free is—advice.

A Rooster born at the crack of dawn, during the Tiger's hours, or at sundown (between 5 and 7 P.M. the hours of the Rooster) is definitely going to be the noisiest of the lot. I personally know of one whose family has long since been considering the use of a muzzle to silence his lengthy discourses. Too bad not one among them has worked up the courage for the task. Night Roosters tend to be the exact opposite. They can be over serious, self-contained and uncommunicative even. These quiet roosters tend to be doubly eccentric, bookwormish, aloof or insulated in their quest for perfection.

All Roosters are perfectionists in one form or another. They will have a sharp eye for details mixed with theoretical flights of fancy. Their ideas sometimes look better on paper than in actual application because they forget to make allowance for human frailties and other varying factors. They have scientific minds and may fail to see why other people cannot exist by fixed formulas as they do.

Yet for all his faults and interfering ways, the Rooster native is usually sincere in his desire to help others and will undoubtedly mean well in all his endeavors. He just comes on too strong because he is so positive in his convictions that he tends to close his mind to the views of others.

If the Rooster's dreams are too farfetched and overambitious, he will suffer many disappointments in life. He must learn to stop reaching for the sky. While he can be practical about difficult matters, the Rooster can also be very unreasonable and difficult over simple things. But it is useless standing between him and his goals. He is the dauntless knight, who recovers at a moment's notice and will go off chasing another rainbow. Who knows, he may succeed at the next try. The Rooster is brave and chivalrous under stress, but sometimes he will carry his heroism far beyond what is required.

The female of this sign is usually more down to earth and less colorful in her aspirations. She is superefficient and will get things done with a minimum of fuss. You can rely on her to have enormous amounts of energy to dedicate to any job she sets her sights on.

One would be hard pressed to find a more helpful woman than the female Chicken, with the exception of a Boar lady. Although this Hen acts like she has been gang-pressed into her labors, the truth is that she loves to conscript herself to a life of involvement and dedication. What would she do with her vast reserves of energy otherwise? Whereas others are only bored, she can actually be frightened when she finds extra time on her hands.

The Hen is more adaptable than the male Rooster and will do well in society. She will have no qualms about being a mere worker, just one of the group, if it gets her where she is going. Routine appeals to her and she is always on schedule if not ahead of it. She is as capable and productive as her male counterpart but will go about performing less offensively. Careful, dutiful and less obtrusive, she could excel in precision work, proofreading, preparing long-range studies or compiling statistics and the like. A meticulous worker, she is also likely to make a very thorough and patient teacher, watchful and protective mother and solicitous wife.

She does have the tendency to harp or constantly remind you of what is next on the agenda, but this should be accredited to overzealousness and not to the fact that she is out to persecute you. One gets the impression that she is out to reform or remake the people she loves. This is simply her way of showing that she cares. She cannot bear to see you make mistakes when she is on hand to prevent such blunders. Consequently, she will help you up every time you stumble, supply you with the right word every time you stammer. Helpful to the extreme, the Hen can drive the objects of her devotion to the limits of sanity.

She will forgive you anything, but not before she gets those hurt feelings off her chest with a strong lecture. After that, she won't harbor grudges and is not vindictive by nature.

The lady Chicken is a simple dresser. She will go for simple, classical and natural outfits that could be appropriate for numerous occasions and which can be complemented by her large array of accessories.

Taking a peek into her handbag could tell you loads more about her character. Besides all those little notes she writes to herself constantly, she will probably have a tape measure and all the dress and shoe sizes of her entire family. She's armed to the teeth with remedies for every illness and other do's and don't's. She is precise and orderly and will enjoy taking charge of distributing or organizing things. It is not beyond her to open the office in the morning and lock up after everyone leaves in the evening. She guards her responsibilities jealously and enjoys with gusto the power her authority confers.

Every Rooster is a reputable worker. He will know how to please his superiors, who in turn will be impressed by his sharp intellect and efficiency. But although he has boundless energy and a driving will to succeed, the Rooster is too cocksure when he is negative and can misdirect his efforts or take on impossible tasks. The irony of it is that the Rooster will find success and money in the most common places. Contrary to his own opinions, he will not have to search far and wide for his fortune. As the Chinese put it, "Chickens can find food even in the hardest ground with their sturdy beaks and claws."

Likewise, if the vigilant Rooster person can bring himself down to earth and apply himself to mundane matters, he can literally dig up gold from his own backyard. He would do well setting up his own business or running the family estate. But wherever he goes, he will be meticulous and competent enough to have everything operating smoothly in no time at all.

The emotions of the Rooster-born swing high and low. He is plagued by an activity-oriented and inquisitive mind. His probing ways keep him chained to his objectives. Once he sets out to prove a point, he will not leave a single stone unturned. He makes an excellent investigator: there is a bit of Sherlock Holmes in every Rooster.

With his many administrative abilities and natural passion for work, the Rooster will start out young and be successful early in life. What he needs most in everything he undertakes is restraint, moderation and a firm hand to direct his irrepressible energies. No matter how competent he is, he must realize that he cannot take the world by storm in a single day and reprogram everyone else in it to do things his way. In short, the Rooster-born can achieve the most astonishing task with aplomb and then become eccentric over the last detail.

The Rooster loves praise, is allergic to criticism of any kind and can be very selfish about sharing the limelight. He will never like to admit he is wrong. He will go to all lengths to discredit his enemies. A good provider, the Rooster person is wonderful to his family and will indulge them anything, provided no one dares usurp his No. 1 spot. It would do well for him to have a large family as he needs a cheering squad to bring out the best in him.

No matter what happens, it will be an advantage that the Rooster is indeed a tireless worker, for he will have to work his way through life. Things won't just fall into his lap. He is the intrepid dreamer, full of ambition and goodwill but destined to succeed in ordinary things. Yet, on the other hand, it will not pay to underestimate his powers. Being fiercely competitive by instinct, he could peck the formidable Snake to death should he set his mind to it.

To sum it up, the colorful but controversial Rooster will never fail to make an impression on you. You will either be enchanted and grow to love him immensely or you will simply be unable to bear the sight and sound of him.

The Rooster will pair off nicely with the wise and intuitive Snake. The Snake in turn will need the effervescent personality and sunny, dauntless outlook of the Rooster to cheer up his life. The Ox will also welcome the sunshine the Rooster could bring into his regimental existence. Both will be compulsive workers although the Chicken is not as Spartan as the Ox. The Dragon will definitely find the grandiose plans of the Rooster very much to his liking, both of them being outgoing, energetic and ambitious.

The Tiger, Sheep, Monkey and Boar will be the next best partners for the Rooster. Put two Roosters together and you know what you will get—a cockfight. With the Hens, there is more likely to be more harmony. The Rooster-born will come into conflict with people born under the sign of the Rat. The Rooster lacks intimacy, the Rat thrives by it. Neither will the Rooster find happiness with the Rabbit-born. The Rabbit is sensitive and will seek to avoid squabbling or inciting his enemies. The Rooster on the other hand is an expert at provoking a fight and can rub people the wrong way by his uncomplimentary remarks. This trait will scandalize and alienate the Rabbit, who cannot bear such glaring directness. The Dog's relation with the Rooster will range from lukewarm to frosty, depending on how wide the gaps are between their different points of view. They could work together when necessary but they are not fated to be joined together in perfect connubial bliss.

THE ROOSTER CHILD

As a child, the Rooster-born will be a self-starter. A good student, fast learner and industrious little soul, he or she will be forever poking around for answers. You can rely on him to pursue his studies, or anything else that attracts him, with self-generated zeal. It will be a joy to teach him, as he is sharp, intelligent and precise. He will have all the tendencies of a bookworm.

The Rooster child will be neat and orderly. He will do things in the proper sequence and is a creature of meticulous and exacting habits that will sometimes really annoy you. He won't be reticent about his opinions either—more of a wise guy around the house. Tough and well-disciplined, he will save the most pocket money among the children. He could be petty about minute discrepancies and will plan the simplest routine with military precision.

This child will probably be the most discriminating critic you can find for miles around. Be glad, even if it hurts to have your ego dented so often. This is because the Rooster is pure-minded and hates hypocrisy. His criticism and clinical observations will just be factual statements and he has no intention of offending you personally. Sometimes he is really astonished why you should get angry when he is trying so hard to point out all the relevant flaws to you. Then again, he really couldn't care less what others think of him. He has to speak his mind as his is a true independent spirit.

The Rooster child will be very demanding of his parents, but in return he will be just as dependable when called upon to do his part. Not one to cry for help, he will detest weakness and dependency in others. If you are slipping, he will be the first to notice and call it to your attention. He can't help it as this is just part of his nature. He tends to be bossy, too, so if you are not careful, your little chick will soon be running your life.

Optimistic and dauntless, the Rooster will never change his course of action even if the whole world condemns him. You may have to watch helplessly as he rushes headlong off a cliff, as he won't take any advice once he has made up his mind. Just keep praying that some of his wild, idealistic schemes work. He is never too practical when it comes to his own life. But one day, who knows, his unheard-of ventures may hit it big. Many millionaires were born in the year of the Rooster and they all have one other thing in common besides money—they were all eccentric.

What is more enervating is the fact that he will be completely blind to his own faults. Don't bother to debate with him; it will be a waste of time as he never admits he is wrong. His is the right way and no Buts about it!

In short, the high-powered and resplendent Rooster will have many splendid talents (which no doubt he will carefully enumerate to you), but he carries with him a whole bag of idiosyncrasies, too. He will never take the middle of the road. With him, you either sink or swim. His simple "love me or leave me" attitude means that if you wish to support him—you must be prepared to go all the way.

THE FIVE TYPES OF ROOSTERS

METAL ROOSTER—1861, 1921, 1981

A practical, exacting and industrious type of Rooster with a flair for captivating others with his brilliant powers of deduction. Investigative, optimistic and idealistic, he will have a passionate attitude toward work.

Metal will make him opinionated and headstrong and he will have a strong need for importance and fame. He could be fastidious about his self-conceived image and cannot subscribe to the viewpoints of others readily. He has the gift of oratory, which he may use to drown out the voices of his opponents. Although he is factual and reasonable, he finds it hard to be totally impartial when his ego is directly challenged.

If he cannot relate well to others or make real efforts to compromise, his talents could be wasted and his genius will go a-begging. Overrationalizing and analyzing could be disastrous. When he is negative, he will even subject a blooming romance to a routine clinical examination. He should curb his urge to overkill.

The Metal Rooster could be inhibited with his emotions despite his outward bravado. He will insist on order in his life and will demand hygienic conditions or even sterile cleanliness in his surroundings.

But while this acquisitive Rooster is attracted to material wealth, he will also be concerned about social reforms. He will feel committed to extend his services and know-how to all humanity and will find fulfillment in solving social problems or instigating reforms for the advancement of mankind.

WATER ROOSTER—1873, 1933, 1993

This is the intellectual type of Rooster who will enjoy cultural pursuits. He has tremendous energy and initiative at his disposal and will seek to use his resources or enlist the help of others to speed up progress.

With Water as his element, he will be given to clear thinking and practicality. You can reason with him, as he will be compliant when faced with insurmountable odds. He is not as austere or self-sacrificing as other Roosters.

Proficient in the use of the written word and a commanding speaker, the Water Rooster can sway the masses and incite willing action from others. He will have strong scientific leanings and will be interested in health, medicine and technology. His mind functions with computerlike efficiency and thus he could lose sight of the main issues when he overstresses details. Systems and procedures fascinate him and when he is obsessed with perfection he could be bureaucratic and trivial.

WOOD ROOSTER—1885, 1945, 2005

An expansive type of Rooster who can be more considerate of others and have a wider outlook on life. Although he is much less stubborn and opinionated, he still has the tendency to complicate matters and get caught in a maze of his own making. He should learn to contain his enthusiasm and to avoid overexerting himself and expecting everyone else to have the same stamina and devotion that he has. No matter how well meaning his intentions may be, prescribing unrelieved clockwork and regimentation may drive his subordinates crazy.

Wood makes him progress-oriented, and when Wood is matched with his virtuous qualities of honesty and integrity, he will excel in his performance and his charts and graphs will amaze everyone.

Open-minded, fair and sociable, he can give unselfishly of himself to the welfare of others. He will seek to contribute to or improve existing social conditions. Desirous of congeniality, he will seek close association with the people he works with and will have an excellent record of reliability. Still, he will be basically a Rooster and he will not water down his biting comments when inflamed and will always work to protect his security. Life will be a dream for him if he does not take on too many high-flying projects all at the same time.

FIRE ROOSTER—1897, 1957, 2017

Possibly a shooting star. With fire as his element, this Rooster will be vigorous, highly motivated and authoritative. He will be able to operate independently and with great precision and skill, although he could also be temperamental, overdramatic and nervous at times.

Strongly principled and single-minded in his pursuit of success, he will display above-average managerial abilities and leadership. The diligent and intense Fire Rooster will abide fanatically by his own views and conduct his own fact-finding tours and feasibility studies.

He will be unmoved and unswayed by the feelings or personal opinions of others, but he will be professional and ethical in his dealings.

At times, he is too inflexible to make workable compromises and will take to putting people and situations under a microscope for observation. If things do not measure up to his expectations, he could assume the role of an Inquisitor or cause major upheavals.

Yet he does have organization talents and in spite of his other shortcomings, this type of Rooster will have the noblest intentions behind his actions. He could project a stimulating and dynamic public image.

EARTH ROOSTER—1909, 1969, 2029

A studious, analytical and probing Rooster who will dig for the truth, mature early and compile his own irrefutable information. Earth ensures that he will be accurate, efficient and careful in carrying out assignments. He will know how to brush aside the trimmings and view the hard, cold facts for himself. With him, you will get the bottom line first.

Unafraid of shouldering vast responsibilities, he will still cling to his Rooster's reputation for not mincing words. He is unpretentious and dogmatic and will have strong missionary tendencies. He loves conducting sermon-on-the-mount sort of meetings, exhorting everyone to work harder and follow his shining example. He can lead a simple and austere existence when he finds his job rewarding. Fanatically systematic, he will keep notes, file data and record everything he does for posterity.

A hard taskmaster, strict educator and much dreaded critic, the Earth Rooster will sow and reap from dawn to sundown and have bushels and bushels of success to show for his efforts if he can bring himself to be practical in his aspirations.

THE ROOSTER AND HIS ASCENDANTS

Born During the Hours of the Rat—11 P.M. to 1 A.M.

Mixture of piquant charm and curiosity. The Chicken is more convivial and acceptable with the Rat in him. Still argues, but in a more pleasant manner.

Born During the Hours of the Ox — 1 A.M. to 3 A.M.

The Ox, with his hooves firmly planted, could bring the flighty Chicken down to earth. But both signs crave authority and can be harsh when given absolute powers. Type that could use a sledgehammer to kill a fly.

Born During the Hours of the Tiger — 3 A.M. to 5 A.M.

Magnetic but a bit incoherent by nature. Could blow hot and cold in the same breath. The Rooster's analytical qualities may be swamped by the Tiger's impervious ways. Result is more misplaced self-confidence than normal.

Born During the Hours of the Rabbit — 5 A.M. to 7 A.M.

A quiet, efficient bird who always manages to get his worm. A Rooster less likely to cause trouble, but an expert at bluffing.

Born During the Hours of the Dragon — 7 A.M. to 9 A.M.

A Rooster who will not let you usurp one iota of his power. The Dragon within makes him ultra-assertive, fastidious and fearless. Will mow down the opposition with the finesse of a bulldozer.

Born During the Hours of the Snake — 9 A.M. to 11 A.M.

A wise and wiry fowl. The Snake makes him aloof and secretive. This Chicken may even learn to mind his own business and keep his opinions to himself.

Born During the Hours of the Horse — 11 A.M. to 1 P.M.

A nifty, practical Rooster with fast and sharp reflexes. Both signs here have colorful and flamboyant tastes, but the Horse could teach the Rooster not to waste time on unfeasible ventures. Result is that his pursuits could pay higher dividends.

Born During the Hours of the Sheep — 1 P.M. to 3 P.M.

An amiable, less assertive and bashful Rooster. The Sheep's coyness could mellow the Rooster's brash ways. A good thing after all.

Born During the Hours of the Monkey — 3 P.M. to 5 P.M.

A crafty but congenial Rooster, who is more purposeful and adept at making conciliatory deals. A happy-go-lucky, successful and plucky Chicken.

Born During the Hours of the Rooster — 5 P.M. to 7 P.M.

A double dose of meticulous efficiency and criticism that few can swallow.

Likely to be very notable, highly eccentric and overly particular. He will be in a class of his own.

Born During the Hours of the Dog — 7 P.M. to 9 P.M.

A calculating, erratic but fair Rooster. The Dog makes him less cocky and opinionated. Still, you must expect great color from this combination of two equally idealistic minds and sharp tongues.

Born During the Hours of the Boar — 9 P.M. to 11 P.M.

A complacent Rooster who will insist on helping you whether you like it or not! His brilliance may be on the surface and he is a social butterfly, but then he is unselfish and quite incapable of dishonesty.

HOW THE ROOSTER FARES IN DIFFERENT YEARS

Year of RAT

A difficult year. The Rooster will be forced to dip into savings as money is scarce or find that other people waste his money. Friends won't be of great help or will let him down when he goes to them for assistance. Headaches at home and health discomforts are indicated, as he works hard to settle his troubles alone. A year for discretion and much moderation.

Year of OX

The Rooster recuperates in the year of the Ox. He recoups lost power and will have the ability to conquer adversities or receive outside help. Good news at home and some traveling. Loss of blood indicated too at this time, so he should beware of injuries from sharp objects. He could also have an operation.

Year of TIGER

An eventful year. The Rooster is lucky with money and his business ventures could produce very fruitful results. Some worries at home, but his general plans go according to schedule. Still he should be careful this year as things tend to happen too fast for proper assessment. He must not be overoptimistic.

Year of RABBIT

A fair time for the Rooster if he remains conservative in outlook. Investments this year are shaky and he should not speculate, as loss of money is indicated. He is also prone to miscalculations and his profits may be eaten away by unpredicted expenses. It would be advisable for him to join forces with others this year instead of acting independently.

193

COMPATIBILITY TABLE FOR THE ROOSTER

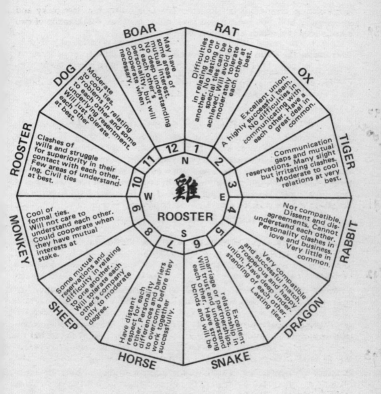

1988 Year of DRAGON

A very good and prosperous year. Success shines on the Rooster this year as he is able to occupy leading positions or is given the power to shape his own destiny. Home-wise and health-wise, there may be frustrations that make him tense and tired. Birth or marriages in his family.

1989 Year of SNAKE

Still a fortunate year for the Rooster, as some progress is indicated and he is lucky enough to retain his good position. No large monetary gains foreseen this year, although he will be able to curtail his losses to an admirable degree. Freak accidents or malicious rumours are also likely this year and he should not take long or unnecessary journeys.

1990 Year of HORSE

A trying time. The Rooster must not expect too much too soon as he will meet many obstacles in his path this year. He will pull through if he is not misguided by favorable preliminary results that could turn sour later on. A time to play politics or employ diplomacy, as he will have to make unwilling compromises with his enemies. His work scene is likely to be quarrelsome or unhappy. Some good news indicated in his family.

'91 Year of SHEEP

A good, protected year for the Rooster. No upheavals indicated as he enjoys glad tidings, regains lost ground and sees some advancement in his career. Troubles may still abound but he is not directly affected. Life is quieter and more settled. He is able to relax or take a good vacation.

'92 Year of MONKEY

A mixed year. The Rooster is faced with financial problems, failure in business or career, or personal suffering at home. He is prone to make errors in judgment, so he must not rely on outside information but investigate everything thoroughly on his own. Things may look better than they actually are.

'93 Year of ROOSTER

A moderately happy year in store for the Rooster. A time for him to make a splendid comeback. He is able to solve his problems with relative ease and he finds influential or powerful people who will support his ideas. He may still be involved in disputes but will emerge unhurt from accidents or other calamities.

Year of DOG

A good year for the Rooster as lost power or position can be restored. Travel or much entertaining is foreseen. His gains will be average but his losses are minimal. Plans are easily realized but his personal life may be clouded by some secret unhappiness or brooding.

Year of BOAR

A disturbing year for the Rooster as worries caused by unexpected difficulties plague him. His home life suffers or he may have temporary setbacks in his career. Trusted associates may also give him wrong advice or encourage him to spend beyond his means. A year to discount good news and plan prudently.

FAMOUS PERSONS BORN IN THE YEAR OF THE ROOSTER

Metal
Prince Philip
Peter Ustinov
Alex Haley
Alexander Dubček
Deborah Kerr
Yves Montand

Water
Crown Prince Akihito

Wood
King Birendra of Nepal
Elton John

Fire
D. K. Ludwig
Pope Paul VI
Grover Cleveland
Paul Gallico

Earth
Edwin Land
Baron Guy Rothschild
Queen Juliana
Peter Drucker
Elia Kazan
Katharine Hepburn
Andrei Gromyko

Chapter 11

The Dog

The martial strains have summoned me
To hear your sorrows,
Still your pain.
I am the protector of Justice;
Equality—my sole friend.
My vision never blurred by cowardice,
My soul never chained.
Life without honor
Is life in vain.

I AM THE DOG.

THE DOG SIGN

Chinese name for the Dog: GOU
Ranking Order: Eleventh
Hours Ruled by the Dog: 7 P.M. to 9 P.M.
Direction of its sign: West-Northwest
Season and principal month: Autumn—October
Corresponds to the Western sign: Libra
Fixed element: Metal
Stem: Positive

THE LUNAR YEARS OF THE DOG IN THE WESTERN CALENDAR

Starting Dates	Ending Dates	Element
February 10, 1910	January 29, 1911	Metal
January 28, 1922	February 15, 1923	Water
February 14, 1934	February 3, 1935	Wood
February 2, 1946	January 21, 1947	Fire
February 18, 1958	February 7, 1959	Earth
February 6, 1970	January 26, 1971	Metal
January 25, 1982	February 12, 1983	Water
February 10, 1994	January 30, 1995	Wood

If you were born on the day before the start of the lunar year of the Dog, e.g., February 9, 1910, you belong to the animal sign before the Dog—which is the Rooster.

If you were born on the day after the lunar year of the Dog, e.g., January 30, 1911, you then belong to the sign following that of the Dog—the Boar.

THE YEAR OF THE DOG

Paradoxically the year of the Dog will bring happiness and dissent in the same boat. The Dog's domestic auspices will bring harmony to home life, patriotism to one's country and unwavering fealty to whatever cause you wish to support.

On the other hand, his rigid willpower and unbending sense of justice will also lead to major confrontations with the weaker side getting the upper hand. It is a year in which controversial issues will be awarded a hearing and unconventional but effective changes will be introduced. Equality and liberty will be advocated by the Dog's noble influence.

We will become more idealistic in our views, shedding some materialism by doing charitable acts or otherwise championing some worthy projects. It is a year in which we will shift away from the pursuit of the almighty dollar and become a little more reflective. A perfect time to reassess our sense of values, polish up our virtues and go on crusades against tyranny and oppression.

In spite of the Dog's dismal outlook, he brings stability because people do not usually dare to challenge his authority when they see how intent he is on keeping the peace. The year of the Metal Dog is more feared than others as he is said to bring war and calamity.

Needless to say, the Dog's resoluteness and intensity will cause clashes, upheavals and rebellions of all sorts, but it will be his good sense and largesse that will also smooth things out in the end. His unselfishness will predispose us to be more bighearted than we normally are.

This will also be a year in which we will wish we could relax more without the cynical Dog constantly casting worries on our minds. Then again, perhaps it will be the Dog's ever-watchful eye that will be the main force in keeping this time calm.

Aside from this feeling of uneasiness, there should be no cause for alarm. We can go about our business as usual since the Dog makes the perfect sentry.

The Dog's year will lend integrity to our intentions and make us act in good faith. Nothing should concern us so long as we stick to the righteous path.

THE DOG PERSONALITY

This may be the most likable sign of all in the Chinese cycle. A person born in the year of the Dog is honest, intelligent and straightforward. He has a deep sense of loyalty and a passion for justice and fair play. A Dog native is usually animated and attractive and will exude sex appeal. Generally amiable and unpretentious, he will know how to get along with others as he is not too demanding. The egalitarian Dog likes to meet others halfway, is always willing to listen to reason and can be counted on to do his share.

If you have a forthright Dog for a friend, you must know that when you are in trouble, all you have to do is dial D-O-G. For no matter how much he or she complains, scolds or feigns indifference, the Dog person cannot ignore a real call for help. At times, the Dog protects the interests of others more avidly than his own. If anyone will bail you out ten times out of ten, he must be a Dog. The Dog-born sometimes sticks to the object of his affection no matter how unworthy the person is. You don't find a Dog leaving home just because he discovers that his master has the proverbial feet of clay. He makes allowances for such frailties and he will probably stick it out through thick and thin. And if he does leave home, well, don't blame him, it must be a truly dismal place indeed! The Dog does not desert easily.

Like his equally humanitarian friend, the Tiger, the Dog seldom directs his wrath at someone personally. He will take you to task over one specific act or offense without hating you entirely or forever. His anger is more of a bright flash. It could come without warning and may die as quickly, too. But it will always be a justifiable kind of anger—without malice, without rancor and without jealousy. When all is said and done and proper reparations have been made, he can bury the hatchet.

Not all Dogs look for fights. It would be more just to say that the Dog person is an open-eyed and open-minded observer, with the objective of preserving social goals and guarding the interest of the public at large.

Once in a while, when the Dog decides to take up a cause he thinks is right, he will emerge victorious. Fortunately, he is not one to champion bad causes because his ideals and morals will be of the highest order. As the symbol of justice, the Dog person is very serious about his self-imposed responsibilities.

Collectively speaking, the Dog is not materialistic and ceremonious;

he prefers plain talk. He usually sees through people's motives anyway, so fancy language just affects him the wrong way. He is a natural lawyer and will listen to your case objectively. But don't pry into his affairs as he will become secretive and withdrawn. The Dog was born with his defense shields up. You will have to gain his confidence gradually and wait for him to open up.

The Dog is reputed to be cynical, but this is a callous generalization. Actually, it is more fitting to say that puppies are universally lovable and irresistible, young dogs are frisky and full of life and only mature or old dogs earn the right to be the diehard cynics of the Oriental zodiac. Staunch public defenders and members of the Old Guard must indeed belong to the elite Dog unit, getting bleary-eyed with disillusionment as the years go by but remaining ever faithful in rallying to the bugle's call. Raving with disgust at how low our morals have sunk, the Dog will still be found pitting his strength against the forces of evil and answering every S.O.S. that comes his way.

Even as young pups, the Dog will be able to spot the good guys and the bad guys. He'll want to be one of the good guys, of course. She will be Joan of Arc and he will be Sir Galahad.

The Dog, whether he admits it or not, will have an inborn need to divide people into fixed categories. To him, you are either a friend or foe; black or white. No mousey grays or other shades of in-between. He has to know how to classify you before he can relax in your company. His decision to trust or not to trust you is often a final one. And if he does suspect you, well, he may not be rude enough to come right out and accuse you without the evidence, but you can be sure he will be watching you from the corner of his eye. However, even snarling, barking, mad dogs have a good idea of how the legal system works and won't come after you without that warrant. But when he's onto your scent and picks up your tracks, it will be difficult to shake him off.

On the whole, the Dog is only violent when stirred or attacked on his home ground. He will work hard when he has to or wants to; otherwise, he has a certain "lie by the fire" kind of laziness. Yet, while he is tolerant of and acquiesent to his friends, he can be critical of and emotionally cold to people he dislikes. Practical, fearless and the owner of one very sharp tongue, the Dog person is ultrarealistic and outspoken. He will make a good judge as he spares no one, not even himself, in the final analysis.

Like the late Chou En-lai, who was born in the year of the Dog, the native of this sign will be loved for his warm charisma and superb insight into human nature. With his astute intelligence and noble character, he makes a good but sometimes reluctant leader. People trust him and hold him in high esteem because of his sense of duty and discretion. The Dog's leadership is unemotional, although altruistic. But he is also prone to bouts of erratic and cantankerous behavior. This may be because he is really an introvert at heart and hates all that pretense on the social scene.

The Dog-born does not care very much about money, but should he have desperate need for it, no one is better equipped to find it. In many cases, he will be born into a good family; if not, he will elevate his status in life by himself without shunning his family or hiding his humble origins.

Even while he puts on a bright and cheerful appearance, the Dog is by nature a pessimist. He tends to worry unnecessarily and will expect trouble to be lurking in every corner. But there are times when his predictions come true. Anyway, it will be wise to note that Orientals as well as Westerners have the same belief that everyone needs a Dog at home to distinguish friends from foes.

You can trust the Dog to hand you the bad news with the good. With his matter-of-fact ways, he may even be quite good at breaking sad tidings, especially to theatrical and overemotional people. It is not that he will enjoy informing people of disaster (whether or not he led a demonstration last week to protest the matter); it will be because it is against his nature to hedge or delay the inevitable. He is a definite person and he has this necessity to give you a definite answer. As for himself, he will be able to face the facts of life, even if he is young and untried.

When he is right, the Dog can be obstinate and unbending. It is hard to influence the unprejudiced Dog once he makes up his mind. He will cut the opposition's arguments to ribbons with his flawless logic and acid wit. His bad temper and hot criticism can do a lot of damage but he only resorts to this when he is getting nowhere with diplomacy and formal protests. The Dog may be pugnacious and quarrelsome but he will take his fights out to the open and rarely stoops to underhanded methods in order to win. He excels as a military man, lawyer, teacher, judge, doctor, captain of industry or missionary. He is one person who can carry on revolutionary activities with a pacifist's views.

The lady Dog will be a thoughtful and capable person who will in all situations be a simple dresser, preferring casual and serviceable clothing. She will opt for a loose and flowing hair style that could frame her expressive face quite dramatically. She can become curt, impertinent and impatient when she is crossed, but on the whole she is unaffected and attentive to the needs of others. Cooperative, unprejudiced and a very good sport, she will enjoy dancing, swimming, tennis or any other lively outdoor activity. A real friend to her husband and children, she will allow them enough freedom to express themselves and choose their own futures without being possessive or interfering.

Dog girls have warm, enduring beauty. Ava Gardner, Sophia Loren, Brigitte Bardot, Zsa Zsa Gabor and Cher are but a few of the glamorous examples of famous females born under this sign.

Although she exhibits a fairly amiable disposition and has a ready smile for everyone, the Dog lady likes to form friendships slowly. You will have to come over to her house for tea (a good sign of acceptance), then invite her over to try your homemade cupcakes. You must discover each other's qualities leisurely. Compare likes and dislikes. Exchange mutual oaths of loyalty. When her sense of equilibrium is satisfied, you will get the royal stamp of approval. Henceforth, your name is engraved in gold in her little black book under the heading Friend (she has another section for the Enemies), and when you call upon her she will come to your rescue wherever she may be.

The Dog person is never without resources, and even when he does not have direct power, he will wield influence on important or decision-making people through his sound advice and remarkable insight. People do lend him their ears, as he champions moderation in all things. Yet the Dog-born is the first to see the perils of being at the top of the power game and is often criticized for his lack of desire for fame and authority. He keeps his aspirations to himself and is modestly prepared to serve others, if that is his duty, or else be left alone to do whatever pleases him most. Moreover, he is not renowned for his patience and has the tendency to snap at others when irked. He will not go out and fall madly in love like the Horse or Tiger, but he will be deeply attached and affectionate to those he loves.

While it will never be easy for the Dog to trust everyone profoundly, as the Boar does, he does his best to bring out the good in his fellowmen. Once you have gained his allegiance, he will place complete faith in you and give you his undivided support. Try criticizing someone who is dear to the Dog, and you will be in for a very strong rebuttal.

Most people born under this sign are tough, in the sense that they can take a lot of stress without cracking up. The Dog's stable mind makes him a good counselor, priest or psychologist. During times of crisis, he can suffer great hardships and deprivation without complaining. He earnestly wishes that the world were a better place to live in, and he will not be afraid to go out and do something about it. Many saints and martyrs were born under the idealistic sign of the Dog.

A Dog who is born at night is reputed to be more aggressive and high-strung than one born during the day. Dogs of all seasons will be well provided for throughout their lives and have need of little.

The Dog will be most compatible with the Horse, the Rabbit and the Tiger. He will have no conflict with the Rat, Snake, Monkey, Boar or another Dog. The Rooster he will have difficulty understanding. The one he will never really get himself to believe in is the overconfident Dragon. Neither can he find it pleasant to tolerate the constant complaints of the indulgent Sheep. Likewise, the Dragon will be enraged when the Dog pours cold water over his grand designs and the Sheep will call the Dog insensitive.

THE DOG CHILD

This child will be friendly, happy and well-balanced. Cheerful and harmonious, he expects little of others and can accept his parents and friends as they are. Open, confident and loyal, he will preceive other people's viewpoints with amazing clarity while still maintaining his own convictions and dignity. He will never allow himself to be bullied and in all probability will put up a hefty fight with the neighborhood tyrant and win the respect of his peers.

Sensible and fairly consistent, the Dog will get his schoolwork done without too much trouble. He will be reasonable when asked to help around the house and will be protective toward younger family members.

Playful and outgoing, he will insist on a certain degree of independence. But the faithful Dog will never stray too far from home. This child will be known and liked for his sense of humor, warmth and candid ways. When offended, the Dog child can turn rebellious, mean and hypercritical. His anger flares and subsides relatively quickly and he will return to his normal equilibrium. He will not keep a grudge for long and can forget and forgive readily.

When he is negative, the Dog is pugnacious, argumentative, caustic and unbendingly opinionated. He is only liberal and fair-minded if not pushed too far. When he feels he has been taken undue advantage of, the Dog will retaliate bitterly and without any compassion. Once he starts to fight, the Dog will not be open to discussion or negotiations anymore. It is better never to challenge this tolerant child to the point of no return. The unassuming Dog can erupt like a volcano.

If the Dog child is rejected or unappreciated, he could be lethargic, insensitive, cynical or plain indifferent to the wishes of his parents. Compliment and encourage him and this child will reciprocate lavishly. Basically, he is cooperative, so there should be no need to cajole or threaten him in any way. Efficient and diplomatic, the Dog will exhibit a lack of prejudice, or at least he will make it a point never to show it. He is inclined to avoid scenes rather than create them.

It will be safe to give him responsibilities or take him into your confidence even at an early age. The trustworthy Dog will not like to be accused of having a loose tongue. He will guard a secret like a sacred trust.

To sum it up, the Dog will always defend what is his. He will have a high sense of values and to him home and family will come first.

THE FIVE TYPES OF DOGS

METAL DOG—1910, 1970, 2030

This type of Dog can be unwavering in his convictions and highly critical of every infraction of the law according to his own interpretation. However, his principles are of the highest kind and fundamentally he is noble and charitable. He will give himself to a lifetime of selfless dedication if he finds an object or cause worthy of his devotion. Yet he can be ruthless when aroused and will pursue his enemies until they are annihilated.

The metal element combined with his lunar sign, which is also governed by Metal, produces a double Metal sign, which is extremely formidable. Tibetans call this combination the "Iron Dog" and look upon its year with much apprehension as it could be either very good or very bad, depending on whether it takes on a negative or positive course.

Likewise, the stern and principled Metal Dog will exhibit the same traits and will exercise strong mental discipline over himself and take things very seriously—expecially when they concern the affairs of his heart or his country.

His loyalty is unquestionable and he has strong political views. Never indecisive, he will pick a side and never desert his affiliations. Consequently, even though he hates injustice and foul play, this type of Dog can resort to extreme measures when he insists that others subscribe to his views.

WATER DOG—1922, 1982, 2042

An intuitive type of Dog, who will be difficult to lead astray. He could be very attractive and a striking beauty if a female.

Water gives him more reflective qualities and he will be sympathetic to the views of the opposite side. However, despite his pleasant personality and democratic stance, he does not establish very strong personal bonds to those close to him and is often too liberal where he should be more firm.

More easygoing than other Dogs, he will tend to be lenient with himself as well as with others, often indulging in self-gratification and adventurous sprees. But because his strong temperament will be toned down by the Water element, this Dog is able to contain his emotions to an admirable degree and will present a calm and charming exterior.

A good counselor, fair judge and legal-minded operator, the Water Dog will be fluid in expressing himself, using psychological approaches that are hard to refuse or refute. He is fated also to have a large circle of friends and his company will be much sought after.

WOOD DOG—1874, 1934, 1994

An enchanting, warm-hearted and even-tempered sort of Dog, who in spite of his candor and wariness of strangers will form close and lasting relationships with those he chooses to befriend and love. Honest, considerate and well-liked, this Dog person seeks intellectual stimulation and will work hard to develop himself.

Wood gives him a more stable and generous nature and he will seek growth, balance and beauty in his environment. He will also be attracted to money and success but will preserve himself from too much materialism. With an aptitude for dealing with vast numbers of people from all walks of life, he or she will act with maturity and common sense.

The Wood Dog will be popular and will gravitate toward refinement and social graces despite his hidden assertive qualities. Energetic and cooperative, he will like to deal in partnerships or ally himself with powerful affiliations.

He is basically group-oriented and will be eager to please as many of his associates as possible. Thus, this type of Dog can sometimes be held back because he refuses to move without the sanction and backing of others. He must learn independence even if it means rocking the boat on occasion.

FIRE DOG—1886, 1946, 2006

A highly dramatic and attractive type of Dog who will be thrown into the limelight by his alluring yet friendly personality. He will be defiant and rebellious when forced to do something against his will, but he will be very popular with the opposite sex. Although he may be the life of the party type, he is still careful to practice what he preaches and will not be spoiled by success and fortune. Fire makes him very fierce when attacked; nor will he make threats he cannot carry out. His bite is just as strong as his bark.

The buoyant and self-assured Fire Dog has great magnetic charm and can convince others to follow his lead. His independent spirit and courage will see to it that he is never afraid of getting involved with others. He will constantly thrill to new experiences and adventures. But he needs a strong shining example to pattern himself after. He will relate better to people older than himself, those from whom he can learn a great deal or whom he can depend on to bring stability into his life.

Fire makes him or her more creative and pure in expression. He will be charged with super willpower and a natural honesty that people find hard to resist. His outgoing character combined with the Dog's basic faith and idealism will help him to succeed in ambitious endeavors and to overcome great barriers.

EARTH DOG—1898, 1958, 2018

This Dog will be an impartial dispenser of sound advice and justice. An efficient and constructive thinker, he moves slowly and with good purpose. He is faithful to his beliefs but will bow to the majority rule. Vigilant and careful, he will appreciate the proper use of money and power and have a fixed scale of values from which he seldom deviates.

Quiet, kind-hearted but secretive, he will understand how to inspire others and instruct them wisely. Yet because of his high moral standards and unfailing idealism, he tends to overperform and may demand excessive dedication and loyalty from others.

A good fighter and an equally good survivor, this Dog is practical and less sentimental. The realistic Earth Dog will value his individualism and self-respect and will speak without reserve straight from his heart. He will not abuse powers bestowed on him and will delegate duties with a keen insight into other people's potentials. He is never totally suppressed by defeat nor overconfident in victory.

THE DOG AND HIS ASCENDANTS

Born During the Hours of the Rat — 11 P.M. to 1 A.M.

Loving but not so giving. Has a monetary angle even when he is moralizing. He is considerate and careful about money—mainly his own.

Born During the Hours of the Ox — 1 A.M. to 3 A.M.

Has brusque but unquestionable veracity. May have a spotless reputation but he is too conservative and dour in many ways. Staunch defender of the faith!

Born During the Hours of the Tiger — 3 A.M. to 5 A.M.

Both signs here are tirelessly active and courageous. However, the Tiger could make the Dog more impatient and critical than he already is. But on the whole this combination could also produce a more stimulated and passionate Dog.

Born During the Hours of the Rabbit — 5 A.M. to 7 A.M.

A Dog who is all for détente. Weighs his pros and cons carefully before taking sides. Apt to be lighthearted and will not like baring his fangs.

Born During the Hours of the Dragon — 7 A.M. to 9 A.M.

A very idealistic Dog who will be a miracle worker or missionary. He will

209

COMPATIBILITY TABLE FOR THE DOG

BOAR — No serious clashes. Personality struggles for dominance. No struggles for dominance. Acceptable and agreeable to a certain degree. A moderate relationship.

RAT — Have respect and admiration for one another. No serious differences or personality clashes. Could have good teamwork in common aims.

OX — Do not have many areas of similar interest. Some communication gaps and unsympathetic feelings. Will not relate very well together.

TIGER — Excellent match. No difficulties in communication in this union. Will achieve success and prosperity in love or business relations.

RABBIT — Highly compatible and rewarding relationship. Deep trust and affinity for one another. Will find prosperity and happiness together.

DRAGON — Serious clashes and strong conflicts. Cannot comprehend or trust each other. Highly incompatible. Cannot see eye to eye.

SNAKE — Mutual respect and certain areas of common interest. No conflicts. Will co-operate to a good and large extent. Fairly amicable ties.

HORSE — Very compatible combination and happy successful love and partnerships. Deep affinity and permanent bonds for one another.

SHEEP — Tolerate each other at best. Have very little in common and no special need for each other's company. Incompatible team.

MONKEY — Have underlying respect for each other. No clashes of wills. Good and workable relations in love and partnerships. Will cooperate well together.

ROOSTER — Nothing solid or lasting will result from this relationship. Some resentment and communication gaps. Moderate to cool ties at best.

DOG — No conflicts. Congenial and cooperative ties. Compatible to a good extent. Will work together amicably for common goals.

狗 DOG

truly qualify for sainthood if he can only accept other versions of religion aside from his own. Very dogmatic combination.

Born During the Hours of the Snake – 9 A.M. to 11 A.M.

A Dog with a silent, brooding nature that rarely surfaces. Competent and mentally superior. The Snake in him will bend his sense of justice a little so that he is not adverse to taking shortcuts in order to achieve his goals.

Born During the Hours of the Horse – 11 A.M. to 1 P.M.

A sharp, sunny Dog with electric responses. Never misses a cue and is everyone's best friend—but don't ask him to prove it. He will go merrily on his way if you are too imposing!

Born During the Hours of the Sheep – 1 P.M. to 3 P.M.

Soft-hearted, cuddly Dog who will be artistic, pessimistic and sympathetic in nature. Still, he won't lose his keen sense of fair play but may keep one eye closed now and then to make allowances for your weaknesses.

Born During the Hours of the Monkey – 3 P.M. to 5 P.M.

A Dog with a stretchable conscience and unfailing wit. Amusing, diverse and gay. A splendid interlacing here of character and ingenuity.

Born During the Hours of the Rooster – 5 P.M. to 7 P.M.

A preaching Dog. And, believe me, he would rather preach than practice. Very analytical, and competent to achieve his goals, but it takes him so long to get to the point.

Born During the Hours of the Dog – 7 P.M. to 9 P.M.

A defensive, ever-alert Dog. Constantly looking for causes to fight, rights to wrong and infidels to save. Has an open and honest nature, but is a committed revolutionary.

Born During the Hours of the Boar – 9 P.M. to 11 P.M.

A burly, sensuous and emotionally charged Dog. Will go all out to censor others while still hooked on some pretty rich indulgences of his own.

HOW THE DOG FARES IN DIFFERENT YEARS

Year of RAT

A very fortunate year. The Dog can be successful in business or will receive additional income from some investments. His health is good but there will

be some problems in his home area or with young children. He shou
lending money this year.

Year of OX

A year of uncertainties for the Dog-born. He may suffer from hasty decisions
or may have to make difficult concessions. Friends or associates tend to
misunderstand him or take offense easily. His good intentions are misread
and he must avoid confrontation at all costs. Loss of power or additional
expense is indicated this year.

Year of TIGER

A moderately happy year. No serious disputes at home or office. Some
romantic squabbles predicted but they will do no permanent damage. The
Dog's net results this year will be mixed and he will be confused by
conflicting reports. Friends and family will make too many demands on his
time.

Year of RABBIT

A favorable year for the aspirations of the Dog. He can start his own business
this year or go into a partnership. He will be able to advance his position and
can reorganize things for the benefit of others. Problems are solved with a
minimum of complications.

Year of DRAGON

A difficult year in store. The Dog will have to strive very hard to maintain
his former status and may have to fight off the competition constantly.
People take advantage of his weak position and he is susceptible to infections
and contagious diseases. A time to lie low and join forces with others instead
of acting independently. He will receive good news in the winter.

Year of SNAKE

A very good year. The Dog will still have to work hard but he will receive
due recognition of his efforts. He will be lucky in his business investments
and will have the support of the right people. A year for him to take things
easy and enjoy his family life more. He will also benefit a lot from good
advice or tips given to him at this time.

Year of HORSE

A year of expansion and progress for the Dog. Promotions and real financial
gains are indicated and he will be at the peak of his power and luck. Some
unhappy news at home or loss of a small belonging is indicated. He will
entertain or travel a lot this year. This is a time in which the Dog will have to
use his mind a lot.

Year of SHEEP

A moderate year for the Dog. Anxiety and worries beset him. He can prevent losses and resolve differences if he holds his tongue and refuses to lose his temper. A year for him to be patient and conservative.

Year of MONKEY

A fair year. It will be hectic and not as fruitful as the Dog expects, but there will be good news or celebrations at home. Extra expenses, more traveling than usual or a change in residence are also foreseen. New friends and important people will fete him.

Year of ROOSTER

A mixed year for the Dog native. Problems with health, romance, government or superiors are indicated. Friends are not helpful or understanding and he finds it hard to get back money due him. He will suffer temporary loss of position and credibility.

Year of DOG

A protected year. Problems and health upsets are few and the Dog will be able to increase his knowledge, spend time for study or meditation or regain lost credibility. He will have some achievements in his career but no large profits or return on investment.

Year of BOAR

A calm year. The Dog person could make some gains through speculations or reap unlikely benefits. Results cannot be as good as he wishes due to delays and additional expenses. A year to cultivate new and influential friends or contacts.

FAMOUS PERSONS BORN IN THE YEAR OF THE DOG

Metal
David Niven
Chiang Ching-kuo

Water
Itzhak Rabin
Charles Bronson
Pierre Cardin
Zsa Zsa Gabor
Ava Gardner
Norman Mailer

Wood
Voltaire
Sir Winston Churchill
Herbert Hoover
Elvis Presley
Ralph Nader
Brigitte Bardot
Sophia Loren
Carol Burnett

Fire
King Carl Gustav
Ilie Nastase
Cher
Liza Minelli

Earth
Golda Meir
Chou En-lai

Chapter 12

The Boar

Of all God's children
I have the purest heart.
With innocence and faith,
I walk in Love's protective light.
By giving of myself freely
I am richer and twice blest.
Bonded to all mankind by
     common fellowship,
My goodwill is universal
And knows no bounds.

I AM THE BOAR.

THE BOAR SIGN

Chinese name for the Boar: ZHU
Ranking order: Twelfth
Hours ruled by the Boar: 9 P.M. to 11 P.M.
Direction of its sign: North-Northwest
Season and principal month: Autumn—November
Corresponds to the Western sign: Scorpio
Fixed element: Water
Stem: Negative

THE LUNAR YEARS OF THE BOAR IN THE WESTERN CALENDAR

Starting Dates	Ending Dates	Element
January 30, 1911	February 17, 1912	Metal
February 16, 1923	February 4, 1924	Water
February 4, 1935	January 23, 1936	Wood
January 22, 1947	February 9, 1948	Fire
February 8, 1959	January 27, 1960	Earth
January 27, 1971	January 15, 1972	Metal
February 13, 1983	February 1, 1984	Water
January 31, 1995	February 18, 1996	Wood

If you were born on the day before the start of the lunar year of the Boar, e.g., January 29, 1911, you belong to the animal sign before the Boar—which is the Dog.

If you were born on the day after the lunar year of the Boar, e.g., February 18, 1912, then you belong to the sign following that of the Boar—the Rat.

THE YEAR OF THE BOAR

A year of goodwill to all. An excellent climate for business, and industry in general will prevail. People will be more free and easy on the whole and the complaisant attitude of the Boar will generate a feeling of abundance. But in spite of the favorable auspices here, like the Boar we will hesitate, waver and undermine our own abilities when opportunity calls.

The Boar's year is one of plenty. *La dolce vita* is very much advocated and practiced by the sensual Boar. If life is worth living, it must be lived to the hilt. Such is his motto. The Boar is as lavish with gifts as he is with affection. He takes pride in being chivalrous and extravagant. It would be ill-advised to overspend this year or make sizable investments without thorough investigation. We may also come to regret impulsive acts of generosity made on the spur of the moment.

The fortunate Boar carries with him contentment and security. This is one year in which you could be happy without having or needing a lot of success or money to make it so. There will not seem to be many hurdles to overcome and the placid Boar radiates a sense of well-being. Still, a great deal of prudence is recommended in money matters, as the Boar is always susceptible to swindlers.

This year will find us entertaining a lot more than usual and getting ourselves involved in all sorts of charitable and social functions. We find it a lot easier to make friends in the Boar's tolerant and expansive atmosphere.

Watch out for excesses, though, as the Boar tends to overindulge himself in anything when given the opportunity. Weight watchers will have a tough time and may face losing (or rather, gaining) battles.

THE BOAR PERSONALITY

This is the sign of honesty, simplicity and great fortitude. Gallant, sturdy and courageous, a person born in this year will apply himself to an allotted task with all his strength and you can rely on him to see it through. Outwardly, he may appear rough-hewn and jovial, but scratch the surface and you will find pure gold.

The Boar is bound to be one of the most natural people you could come across. The original nice guy, winner of the "Charlie Brown" award, he will never hit you below the belt. The Boar person is popular and sought after because, like the Sheep and Rabbit, he seeks universal harmony. No doubt he will have fights and differences with others, but he will not carry grudges unless you give him no choice. He doesn't like to add fuel to the fire in a confrontation and will usually let bygones be bygones. The lenient Boar will always take the first step forward and establish excellent rapport with others. If he fails, it certainly won't be for lack of trying at his end. He will be blessed with great endurance. He can work steadily on one thing at a time with incredible patience and will make an excellent and exact teacher.

However, he is equally reputed for his wanton pursuit of pleasure, and even depravity, when he emphasizes his negative traits.

In his life, the loyal and thoughtful Boar will make lasting and beneficial friendships. He enjoys gatherings of all kinds, giving parties and hosting fetes, joining clubs and all kinds of associations. A quiet organizer, who hates arguments and bickering, he is capable of bringing people of all sides together. His credibility and sincerity are his best assets. Yet, he can be a bit too affable and condescending at times, and he also expects others to tolerate his weaknesses.

The Boar will not dazzle you like the Dragon, nor bewitch you like the Monkey or Tiger, nor mesmerize you like a hypnotic Snake. He will simply grow on you until you cannot do without him. The solicitous Boar is synonymous with diligence and shining, old-fashioned chivalry. He won't mind taking up the burdens of others; he won't rebel at staying in the background or even supporting the whole cast with his incredible strength. He is the kind of person we tend to take for granted until he leaves us to fend for ourselves—totally stunned by our dependency on him.

It will be easy to trust the kindly Boar. He rarely has ulterior motives. As a matter of fact, he is too innocent and naive, and as a result, he is the favorite victim of swindlers. Still, the guileless Boar is fortunate in the sense that he will always find people to help him even though he does not go around begging for favors. He would prefer to be on the giving end, and when he is in a position to help you, you can be sure he will extend his hand. Fortune will favor him in many respects because of his all-round goodness and faith in his fellowmen. The Boar believes in miracles and miracles will happen to him.

Calm and understanding, the Boar is a genial fellow who can and will tolerate a lot of nonsense from his friends. He is quick tempered too, but since he hates quarreling, he will end up giving his opponents the benefit of the doubt. All told, he is one of the most accommodating guys you could find.

A person born in this year will be a great fund-raiser. He will have a penchant for social work and charity because a spirit of selflessness prevails over such functions and because he seeks to identify with as many people as possible.

When the world is cruel to you and fate has dealt you a stinging blow, run to a Boar. Author of the Good Neighbor policy, he will welcome you and your troubles with open arms. He is a good listener and even when you are definitely in the wrong, he will never have the heart to tell you so. He will do what he can without rubbing any salt into your wounds. He'll even get others involved. He'll call upon his Masonic brothers or hold a fund-raising dinner to help pay your debts. The Boar doesn't mind commitments. He's made for them. He has a good strong back and the biggest heart that can be found. These are no mean virtues by any standard and pretty hard to come by wherever you go. With a Boar, it is simply, "ask and you shall receive."

Now, to be perfectly fair, we must see the other side of the coin. While the Boar may be generosity itself, he also adheres to the "what's mine is yours and what's yours is mine" maxim.

When your Boar friend comes calling, he will help himself to your food, your wine, your clothes, your new golf set, your latest camera, your car, etc., with relative ease and childlike simplicity. Telling him off could be a problem. He will respond with great disbelief and hurt. He won't understand or accept your one-way street mentality.

Ms. Boar will be either spotlessly clean or terribly untidy. All Boars tend to come in these two categories and there are only rare cases of in-betweens. Nonetheless, she will be very personable and modest. She will devote every ounce of energy she has to the objects of her affection and ask for very little in return. You will be able to identify her by her remarkable purity of expression and trusting ways. Yet, although she loves with total abandonment, she will show a prefer-ence for anonymity or even secrecy. She can worship someone at a distance for years or serve him with passionate devotion without his knowing about it. She could play the perfect hostess to her husband's cronies and spoil the children by constantly answering to their beck and call—not to mention picking up after them all the time. But she won't mind, and when she does complain, it will be mild. Actually, she loves tending to her family and will look upon them not as burdens but as her pride and joy. With her, it will be a labor of love. Wherever she presides, people will congregate in an atmosphere of happiness and contentment.

Defenseless against deception, the Boar person likes to trust everyone and will believe almost anything they tell him, even if they are strangers or people he knows superficially. Needless to say, the Boar and his money are easily parted. The unsophisticated Boar should avoid handling finances. With him, it could be, "easy come, easy go." He is soft-hearted and too sympathetic to hold the purse strings.

By nature, the Boar is a materialist, yet he loves to share whatever he has. The more he gives, the more he seems to have. Unselfish and unassuming, he is surrounded by an ever-widening circle of friends whom he will allow to take advantage of him. He has equal need of them, too, as the sociable Boar must always feel part of the gang and enjoys footing the bills and being looked up to.

On the other hand, he is also thick-skinned and can dismiss insults and unpleasantries with a shrug. He does not like to look too far beyond tomorrow. It may be these traits that will help him recover quickly from the misfortunes that may befall him. The gregarious Boar just does not take calamity all that seriously.

Behind the sweet and reasonable facade of the Boar, there hides a remarkable power of resoluteness. He can take the seat of authority any time he pleases, but the Boar is his own worst enemy. His scruples always get the better of him and serve more as a hindrance to his progress than anything else. On the other hand, when he is pushed to the limit, he can respond savagely and turn into a raging foe. He can summon up tremendous energy and perform Herculean feats.

While the Boar may appear gullible, he may be smarter than you dream. Actually, he knows how to care for his interests in an inoffensive manner, and by allowing you to take him for a ride, he may just be giving you enough rope to hang yourself. The Chinese saying "What is yours will always find a way to come back to you" applies to the Boar's policy in full force.

Anyway, being of scrupulous makeup, the Boar will rarely be a trickster or thief. He is all too uncomfortable with ill-gotten gain and will be haunted by severe guilt feeling over the slightest transgression.

Once the Boar is driven to litigation—everyone loses. He may be barricaded by an army of lawyers or even held incommunicado by those familiar with his forgiving nature. He doesn't really hate you and personally regrets being the instrument of bitterness, but once his legal advisors have set the wheels into motion he is forced to go along with the suit. Even when he does win, he may be plagued by remorse for the rest of his life. Tangling in lawsuits will get the Boar dragged deep into the mud of the legal pit. His involvements in legal cases are often doomed to be long and complicated.

Being a sensuous creature, the Boar has strong passions. Endowed with extraordinary vigor and stamina, he is admired for putting his heart and soul into his work. Then again, his very strength could turn out to be his undoing. Because of the fact that his virility and vitality are above average, the Boar will love to savor the good things in life without restriction. If he is unable to check his enormous appetites and practice self-control, the Boar will be corrupted or debased by people who know how to exploit his frailties.

The honest Boar loves with all his heart. He is very considerate as a rule and does not know how to camouflage his emotions. In a love affair, he or she is most likely to end up as the injured party. He could carry the torch for years to come.

His main fault will be his inability to say "No" firmly to himself, his family and his friends. In some cases, he will oblige others by making concessions that it would be wiser to avoid and end up in a heap of trouble. However, when difficulties result, he will bear the blame and burden uncomplainingly. He will become bankrupt at least once in his life, but he will always manage to make a comeback, brighter and bolder than before. The secret of his success lies in his good faith, generosity and resilience.

The Boar will elect to work hard in life, and he will play just as hard, too, so long as he can use up his bountiful supply of energy. With his basic aptitude and conscientiousness, he will triumph and provide well for those about him. His life is fated to be blessed with all he will need and the money, power and success that comes to him will be unselfishly shared with one and all. With his robust and free-spending ways, the burly Boar will always be found living it up. He is the perfect friend, forever willing to do you another favor, or lend you another dollar. Maybe this explains why he is so lucky! At times, it seems he owns the Horn of Plenty.

Although intelligent and well-informed (everyone will somehow tell the Boar his secrets), the Boar person is not deep. He accepts things at face value and would rather conceal the misgivings he has about others in order to keep the peace.

But it is also said that the Boar has a fatalistic streak to his nature, and when he has nothing further to lose, he could turn into the most negative and debauched of creatures, throwing himself into an abyss of self-gratification and eventual destruction.

Most of the Boar's problems stem from his overgenerous character. If he could contain his basic urge to do too much for others and to promise more than he can deliver, he should have few major upsets.

The Boar will have a happy life when he shares it with the quiet and sagacious Rabbit or the gentle Sheep. He will also get along well with the Tiger. The Rat, Ox, Dragon, Horse, Rooster and Dog will make secondary teammates and have no serious conflicts with the Boar. He may not find the company of other Boars too stimulating, but will be able to take things in stride. Most of his problems will arise from his dealing with the Snake and the Monkey, for he will be no match for their cunning and wit.

THE BOAR CHILD

The Boar child will be self-reliant, sociable and easy to deal with. Dependable and determined, he will lead in school activities and acquire prestige by his perseverance and dedication. This youngster will be courageous in the face of great odds and he will not whimper or complain. As a matter of fact, he will be endowed with a remarkably strong body and can withstand a good deal of pain and suffering without crying.

The Boar, like the Rat, will have a hefty appetite and you won't have to force him to eat or pamper him like the Sheep child. He will work hard cheerfully and will not be easily depressed or discouraged. His placid exterior masks his passionate nature. The amorous Boar finds it difficult to be casual or detached in his affections. If he loves his parents, he will worship the very ground they walk on; if not, he will punish himself with remorse and guilt instead of blaming anyone else. He will not need as much attention as other children but he must be assured that he will have your support when he seeks it.

The Boar child has a certain individualism of his own. He will allow you to be the boss so long as you do not expect him to be your slave. His give-and-take attitude will make him popular around the neighborhood. He strives more for the fun of winning rather than for the rewards. Often, he may not treasure his belongings and may give things away easily.

In spite of his excellent ability for organizing group effort, smoothing out rough edges and calming fiery natures, the Boar will have trouble taking sides, questioning other people's motives or restraining himself from indulging in his rich tastes and love of comfort on the sly.

This is one child who can take reproach with a positive frame of mind. Setbacks can instill him with renewed vigor. Whenever he instigates changes, he will always be able to convince everyone involved of their necessity. The Boar child will put all his strength, conviction and dedication behind anything he undertakes.

With his soft approach and gentle persuasiveness, the Boar can and will inspire others to do his bidding. It is he who needs more discipline if his talents are not to go to waste. He may excel at planning functions, projects and other people's activities, but he is lazy about applying the same rules to his own daily life.

Whatever you do for him, the Boar will pay you back double. This goes for the bad as well as the good. He is totally blind to the faults of his loved ones and is filled with immense loyalty to his friends. His instinctive understanding of another person's emotions or needs will at times make him seem wise beyond his years.

Whatever he does, you will find this child constantly looking for more ways to work off his huge supply of energy. Wherever he is, you will find a lot of togetherness. He loves to seal relationships with a special glue of his own. In him, you will see unselfishness and a truly great passion for living.

THE FIVE TYPES OF BOARS

METAL BOAR—1911, 1971, 2051

A proud, passionate Boar with overpowering sentiments, who values his reputation. Intense and more dominating than others, this type of Boar often has excessive appetites and could lack refinement or tact.

He exerts less control over his personal life and is very sociable and extroverted. Openly demonstrative with his affections and pureminded, he underestimates his enemies and overestimates his friends.

He is not likely to be secretive and will be direct and trusting, even credulous.

Ambitious and forceful, but not always objective, the Metal Boar could be a dangerous opponent, as he can be violent in expressing his anger or resentment.

This type of Boar will not concede defeat graciously. He is not a quitter and can be relied on to have immense powers of endurance. An active doer blessed with great positive strength, the staunch Metal Boar will have enough vigor for ten.

WATER BOAR—1863, 1923, 1983

A persevering and diplomatic Boar with all the qualifications of an outstanding emissary. Perceptive at discovering people's hidden desires, he will be resourceful in bargaining with his opponents. Still, Water makes him look for the best in others and he often refuses to believe their evil intents until the last moment. This type of Boar has a touching faith in his beliefs and loved ones. A believer in miracles, he can be used by others if he is not careful.

The cordial, peaceful and earnest Water Boar will be a great party-goer. He will stick scrupulously to the rules of the game, showing his goodwill by meeting others more than halfway.

Still true to his Boar nature, he will have his basic passions and outpourings of love. When he is negative, he can be preoccupied with sex, enjoyment of rich foods, excessive drinking or indulging in other expensive luxuries at the expense of others.

WOOD BOAR—1875, 1935, 1995

The Wood Boar can manipulate others with expertise. Although he is interested in his personal gains, he will also be inclined to devote a lot of his time to charitable organizations and is excellent at running social functions and club activities. He loves to help all those who come in touch with him and will try his best to get along with everyone. He is a splendid promoter; thus he will be good at getting financing for his business deals.

Extremely good-hearted, he will recommend clemency even for the most unworthy and is often not choosy about whom he associates with. Consequently, his unworthy friends could dupe him or drag him

THE FIVE TYPES OF BOARS 223

down into the mud with them if he is too much in their company.

Yet he will also be rewarded for the confidence he places in people and he will assume important positions because of his gift in bringing people together.

Wood makes him expansive but still scrupulous enough to operate by accepted modes. He will seek to be connected with the right people and will undertake ambitious corporate ventures.

A persuasive talker, the Wood Boar will love to entertain and set up a congenial atmosphere wherever he goes. His positive and bright ways will encourage people to support both his vices and virtues.

FIRE BOAR—1887, 1947, 2007

Fire will conduct powerful and intense emotions to this courageous Boar. He will display stouthearted heroism in all his endeavors and could follow his plans through with pigheaded determination.

He could reach the highest level of achievement or fall to the lowest depths of degradation, depending on which path he chooses and how tight a rein he has over his immense energy and sensuality.

The Fire Boar will never fear the unknown; intrepid, optimistic and trusting in his own innate ability, he will try his luck at anything and succeed against vast odds. He is motivated by love and will try to accumulate wealth in order to provide a gracious life style for his all-important family. He doesn't mind doing favors for anyone, even strangers, and will be famous for his generous handouts to friends.

When he is in his negative state, this Boar can be willful, bullying and guilt-ridden, but generally he is characterized by largesse and lack of prejudice. He will favor manufacturing or labor-oriented enterprises because he will enjoy employing a large number of people if given the opportunity.

EARTH BOAR—1899, 1959, 2019

A peaceful, sensible and happy type of Boar who may have enough sense to benefit himself. The Earth element makes him productive and he will like to take on financial responsibilities or related activities and plan for his own future.

Renowned for his steadiness and patience, he will tie himself mercilessly to an objective until he attains it. His willpower will enable him to endure stress and carry burdens well beyond the capacity of others.

Devoted both to work and family, the Earth Boar will show a diligence and drive that will be hard to surpass. He will not be authoritarian; he will push himself but not others.

Although this person may be portly because of his fondness for food and drink, he has an ability for not worrying himself too much over his problems. His ambitions are reasonable and not above his reach. Therefore, he will find the security and material success he craves.

A kind, thoughtful friend, reliable associate and helpful employer, the Earth Boar will steer clear of troubled areas and look for tranquility and domestic harmony in his life.

THE BOAR AND HIS ASCENDANTS

Born During the Hours of the Rat — 11 P.M. to 1 A.M.

With the Rat behind him, this is a Boar that is better equipped to make investments and assessments. He is less likely to be left high and dry. Both signs here are very sociable and know how to make the most out of carefully cultivated friendships.

Born During the Hours of the Ox — 1 A.M. to 3 A.M.

A strong-tempered Boar with more precise habits and opinionated views. The Ox will see to it that he does not get too carried away by his sensuality. Can be relied upon to watch his waistline.

Born During the Hours of the Tiger — 3 A.M. to 5 A.M.

A daring, bighearted and athletic Boar. Fine performer and organizer. Both signs here are basically led by emotions and this makes him easily influenced by others.

Born During the Hours of the Rabbit — 5 A.M. to 7 A.M.

An easygoing but sagacious Boar who will not carry any more burdens than he has to. A great party man, too—but he also never forgets to collect his commissions. Not as obliging as he says he is.

Born During the Hours of the Dragon — 7 A.M. to 9 A.M.

A strong, dutiful Boar with immense devotion to those he loves. Both signs here are strong but innocent. His successes will only be equaled by his failures.

Born During the Hours of the Snake — 9 A.M. to 11 A.M.

A meditative and more stealthy Boar who will pursue his goals with more consistency. Here the Snake could relax the Boar's scruples and make him take what he wants. He may also have an oblique way of looking at justice.

Born During the Hours of the Horse — 11 A.M. to 1 P.M.

A Boar with more mettle. For once, the Horse should be commended for making the Boar more selfish and inconsiderate in order to achieve personal profit and recognition.

Born During the Hours of the Sheep — 1 P.M. to 3 P.M.

A compassionate and sentimental Boar. Too polite and easily conned. Will work hard for others or be overly generous. Attracts parasites as well as influential supporters.

Born During the Hours of the Monkey — 3 P.M. to 5 P.M.

Will not be led up the garden path. A Boar who conceals greed under his friendliness. The Monkey here will be able to spot the tricksters and protect the Boar from his own naiveté.

Born During the Hours of the Rooster — 5 P.M. to 7 P.M.

An unorthodox and impractical Boar with all good intentions. Performs splendid tasks for free and is absurdly tenacious in unrewarding exercises. The Rooster is too quixotic and the Boar is too oblivious of his true worth.

Born During the Hours of the Dog — 7 P.M. to 9 P.M.

A direct, logical and less sensuous Boar who will be guided by the Dog's sound judgment. Will never tolerate deceit. If you trick him, he will come after you with a posse and you can be sure he has swarms of tough friends.

Born During the Hours of the Boar — 9 P.M. to 11 P.M.

A rough diamond. Still waiting for expert hands to cut and polish. All his fine qualities are intact and just waiting to be discovered. Look more closely, please.

HOW THE BOAR FARES IN DIFFERENT YEARS

Year of RAT

A year of uncertainties for the Boar. Things are unsettled at work and at home and he may lose something he presumed he gained. He will manage to surmount difficulties but worries weigh him down and adversely affect his progress and chances for success.

COMPATIBILITY TABLE FOR THE BOAR

BOAR — Underlying clashes for personality and struggle and dominance. Will not try hard to resolve their differences. Not very compatible.

RAT — Moderately happy or at least peaceful relations. No personality clashes. Share some common interests. Fairly compatible.

OX — No strong conflicts. Compatible to a certain extent. Acceptable but moderate relations. No permanent bonds.

TIGER — Sympathetic and have mutual interests at heart. Happy and compatible to a good degree. Can work as a team.

RABBIT — Successful match to some degree. Both will be cooperative to each other's goals. Good communication and no major conflicts.

DRAGON — Workable and tolerant relations. No differences that cannot be reconciled. Can and will cooperate for mutual benefits.

SNAKE — Deep animosities and lasting conflicts. Will not be able to communicate or understand one another. Highly incompatible.

HORSE — Mutual interest in some areas. Compatible only to a moderate extent. No clashes of will but no special attraction either.

SHEEP — Have a good comprehension of each other. Will relate very well in marriage or partnership. Compatible and happy match.

MONKEY — Fairly civil union. No great difficulty in tolerating each other. Have similar interests and can relate to each other.

ROOSTER — Moderately favourable relationship in love and business. Will cooperate when necessary but cannot communicate well.

DOG — Mutual respect for one another. No underlying clashes or struggles for dominance. Agreeable ties in love and partnership.

豬

BOAR

12 1 2 3 4 5 6 7 8 9 10 11

N E S W

Year of OX

A good year for the Boar. Good prospects are evident and the Boar is able to tap hidden resources or start his own business. His gambles or hunches could pay off handsomely. Problems are not large or troublesome but there could be complications in romance or family affairs.

Year of TIGER

A tough and trying year. The Boar will encounter difficulties that he may have to face alone. A difficult time for him to borrow money or get back money due him. He may have many unexpected expenses or be forced to pay fines, legal fees or extra taxes. He must be very careful of trusting his associates at this time and attend to important affairs himself.

Year of RABBIT

A fair year for the Boar with some modest results. Obstacles still crop up but there will be no major upheavals. He makes some financial gains and is able to consolidate his position to a good degree. Home life is calm and happy. Much entertaining and socializing foreseen.

Year of DRAGON

A smooth year. The Boar will win the support of powerful people and be able to please his superiors. He will gain the recognition and respect of his coworkers. Family life is smooth but he could expect some health upsets or loss of personal belongings.

Year of SNAKE

A hectic and uneasy time for the Boar, although moderate success can be expected. He will be occupied with travel, aggressive speculation and joint ventures. He will also receive some sad news and have problems with the opposite sex. Setbacks will result mainly from overspending or extravagance.

Year of HORSE

A good year for the Boar if he avoids speculation or entrusting his money to newfound friends. Benefits formerly withheld from him will now come from all directions and past problems turn into blessings in disguise. Fortunate and prosperous year for his family and career.

Year of SHEEP

A fair year for the Boar, as his financial position is at a standstill or loss. He will have no serious health problems or big upheavals. His gains will be in the form of knowledge, more professional training or career development. A time to plan for the future and seek out new opportunities to explore.

Year of MONKEY

A moderately satisfying time for the Boar. He will suffer from a lack of money or support and various domestic and personal problems will occupy his mind. Results are not entirely favorable but he will be able to borrow money or join forces with other people and solve his difficulties.

Year of ROOSTER

A busy and fair year. The Boar's domestic scene is calm but his advancement will be curtailed or interrupted. He spends a great deal of time and effort to overcome obstacles and must be patient with negotiations that are complicated and involved.

Year of DOG

A frustrating year likely for the aspirations of the Boar. He will be disappointed if he expects too much. Difficulties arise from many directions and could be the results of his past neglect, miscalculations or errors in judgment. He must be careful where he places his confidence and take criticism constructively.

Year of BOAR

The Boar's life will stabilize this year as gains and some progress are foreseen. He may still experience some friction at work or at home but no serious setbacks are indicated. He may have some persistent health problems or infection that he should attend to. New friends and opportunities dominate the winter months.

FAMOUS PERSONS BORN IN THE YEAR OF THE BOAR

Metal
Hubert Humphrey
Ronald Reagan
Lucille Ball
Merle Oberon
Rosalind Russell
Prince Bernhard

Water
Prince Rainier
Lee Kuan Yew
Maria Callas
Henry Kissinger

Wood
Françoise Sagan
King Hussein
Julie Andrews
Bibi Andersson
Woody Allen

Fire
Field Marshal Montgomery
Chiang Kai-shek
Andrew Jackson

Earth
Ernest Hemingway
Humphrey Bogart
Alfred Hitchcock
John D. Rockefeller
Al Capone

Chapter 13
The 144 Marriage Combinations

RAT HUSBAND + RAT WIFE

A bit too much togetherness. They may both be too conscientious and domesticated. When they are too alike, they could suffer from overexposure to each other's personality. Mr. Rat could be more easygoing than Mrs. Rat here, who may have an inclination to be fussy and bossy. Two worldly and calculating signs who may watch each other rather intently and not like the close-up picture they see.

RAT HUSBAND + OX WIFE

A happy combination. The affectionate Rat husband will be very attractive to his security conscious wife. He is a good provider, which is the chief requisite in her book. She, on the other hand, is more than dutiful, competent and reliable. She will love attending to all his needs and will keep his house in order. Under this arrangement, they will no doubt admire each other's qualities and each will do more than his or her fair share. The ardently demonstrative Rat could make the Ox lady more responsive and less obstinate.

RAT HUSBAND + TIGER WIFE

He is success-oriented and a home and family man. She is affectionate and generous but very unconventional. They will have a lot in common as they are both sociable, active and have many interests. He will seek power and riches and she loves the prestige and recognition it provides. However, he could be resentful of her unpredictable manners and she may criticize him for being niggardly at times. But both are basically optimists and will try to work out their differences or call it quits.

RAT HUSBAND + RABBIT WIFE

This match may not bring out the best in each party. Both are charming and pleasant but not selfless and dedicated individuals. They could be friendly and sincere but constant coexistence may create a strain on both of them. He is possessive and romantic and she tends to be too passive in her response to him. Expectations on either side may be greatly reduced in the final accounting.

RAT HUSBAND + DRAGON WIFE

These two share courage and determination and will find a bright and rewarding future together. They will not try to restrict each other unduly and the Rat will find his Dragon wife an admirable companion if she is not overbearing. Both are very competent and have enough self-assurance to trust the other. They will look at the brighter side of life and enjoy a very gratifying relationship.

RAT HUSBAND + SNAKE WIFE

A union made up of two possessive partners who are realistic enough to make all the necessary adjustments if they find much to admire in each other. The Rat man will value the Snake's brilliance and tenacity while she finds him ambitious and clever enough to set up house with. Of these two materialistic and performance-conscious parties, he may be the more adaptable and easygoing. She is cautious and he could rely on her excellent ability to sniff out those traps. The Snake also finds the Rat's devotion very touching and will respond passionately.

RAT HUSBAND + HORSE WIFE

Both have independent and active spirits. But he will be very irked by her restlessness and inconsistency. She, on the other hand, will be unhappy and nervous with all his bickering ways. They cannot appreciate each other's way of thinking and may not try hard to work together.

RAT HUSBAND + SHEEP WIFE

The Rat may not like setting up house with an oversensitive and impractical Sheep lady. She, on the other hand, will respond only when she is pampered and indulged. The prudent Rat may conclude that she is too expensive to maintain and she may find him too calculating and greedy to suit her tastes. Neither of them is openly combative but they could harbor deep resentments and be very frustrated and dissatisfied by doing so.

RAT HUSBAND + MONKEY WIFE

Strongly compatible as he will fall for her charm and ingenuity and she will find his go-getter attitude very admirable. They are both achievement-conscious and will push each other up the ladder of success. They are not hypersensitive and can accept each other's faults with understanding. They could work together or choose separate paths or careers without any trouble. Likewise, they will be able to smooth out any rough spots in their relationship.

RAT HUSBAND + ROOSTER WIFE

Will not blend together well. She appraises him critically and finds him wanting. She means well and feels obligated to call his attentions to all his shortcomings. He finds her eccentric and overly analytical ways very annoying. He cannot avoid resenting this and feeling hurt. He wants a doting wife, not a psychiatrist. She is surprised he is resentful and labels him ungrateful.

RAT HUSBAND + DOG WIFE

Both are peace-loving and independent. He can be hard-working and energetic and she will be loyal and tactful. The Dog wife is warm and responsive and the Rat husband is charming and equally affectionate. The danger in this match is that they may both do too much compromising and end up with a too bland relationship that makes them uninterested in each other.

RAT HUSBAND + BOAR WIFE

Both have a great zest for life. They will find each other attractive physically as well as mentally. But both signs are too optimistic and imprudent and they may just push their luck too far. Neither has enough willpower to apply the brakes and provide a stabilizing force to the union. They need something concrete to seal the marriage.

OX HUSBAND + RAT WIFE

He is always dependable enough to bring home the bacon and she is loving and doting enough to cook it just the way he likes it. Very satisfying and rewarding union. He is strong and silent and loves being fussed over and admired by his outgoing wife and she is content with the security and stability he provides. Both will have few complaints.

OX HUSBAND + OX WIFE

Both members of this team are serious and industrious to a dismal extent. Neither is lively enough to provide some respite from all that work they have planned. An extremely reserved and civil union of two security-conscious subjects who are both pessimistic and strong-willed. They may end up showing each other too much of their negative sides.

OX HUSBAND + TIGER WIFE

He is interested in personal success and achievement; she is interested in herself before anything else. He is practical, well-organized and stable; she finds him too predictable and dour. The Tiger wife can be very temperamental if she feels neglected, while the Ox cannot stand tantrums and will not tolerate her fussing over nothing. They are on different wavelengths. The reserved Buffalo will be shocked by the Tiger's unrestrained and passionate display of emotions. She on the other hand will be frustrated by his coldness and may need a more warm-blooded and responsive partner.

OX HUSBAND + RABBIT WIFE

The Rabbit finds the Ox steady, realistic and dependable while the Ox sees her as sociable, sympathetic and feminine. However, he can be very exacting and will criticize her for her lack of discipline and she will respond by becoming withdrawn and oversensitive. But getting to know each other may be well worth an effort in this marriage, as both of them could sustain a satisfying relationship if they can adjust a bit.

OX HUSBAND + DRAGON WIFE

Will not be an entirely harmonious union. He is slow and deliberate, too methodical for the pioneering and dynamic likes of the fiery and excitable Dragon woman. He could make her more persevering, but she will still be imprudent and daring at times. It's possible she can enliven him with her optimism or drive him further away. He can be a cold and unemotional loner while she needs fun, friends and variety. Both these strong personalities will have to respect and admire each other a great deal before they agree to make any adjustments to each other.

OX HUSBAND + SNAKE WIFE

A very enduring and happy combination. The Ox has high standards of achievement and the Snake wife is equally ambitious and materialistic. She will be appreciative of the luxury and comforts he can provide. He finds her very well mannered and presentable—and astute in financial matters as well. Both will be happy fulfilling their part of the relationship. He will be a source of strength for her and she will be his pride and joy.

OX HUSBAND + HORSE WIFE

Not many favorable aspects for this match. She is carefree and uninhibited and he is industrious and down to earth. He wants a well-organized and pleasant home and she is too restless and busy to stay pinned down. She needs freedom and diversion. He cannot comprehend her instability and lack of devotion to him. Difficult for either to find complete harmony.

OX HUSBAND + SHEEP WIFE

She can organize an artistic and comfortable nest for him while he acts as her defender. But he is prudent and persevering while she is sentimental and capricious. He accumulates and she spends. The Ox is strong and decisive; she is weak and insecure. She loves being sheltered and reassured, but Mr. Ox may not be so obliging as he expects a great deal from others and his Sheep wife will become depressed when he exacts too much discipline and self-denial from her. Both may find the going rough at times.

OX HUSBAND + MONKEY WIFE

Both are self-assured and know what they want. And what they want may not be each other. He is simple, serious and matter of fact. She is attractive, complicated and self-centered. They both love success and money but they have entirely different ideas on how to attain success and how to spend the money. Mrs. Monkey is quite accomplished and independent and not as security-minded as he. She could find him becoming tyrannical when she takes his orders lightly while he cannot quite get her to pay him the respect and admiration he craves. If he flaunts his authority, she will enrage him—by laughing in his face. Neither will ever succeed in subordinating the other.

OX HUSBAND + ROOSTER WIFE

Both are hard-working and industrious. He values self-respect and devotion to duty and his competent and conscientious Rooster wife will certainly win his admiration. They both love analyzing and organizing, and neither is too easily hurt or sensitive about criticism. They can be objective and methodical in managing the office as well as the household. Both love simple pleasures and intellectual pursuits and will excel in specialized fields. She doesn't mind his exacting nature as she is very attentive to details; he on the other hand will take her criticism constructively and not feel reproached. A happy and contented pair.

OX HUSBAND + DOG WIFE

He looks for money and prestige; he abhors dependency. She is generous, open-minded and a loyal ally. But he could be too Spartan and domineering for his friendly and communicative wife. She will be tough, outspoken and touchy if he pushes her too hard. She could find him too rigid and aloof for her tastes and he may find her questioning mind and cynical logic hard to swallow. Otherwise, they might enjoy each other's company.

OX HUSBAND + BOAR WIFE

They will make the best of each other's outstanding qualities. He is serious, well-mannered and success-oriented while she is patient, self-sacrificing and devoted. He is hard-working and she is trusting enough to support and encourage him every step of the way. Her tastes may be richer than his and she is more sensual and demonstrative. However, she will be understanding of his needs and help make him less reticent and stubborn.

TIGER HUSBAND + RAT WIFE

Not much togetherness in this marriage. He is too hot-headed and imperious for the domesticated and sentimental Rat. She can be considerate and thoughtful only when appreciated and he is too impatient and involved with himself. He finds her petty and too possessive and demanding. Both parties will be dissatisfied with the other's performance.

TIGER HUSBAND + OX WIFE

A clash of temperaments. He is the nonconformist, the activist and the defiant rebel. She loves tradition, respects authority and is conservative in her behavior. They are two stubborn individuals who are 180 degrees apart. It will be difficult for them to find common grounds to equate their varying outlooks on life.

TIGER HUSBAND + TIGER WIFE

They are both attractive, vibrant and charming and may have a great deal in common. However, both are equally rebellious, stubborn and quick on the draw when displeased and there could be a strain in their household from bruised egos. Both need a lot of personal freedom. They may be able to patch up their differences as they have excellent senses of humor, but the family budget may have a perpetual hole in it as these are two big spenders.

TIGER HUSBAND + RABBIT WIFE

The demure Rabbit may be attracted to the rugged and appealing Tiger man but when she takes a closer look she may be frightened by his impulsiveness and daring. He on the other hand cannot appreciate her moody and worrying nature. She is rational and opportunistic while he is led by his feelings and has little need for diplomacy and tact. She is polite and sensitive. He is loud and spontaneous. Both will have to make a major effort to put up with each other's idiosyncrasies.

TIGER HUSBAND + DRAGON WIFE

Both are energetic, ambitious and brave. They could overstimulate each other in the process. With both of them being innovative and daring, there may be no one left to finish the job after their mutual initial enthusiasm fades away. The Dragon wife has aspirations for leadership and will fight the Tiger for dominance. He will let her get away with some things so long as she does not restrict his actions and expect him to be docile. They will only cooperate successfully after much adjustment on both sides.

TIGER HUSBAND + SNAKE WIFE

Each will question the other's motives and only notice the negative traits. The wise and practical Snake will find the Tiger husband directly opposed to her sensible course of action. He finds her jealous, overpossessive and too philosophical. She cannot comprehend his love for courting disaster. She may be financially shrewd but he is overgenerous and a spendthrift. They cannot accomplish very much together.

TIGER HUSBAND + HORSE WIFE

Well-balanced and harmonious pair. They are both outgoing, fiery and spirited. But while the Tiger fights for a cause, the practical Horse wife will direct both their energies to more rewarding pursuits. He will like her quick and intelligent mind and she can steer him toward worthwhile objectives. Neither is domesticated enough to be too possessive. He is thoughtful and affectionate when humored, and she is flexible enough to put up with his unpredictability. They will have a passionate relationship and much need for each other's company.

TIGER HUSBAND + SHEEP WIFE

He is outgoing, involved and vivacious. She is domesticated, sensitive and clinging. He will be companionable but cannot devote himself exclusively to her needs and finds her too dependent and indecisive. She is basically understanding but could wallow in self-pity if she finds him curt, impatient and unconcerned about her trivial complaints. Each will have to adjust to the other's ways before they can make this marriage work.

TIGER HUSBAND + MONKEY WIFE

They live in different worlds. Although they are both sociable, energetic and outgoing, the temperamental Tiger will dislike the competitive Monkey because she is too intelligent and too sure of herself to be intimidated by his loud dramatics. He is productive and forceful only when given the center of the stage. If the Monkey lady demands equal billing, he could feel hemmed in and very resentful. Both are lavish spenders but the Monkey is more prudent and clever about finances. This mixture of two inconstant and self-possessed personalities is just too overwhelming to do either of them any good.

TIGER HUSBAND + ROOSTER WIFE

She is too smart, well-informed and critical to put up with the dynamic but overreacting Tiger man. He is upset by her nagging and faultfinding ways and her love for detail. He is openhanded, generous and outspoken while she is efficient, thrifty and methodical. He is idealistic where she is a keen intellectual. One is unconventional and ruled by his heart, the other is eccentric but ruled by her head. Both are very engrossed in themselves and will be unhappy and irritated by the other.

TIGER HUSBAND + DOG WIFE

An ideal marriage combination of two charming, attractive and humanitarian signs. He is passionate and animated. She is loyal, understanding and helpful. The Tiger is impulsive and impatient; the Dog is logical and clear-headed enough to advise him without getting personal. He admires and respects her loyalty and good sense and she will not try to monopolize his affections. Each is warm and responsive to the other's needs without invading his or her privacy. A very satisfactory arrangement for both sides.

TIGER HUSBAND + BOAR WIFE

These two dedicated and inspired individuals will work more energetically for the goals of others than their own. Together they will make a happy team; the Boar will be tirelessly devoted to the idealistic pursuits of the Tiger, and he will admire her courage and stamina. Although she can be trusting and congenial, she will make him more materialistic because of her taste for luxury. They are both sensual, uninhibited and passionate in love. Both can brush aside little differences and will enjoy journeying through life hand in hand.

RABBIT HUSBAND + RAT WIFE

The Rat is sociable, active and crafty. The Rabbit has a mild disposition and is not inclined to strenuous activity and involvement like his gregarious and entertaining wife. But both love home life and are realistic about their goals. She can be devoted and outgoing enough to brighten up his moods. A responsible and good match.

RABBIT HUSBAND + OX WIFE

The Rabbit is gentle, sagacious, receptive to ideas and the feelings of others. The Ox wife may be lacking the emotion and sensitivity to understand his refined personality. He can be acquisitive, indulgent and selfish. She can be pragmatic, but virtuous and well-disciplined. Both could supply each other with missing attributes if they sincerely care enough to cooperate.

RABBIT HUSBAND + TIGER WIFE

The Rabbit is imaginative and docile, inclined toward mental and creative endeavors. The lady Tiger is dramatic, sensuous and electric. She may be too strong and colorful for the quiet and impeccable Rabbit. On the other hand, she finds him impersonal and lacking in emotions. He could help her solve her problems but she may be too inattentive to listen. She could build up his confidence and assertiveness but he is not too keen on her method of teaching. They tend not to mix well together as, in the final analysis, what one likes, the other shuns.

RABBIT HUSBAND + RABBIT WIFE

Will cohabitate peacefully and quietly. Both are calm and intelligent enough to do whatever is practical and necessary. However, they can only gratify each other to a point, as they tend to perform what is essential and not much more. This is because the Rabbit is basically not selfless and serving. Matrimony for them will have to be a well-thought-out affair with equal sharing of responsibilities. There will be some snags when either one starts to think he is bearing a little more of the weight than he should. They are both gifted and intuitive but may neglect to encourage each other.

RABBIT HUSBAND + DRAGON WIFE

She is independent, vivacious and cheerful. He is capable but introverted and calculating. She could lift his spirits and make him more ambitious in his objectives. He could teach her a thing or two about diplomacy and fine manners. He doesn't mind her assuming the dominant role because he knows in the end she will seek his excellent advice. He is competent and kind and she has a backbone strong enough for both of them. A realistic and positive combination in marriage.

RABBIT HUSBAND + SNAKE WIFE

They are compatible to a good degree if they can enhance each other's stronger points. He has great potential, vision and tact. She is always determined to succeed and approves of his materialistic aims. Although they will both have the same refined tastes and inherent love for ease and beauty, the Snake could be too ardent and demanding for the Rabbit's superficial type of involvement. On the dark side, both are philosophical and meditative and all lines of communication could be severed should they decide to be negative.

RABBIT HUSBAND + HORSE WIFE

They may find it difficult and apt to consider things very carefully before passing judgment. She is governed by her emotions and intuitions. They are both too practical or too self-absorbed to make any great effort at adjusting to each other. She is bored by his deliberation and sensitivity; he finds her thoughtless, inconstant and mercenary. One prefers rest and solitude; the other is constantly on the go. This union could never work at such different paces.

RABBIT HUSBAND + SHEEP WIFE

Each is receptive to the vibrations of the other partner. The Rabbit appreciates her compassionate and sensitive ways and she finds him kind, astute and sagacious enough to make their decisions. Her dependence could make him feel more important and purposeful. He is a good listener and she needs sympathy and advice more than action. Both are romantic and affectionate and will enjoy domestic bliss.

RABBIT HUSBAND + MONKEY WIFE

Some hostilities may develop in this sort of a marriage. She is gay, self-assured and proud of her accomplished wit. He may feel humbled by her and she will hate his anxiety and brooding. Both have the ability to see through others and when they look into one another, they may not find anything that fascinating. These two realistic individuals will not cooperate unless both have something substantial to gain from such a commitment.

RABBIT HUSBAND + ROOSTER WIFE

He would like to be catered to and served rather than serve. She is too straightforward, meticulous and efficient to put up with his whimsical requests. Both are knowledgeable but eccentric. He broods in dark silence while she will make up a long list of his faults and publish it. They could make life very uncomfortable for each other.

RABBIT HUSBAND + DOG WIFE

A beneficial and very agreeable combination. Both parties will only make reasonable demands on each other and come out feeling satisfied and fulfilled. The Dog will be loyal and affectionate to the Rabbit even when he is indifferent and moody. She admires his suave and diplomatic ways and he can rely on her support and logical assessment of situations. She is the more positive of the two and will encourage and pep him up when he is depressed. On the other hand, he is always considerate and sensitive enough to know what is bothering her.

RABBIT HUSBAND + BOAR WIFE

These two will be interesting and sympathetic to each other. He is talented and astute and can negotiate his way out of trouble. She admires him for his aplomb and refined ways and will meet him more than halfway. She is dependable, generous and obedient and he will find her devotion very touching and will be drawn to her unselfishness. Neither of them is given to faultfinding; rather they will be content to count their blessings, especially in such a rewarding union.

DRAGON HUSBAND + RAT WIFE

The Dragon will find his wife's loyalty and optimism endearing. The lady Rat will follow her hero to the ends of the earth. He is magnanimous while she is thrifty and resourceful. He could make a lot of money and blow it but she is likely to have stored some of it away for a rainy day. She is talkative and lively but always agreeable to letting him play the boss. A fruitful and lasting union.

DRAGON HUSBAND + OX WIFE

Both are dutiful but stubborn. This factor could make or break the marriage. He works for glory and recognition while she has to see the material benefits. If his ventures do not turn up hard cash, she could be harsh and unsympathetic. He is exciting and extroverted while she can be too conforming and conservative. He needs love and admiration; she can be cold and undemonstrative. A good deal of compromising needed. But if both parties try hard and succeed, they will be immensely proud of and dedicated to each other.

DRAGON HUSBAND + TIGER WIFE

Not a quiet, conventional and uneventful marriage at all. Both partners are progressive, pioneering and active. They could provide each other stimulating company if they understand their basic individual need for freedom and expression. The Tiger wife may respect and adore her Dragon spouse but will never give up her own identity. He will be in trouble if he tries to give her obedience training. Both are quick-tempered and will resist being dominated. An adventurous marriage if they can maintain a workable balance.

DRAGON HUSBAND + RABBIT WIFE

She needs his strength and daring while he relies on her competence and companionship. He is forceful and outspoken; she is indulgent but tactful. She will manage an artistic and restful home for him. She is adaptable but moody and defenseless; he serves as her warrior and protector. A good marriage if they strive for their common welfare, not allowing petty or calculating concerns to interfere.

DRAGON HUSBAND + DRAGON WIFE

Not a very peaceful arrangement unless they first agree on their goals.

Both are individualistic, strong-willed and aggressive. Mrs. Dragon will not like to be overshadowed; in fact, she may be more assertive than he. Mr. Dragon is masterful and expects to have control, but in this case he may have to surrender some of his rights. Both partners will be wise to maintain their own careers to avoid suppressing each other.

DRAGON HUSBAND + SNAKE WIFE

A fulfilling and stimulating relationship if these two diverse personalities can adjust to each other. He is active, impulsive and domineering. She is sensual, unhurried and a lover of ease. As he is always geared to work and success, she can impart to him some of her tenacity and common sense. She may have a finer business acumen than he or will at least handle the family finances well. They can both build a sound foundation for their home.

DRAGON HUSBAND + HORSE WIFE

The Horse lady will be clever and resourceful enough to stretch whatever income Mr. Dragon brings home. But the serious Dragon may find her restless and not too crazy about a steady diet of housework. Life will be more fruitful and delightful for both if they live in the city and Mrs. Horse keeps a job as well as manages her home. Actually, both parties perform better when given variety and freedom. The constantly aspiring Dragon will find his wife's practicality very profitable, while she finds him strong and reliable.

DRAGON HUSBAND + SHEEP WIFE

May not turn out to be such an appealing pair. They will live harmoniously only after much effort. He is adventurous and independent while she is ruled by emotions and her moods. She loves home and family but he may not care to be so domesticated. She cries easily and he finds it hard to express the sympathy and gentleness she craves. He is ambitious and decisive where she is artistic and intuitive. He is the knight in shining armor who will love helping a lady in distress, but not if she is going to make a habit of it.

DRAGON HUSBAND + MONKEY WIFE

An ideal match romantically and mentally. He is drawn to her magnetism and she admires his leadership. They are both ambitious and above-average performers. They will shine together beautifully. Combined, these two will look for new worlds to conquer and explore. Both are socially inclined and will probably maintain a beautiful home and entertain a lot.

DRAGON HUSBAND + ROOSTER WIFE

Could achieve a great deal of togetherness but will have to smooth out some rough edges first. Her discriminating and at times callous remarks could often deflate his super ego. He is dynamic and full of energy while she is efficient, economical and critical. Both will be happier if they agree on what areas each should control. Mentally they are on equal intellectual levels but they should not try to overpower each other with their accomplishments.

DRAGON HUSBAND + DOG WIFE

Many disputes because of the wide gap in basic temperaments. They are both aggressive and forceful but in different ways. He loves freedom and will act independently while she demands cooperation and unflagging loyalty. Subconsciously each may be trying to attain the attributes of the other that he or she lacks. However, they don't have the basic understanding of how to go about it. Both signs are proud and willful when challenged. Neither will want to give in easily or lose face. A great many modifications needed for this marriage to work; perhaps too many.

DRAGON HUSBAND + BOAR WIFE

A successful and stable union. The Boar wife will always encourage and support her ambitious Dragon mate. He is impulsive while she is patient and enduring. He is a fighter and she loves to be the peacemaker. They will have no trouble cooperating for the same goals. She will devote all her energy to whatever he undertakes. He can have the limelight so long as he makes her feel needed. He is the daredevil and she will uncomplainingly help him up every time he falls. Both will be intensely romantic.

SNAKE HUSBAND + RAT WIFE

An aspiring and covetous pair who will never stop moving upward. This could be a profitable union if they have the right attitude and agree on fixed priorities. The Rat girl is sociable and very charming and will dote on her ambitious but introverted spouse, although she craves more togetherness than he is prepared to give. Both are resourceful and shrewd enough to make their marriage a big success provided they do not let their petty jealousies get in the way. They should not keep secrets from each other.

SNAKE HUSBAND + OX WIFE

Both parties here are cautious and selective and will find that they made a good decision in choosing each other. They are both down to earth and dignified and share the same beliefs and driving ambition. He is tenacious and scheming; she is disciplined, orderly and protective of family and home. They can both rely on each other in a crisis. In a marriage such as this one, the Snake will learn to confide in the tight-lipped Ox and she will stand by him against all adversities. They can look forward to a happy life together.

SNAKE HUSBAND + TIGER WIFE

A difficult and upsetting relationship for both sides. They cannot understand or overlook each other's frailties. Both signs are passionate and deeply suspicious. They cannot ever really trust each other. The Snake is refined, intellectual and constant. The Tiger wife is altruistic, lively and idealistic. The self-contained Snake finds her too unconventional, stimulating and outspoken. She, on the other hand, is resentful of his secretiveness, aloof behavior and intense ambition. They speak entirely different languages and cannot communicate.

SNAKE HUSBAND + RABBIT WIFE

The Snake is forceful and dominant and the well-bred Rabbit will be receptive to his way of thinking. Both share the same exclusive and refined preferences and these two can strike a harmonious chord mentally and romantically. However, these signs are also basically not so obliging. They may neglect each other in their search for self-expression and gratification of their desires. However, the Rabbit is not as possessive as the Snake and will not mind very much if he gets wrapped up in his work or cannot pay her too much attention. She will be content so long as he provides her with a lovely home and pays all the bills. A relatively peaceful combination.

SNAKE HUSBAND + DRAGON WIFE

He is loving but possessive and complicated. She is generous, open and excitable. He is careful and deliberate in his actions. She may have to struggle with him to put across her views. Some friction is bound to develop in the marriage but secretly the Dragon female longs for someone wiser and more dominating than herself. The Snake will not only provide a stabilizing force for the union but he will admire the ambition and enthusiasm of his Dragon wife. Together they could surge forward with greater determination. A helpful and constructive alliance.

SNAKE HUSBAND + SNAKE WIFE

Both will be on the same wavelength and communicate well together especially when they are involved with the same project. They won't cling to each other too much, as they are both independent thinkers. In their search for power and success, they can be relentless and enduring. Usually their mutual ambitions seal them together. If jealousy does not get in the way, they could accomplish a great deal.

SNAKE HUSBAND + HORSE WIFE

Each has a different approach to life. He is cautious, tenacious and strong-willed—his goals are long-term. She is adventurous, mercurial and impatient. She cares more for the joys of the moment. He is consistent in his endeavors; she is impulsive, quick-witted but inconsistent. He finds her irresponsible and hard to keep up with, while she dislikes his serious, calm and deliberate mental deductions. Not a very satisfying union for either.

SNAKE HUSBAND + SHEEP WIFE

Companionable only to a certain extent. The lusty Snake may like to get wrapped around the object of his affections but he won't like it when the Sheep clings to him indefinitely. He will feel trapped. The realistic and efficient Snake is basically an achiever. The Sheep is sensitive, sentimental and docile. He will sacrifice a great deal to realize his ambitions. She is self-indulgent and may be easily discouraged when the going gets rough. He is highly intelligent and she is highly emotional. They may find it hard to bridge the gaps in their relationship in times of difficulty.

SNAKE HUSBAND + MONKEY WIFE

Will not go well together at all. A battle of wills and wits. Both are scheming and competitive. The Monkey could easily incite the Snake to anger and he on the other hand is not forgiving and will retaliate swiftly. She is opportunistic, insensitive and competent enough to challenge him; he is equally ambitious, conniving and set on having his way. A tug of war might occur to determine who is smarter. They seem to bring out the worst in each other and in this alliance neither may emerge with any benefits in the end.

SNAKE HUSBAND + ROOSTER WIFE

These are two brainy, calculating and very performance-oriented signs who will prefer power and money in the bank to holding hands romantically in rags and poverty. She is the efficient and perfect housekeeper. He is the brains behind each financial deal. They will share the same dreams for prestige and material security. The Snake is philosophical enough to put up with the Rooster's rambling and eccentric ways. In the end, he will still rely on his innate wisdom to make the decision. On the other hand, she is happy that he understands her and allows her to let off steam and run his life to a certain extent. In this combination each will be able to expend energy productively; they will have a strong spiritual and mental affinity for each other.

SNAKE HUSBAND + DOG WIFE

The Snake is power-hungry, cool and deliberate in his actions. The Dog is affectionate, loyal and fair. They may have mutual admiration for each other. But she will support him only to the extent her principles allow. He expects total commitment and adheres to the belief that the end will justify the means. Both have strong convictions. They may clash if she finds him straying from the righteous path. He must make hay while the sun shines and cannot understand why her conscience is so easily offended. She is not materialistic and cannot comprehend his fascination with wealth and power. Their disapproval of some of each other's ways may prevent a close relationship.

SNAKE HUSBAND + BOAR WIFE

The Snake has unfailing determination and willpower. The Boar is easygoing and community spirited. He feels that she will not be able to understand him or further his career because of her indulgent and compromising attitude toward others. He is mystical, sophisticated and deep. She is simple, trusting and naive. He finds her scruples unappealing and has no use for her goodwill unless there is a special motive behind it. She is incapable of figuring out his complex and doubting mind. The Snake could be aloof and uncaring for the Boar's sweetness and sincerity and the Boar's feelings will be hurt. Their diametrically opposed personalities cannot provide either with much happiness.

HORSE HUSBAND + RAT WIFE

He requires physical as well as mental freedom. She is levelheaded, industrious and affectionate. She will be content to stay in a close-knit family; he must constantly explore uncharted seas. She is resourceful and thrifty. He is adventurous, flirtatious and changeable. They will not see eye to eye on how things should be done because of the differences in their temperament. The Rat views the Horse as selfish and inconsiderate. He finds her too bossy and possessive. After careful appraisal, neither may find each other appealing enough to join forces permanently.

HORSE HUSBAND + OX WIFE

Not very good prospects for happy cohabitation here. He is too versatile, high-strung and outgoing for the organized, proper and dedicated Ox woman. He is always giddy with excitement and she is too sober to share his zest. He finds her very respectable but too undemonstrative and rigid. She feels she cannot depend on him because of his lighthearted and unpredictable moods. He finds her humorless and difficult to work or play with. Her man must be more disciplined and responsible. These two have very little in common.

HORSE HUSBAND + TIGER WIFE

There will be a spirit of unity between these two signs. They are bonded to each other by the same animated, lively and passionate outlook at life. He is captivated by her vivacious personality and she is greatly attracted to his colorful, vibrant and self-assured manners. Both are active, affable and appealing. The Horse can manage to keep the money coming in and the Tiger is at her best as his radiant and charming hostess. Since they share the same philosophy, they will gravitate toward the same goals. Much togetherness can be achieved in this marriage.

HORSE HUSBAND + RABBIT WIFE

These two parties may not find accord in such a relation because of the differences in their personalities. He is annoyed by her detached, cautious and impeccable ways. She can be affectionate, inspired and very personable once he can reassure her that he is a dedicated and capable provider and family man. But he does not care to have her or anyone else anchor their hopes all on him, so off he goes in whatever direction he pleases. No doubt he will perform well but the tender Rabbit cannot stand uncertainty and insecurity. As a result, both will be discontented and unhappy.

HORSE HUSBAND + DRAGON WIFE

Moderately rewarding partnership. He is versatile and ingenious while she is always enthusiastic about taking on new and exciting projects. If she is not engrossed in her own profession, the Dragon lady may want to transfer her idealistic views and objectives to her high-spirited, adventurous and equally outgoing spouse. He is perceptive enough to judge the chances for success in their venture, while she is persuasive and powerful enough to deal with his inconsistencies. They will both lead a brisk and roving life as neither are domestic enough to stay meekly at home.

HORSE HUSBAND + SNAKE WIFE

An unlikely match. Both are mentally agile and realistic. But while he is mercurial and needs freedom and variety, she can be resistant to change and resentful of his rash and self-centered ways. She may be too determined, private and refined for his strong preferences, and in turn the Snake woman may not find the Horse appetites persistent enough to be worth her while. They both have to be very unselfish to make this marriage work.

HORSE HUSBAND + HORSE WIFE

Teamwork and cooperation are possible because they can work at similar speeds. It would be better if they were born in different seasons so as to provide more variety to their relationship. Both are passionate but independent and restless. Their witty, lively, materialistic and adventurous personalities may make life very hectic but this does not guarantee that they will get anywhere unless one of them is skillful enough to control the other. They may not be able to build a solid foundation for a home, as they are both bored by routine and restrictions.

HORSE HUSBAND + SHEEP WIFE

She is delicate, sensitive and kind-hearted. He is cheerful and practical enough to inject humor and purpose into her life. He can be easygoing with the gentle Sheep, who is compassionate enough to overlook his selfishness if he can liven up her moods and teach her the quickest route around her magnified problems. He will be grateful for a pleasant and warm home and will find the Sheep concerned enough about him to adjust her way of life to his inherent needs. Each will complement the other and this could be a very happy marriage indeed.

HORSE HUSBAND + MONKEY WIFE

Both are adaptable and intelligent enough to leap over obstacles barring their progress. But their very similarities may breed mutual contempt. Because, just as he is practical and opportunistic, she can be equally unscrupulous. She is versatile and adroit and he may irritate her by his shrewd and mercurial movements. The Monkey is bright and beguiling while the Horse is equally witty and persuasive. They may end up trying to con each other into submission.

HORSE HUSBAND + ROOSTER WIFE

Incongruous but sometimes workable arrangement. He is witty and skillful while she may be frank, knowledgeable and zealous. He could start something magnificent and then dash off when he gets bored. The efficient Rooster will complain and no doubt criticize his lack of dedication, but she will sort out the details and finish the job. He is too high-spirited and detached to be really annoyed by her outspoken and faultfinding ways. He may not even stay around long enough for her to finish the lecture. He is the colorful and vigorous performer and she is the most capable of administrators. Neither is too sensitive to be greatly disturbed by the faults of the other if they find the union productive enough.

HORSE HUSBAND + DOG WIFE

A lasting and cooperative match. Both are animated and demonstrative persons who can find real joy in their union. The Dog is loyal, honest and sincere enough to follow the Horse's excellent vibrations. She will be impressed by his intelligent, high-spirited and perceptive ways, while he loves her sense of humor, reason and logic. The Dog is realistic enough to understand and accept the Horse's shortcomings, while he will not take offence at her curt, observant and straightforward manner.

HORSE HUSBAND + BOAR WIFE

He is persuasive, magnetic and appealing and will be able to convince the compromising and good-natured Boar to concede to his wishes. She is kind-hearted and sociably inclined enough to enjoy activities with the gay Horse, but then again, she is a devoted soul and craves for more togetherness and affection than the self-centered horse can provide. He, on the other hand, is not amused when she is too conforming, and considerate enough to please everyone else besides him. Both may have some difficulty coming to terms with each other's weaknesses.

SHEEP HUSBAND + RAT WIFE

Both are charming and capable of great warmth and tenderness but that is where the similarities end. The Rat is resourceful, inquisitive and hard-working. The Sheep husband is likely to take life too easy for his industrious spouse. She saves and treasures money, while he splurges and indulges his whims. She is alert, practical and levelheaded. He is creative but emotional and sometimes indolent. She can be fussy and faultfinding when irked. He finds her too shrewd and conniving to communicate with. There may not be a great deal of give and take in this union, since the partners have difficulty understanding each other.

SHEEP HUSBAND + OX WIFE

The Sheep is artistic and leisurely. He must savor and enjoy life as he pleases. The Ox lady is dutiful enough to keep house and take good care of her family, but she will not relish complying with his indulgent and impractical demands. He must be loved and appreciated to bring out the best in him. She expects order and discipline and will tend to be too commanding for the Sheep. She is resolute and uncompromising and feels she must make optimum use of her time and energy. He is artistic and must wait for the right mood to strike him. She is impatient and scornful of his soft ways and he is thoroughly adverse to regimentation and being pushed around. Drastic changes needed for both sides to cohabit peacefully.

SHEEP HUSBAND + TIGER WIFE

The Sheep is a domestic soul and needs affection and understanding. The Tiger lady is temperamental and unconventional. He is easily hurt by her sudden bursts of fury and dramatic scenes. He is genteel and needs a quiet and comfortable home, while she is all for a fast life and cannot put up with his unhurried and worrying ways. She is too strong for his liking. He is too weak to handle her effectively. Both may end up displeased in this combination.

SHEEP HUSBAND + RABBIT WIFE

These two personalities may be compatible to a very high degree. If the astute and inscrutably suave Rabbit wife takes the lead, she can help the Sheep to perform great things with his inherent talents. The Rabbit is gentle enough for the sentimental and, at times, passive Sheep, but she is decisive and shrewd where he tends to be too generous or compassionate. She will provide him with the right environment to work well in and he will be grateful for her guidance and subtle way of steering him onto the right path. Both are sensitive to and solicitous of each other's moods. In this marriage they could accumulate more than just love and happiness.

SHEEP HUSBAND + DRAGON WIFE

Moderately workable arrangement. The Sheep could be fascinated by the Dragon's brilliance and dominant ways. She, on the other hand, could be drawn to his kindness, devotion and sincerity. On the darker side, the Sheep may be too timid to try out the Dragon's superambitious undertakings and she may find him too reserved and unadventurous to meet her scale. He will be able to depend on her for encouragement, but she could push him beyond his level of endurance. A trying time for both in this union.

SHEEP HUSBAND + SNAKE WIFE

Things will not be completely idyllic in this marriage, but it could work out if both sides make sincere efforts. Both of them are materialistic and receptive to beauty and refinement; these aspects could seal their union. However, the Sheep lacks the perseverance of the scheming Snake. She, on the other hand, could be too secretive and distrustful for the sensitive nature of the Sheep. She is calculating and guided by her wisdom where he is emotional and led by his artistic inclinations. They could disapprove of each other in some areas and succeed in others. The Snake's unfaltering determination could be a valuable asset for the Sheep to cling to.

SHEEP HUSBAND + HORSE WIFE

He is domesticated and home-loving enough to provide a secure base for the restless Horse lady. On the other hand, she is happy and affable enough to complement his depressed moods. He may be jealous and possessive while she is independent and impulsive. But the Horse is not sensitive enough to take the Sheep's self-pitying ways too seriously. She is capable, delightful and quick at catching on to delicate signals. He could curb her freedom by providing her with enough variety and attractive options to stay and spice up his life. A strong and possibly enduring marriage.

SHEEP HUSBAND + SHEEP WIFE

The Sheep cares deeply for the welfare of his family, but in this combination the Sheep wife may turn out to be the stronger of the two. Both love luxury and dependency too much but they could succeed as a unit if they combine their strengths. He will assume responsibility when there is no one else around to do so, and she loves to be the power behind the scenes. Both are good homemakers and compassionate enough to put up with each other's weak points. They should be careful about being too protective or indulgent with their children.

SHEEP HUSBAND + MONKEY WIFE

No deep or permanent attraction here, as the Monkey is too intricate and egotistical for the Sheep. He is more subdued in taste and action and her expertise and craftiness will upset and worry him. He cannot keep up with her inconsiderate demands no matter how good-natured and obliging he may be. She is clever and appealing and will lead him about once she discovers his weak points. He is creative, pure-minded and compassionate but these qualities will go unappreciated since the Monkey prefers someone more conniving and shrewd.

SHEEP HUSBAND + ROOSTER WIFE

He is kind-hearted and considerate enough to make a sincere effort at anything. She loves to investigate, analyze and administer other people's lives. He is pessimistic and subjective; she is optimistic and objective. Her energetic and dauntless attitude could scare the sensitive and unobtrusive Sheep. He finds her too meticulous, argumentative and sharp for his taste. She, on the other hand, will say it is difficult to deal with one as sentimental and self-indulgent as he. They have vast dissimilarities in their basic outlooks, which may prevent them from enduring each other's peculiarities easily.

SHEEP HUSBAND + DOG WIFE

This relationship will probably not work as the Dog is too realistic and will naturally criticize the Sheep's indulgence and enumerate his weaknesses, thus making him more pessimistic than ever. She is reasonable and affectionate enough, but not always willing to resort to the little white lies necessary to placate his touchy feelings. He needs a lot of compassion and support to be able to put his best side forward. She is unsympathetic and hardy and can be irked by his complaining and self-gratification. Not much congeniality here as each tends to bring out the other's negative traits.

SHEEP HUSBAND + BOAR WIFE

A sound marriage because of the obvious lack of friction. Both do not mind making concessions and like to have their activities centered around their home. The Boar is gregarious and not as sensitive as the Sheep, who may take offence easily because of his reticent nature. She is less extravagant than he and could be more sociable and outgoing, thereby reducing his shyness. On the other hand, he can make up for her lack of refinement and is responsive to her ardent need for warmth and cooperation.

MONKEY HUSBAND + RAT WIFE

These two partners will work most constructively together. She is a happy and competent homemaker, while he is the great strategist that she will be immensely proud of. The Rat could get the enchanting Monkey to settle down nicely and he will adore her industry and parsimony. They will be constantly discovering desirable qualities in each other, and their marriage will be rewarding, fulfilling and financially auspicious.

MONKEY HUSBAND + OX WIFE

Both are too egotistical and forceful to coexist happily. He is an extrovert, a natural showman. She is an introvert and reticent. No doubt both parties have excellent positive sides but they may not have a chance to display them. He has an innate superiority complex and considers her dull and unimaginative. She may be blunt and proud and will not mince words when it comes to pointing out his flaws. They will both have to exercise great control over their basic urges to achieve any kind of rapport.

MONKEY HUSBAND + TIGER WIFE

Not a very harmonious combination and these two may not find much happiness in their union. Both are allergic to restraints of any kind and will not like playing second fiddle to anyone. They are both apt to think only in terms of "I" and are goaded by strong ambition and self-esteem. The Tiger can be arrogant when not given her way and the Monkey is naturally cunning and suave in his undertakings. They could regard each other with doubts and secret reservations. One has to be more masterful in order to control the other. So there may always be a struggle as to who can do better.

MONKEY HUSBAND + RABBIT WIFE

He is a positive and innovative thinker and a captivating performer.

She is very personable and well-mannered, although somewhat super-ficial. Both can be diplomatic and inscrutable about obtaining their objectives. The Monkey needs a lot of attention and compliments to keep him charming and companionable. The Rabbit is drawn toward quiet surroundings rather than active pursuits. He delights in contro-versy; she abhors dissent. They have totally different approaches toward life. In the end, both are realistic about their situation and will either adjust accordingly or seek a better solution.

MONKEY HUSBAND + DRAGON WIFE

One of the best matches, as they will both be able to harness their positive forces and achieve lasting unity and success together. Both are aware, aggressive and very ambitious. The Monkey is practical and crafty while the Dragon has more than enough willpower and energy for two. He will plan while she will set their goals higher each time. He loves challenges and she gives him great reassurance by standing behind him through thick and thin. Both will indulge each other, exchange ideas and work in harmony.

MONKEY HUSBAND + SNAKE WIFE

Both may tend to magnify the frailties of the opposite party. He is lively, outgoing and enterprising while she is persevering, ambitious and sophisticated. No doubt they are in the same big league but they cannot help challenging and at times opposing each other because of their natural jealousy and inborn suspicious inclinations. Both may have to be more sincere and straightforward before they can feel comfortable with each other.

MONKEY HUSBAND + HORSE WIFE

Both partners in this union are versatile, flexible and outgoing. Whether or not they can coexist in a spirit of goodwill will rest largely on their efforts to control their self-centered personalities. Neither is long on endurance, and they will not persevere in working out their differences if one finds the other lagging behind. They are both independent and practical individuals who can cooperate well if they want to, as they possess the same quick mind and keen faculties.

MONKEY HUSBAND + SHEEP WIFE

The Sheep lady loves to play house but she may make too many demands on the wily Monkey. He may be flattered by her attentiveness but still finds her flaws outweighing her virtues. She, on the other hand, is no match for the calculating and evasive Monkey, who may not always take her seriously. The Sheep stands to lose more in this bargain, as the Monkey will exploit her kind and generous nature. Each is on a different wavelength in this union.

MONKEY HUSBAND + MONKEY WIFE

A combination that could be binding if envy does not get in the way. If they can think in terms of "we" instead of "I," they can achieve much together. No problem will be too great for them if they meet it in the true spirit of cooperation. Monkeys can rise above pettiness and jealousy if they learn to share the good with the bad. These two could live in harmony if they are willing to stick to each other and not blame each other in the face of adversity.

MONKEY HUSBAND + ROOSTER WIFE

Both are ambitious and crave acclaim and recognition. These two materialistic and similarly powerful personalities may clash more often than they cooperate if they insist on maintaining their affectations. The Monkey man likes to get things done with a minimum of fuss and supervision. He prides himself on his ingenuity and innate capabilities. The Rooster girl is efficient and fastidious. She's prone to looking over his shoulder and picking up on his imperfections. They try each other's patience and endurance. He cannot stand her questioning and love for argument. She finds him too sure of himself and conceited to pay her much mind, let alone heed the advice she readily dishes out. Both are going to find the ride pretty rough unless they are willing to admit to some of their inherent shortcomings and meet the other halfway.

MONKEY HUSBAND + DOG WIFE

A good marriage with the partners usually favorably disposed to each other. The Monkey is productive enough and generally smart and sociable. The Dog wife will be cooperative and congenial if he expresses genuine desire to work together. He is apt to be more materialistic and ambitious than she and will be pleased if she does not try to overtake or outdo him in performance. She, on the other hand, is captivated by the Monkey's many-sided personality. He finds her a strong and refreshingly unpretentious ally and advisor. She loves his talents but could take a dim view of his envious and conniving traits; he may find her inspiring and fair-minded practices a bit restricting at times. Otherwise, both are well-balanced and intelligent enough to make necessary concessions.

MONKEY HUSBAND + BOAR WIFE

There may be a strong attraction for each in this combination, but the trials of everyday married life could wear it away. The Boar lady is prodding, energetic and staunchly devoted to her loved ones and her goals, but she operates more on blind faith, and in this case the Monkey cannot resist the urge to take advantage of her innocent nature. She, on the other hand, benefits from his financial acumen and guile but is not impressed by his unscrupulous and opportunistic ways. He finds her overconscientious about spreading goodwill about. He could also resent her extravagant generosity at his expense. Both may need extra efforts to put up with one another's frailties.

ROOSTER HUSBAND + RAT WIFE

He is analytical and a perfectionist; she is stimulating, practical and quite brainy in her own right. He is bossy and dogmatic and prone to giving lectures. She is balky about criticism and can be sharp and petty when offended. He lacks the sensitivity and warmth she seeks in a mate. Her resourcefulness and competence make her unwilling to follow his orders blindly. Not a promising match for either party. They tend to agitate each other unnecessarily.

ROOSTER HUSBAND + OX WIFE

An excellent and lasting union for both. He is open, frank and brave and makes up for her reserve and restraint. He is also hard-working and serious enough for the Ox's love of dignity and prestige. His security-consciousness will certainly appeal to the steadfast and resolute Ox lady. In response to his sunny and optimistic ways, the Ox may become less undemonstrative and be prodded on to more achievements. She is likely to be the more prudent and down to earth of the two, and in spite of his noisy and competent discourse, the Rooster will love to lean on his strong and noble Ox wife. They will find each other responsible and dedicated.

ROOSTER HUSBAND + TIGER WIFE

A turbulent and spicy marriage. Both are active and progressive souls but they have wide differences in their personalities. He is too egotistic and eccentric for the colorful Tiger lady and she is too much of a fighter to ever concede defeat in the face of his fastidious criticisms. Under different circumstances, they may be energetic and diligent, but in this combination they may be stubborn and petty.

ROOSTER HUSBAND + RABBIT WIFE

They are unlikely to ever find their ideal love in each other. Their personalities may clash strongly because both are vexed by each other's negative traits. He is outspoken, exacting and overzealous in his cutting criticism. She is an artistic and reticent intellectual who may be a bit self-indulgent and unwilling to work hard. When the industrious and ruthlessly efficient Rooster gets through with her, she may feel like a victim of the Inquisition. Needless to say, the Rabbit will be defiant and uncommunicative. The Rooster's lack of tact and indelicate ways are not intentional, but he cannot avoid hurting the Rabbit, who thrives on sympathy and consideration.

ROOSTER HUSBAND + DRAGON WIFE

An excellent and productive marriage combination. The Rooster is analytical and brainy and will be drawn to the bold and bright personality of the Dragon lady. She will immediately recognize his inherent worth and intellectual prowess. Together they can achieve success in their aspirations. She is purposeful and not easily conquered or frightened into submission by his bossy aggressiveness. She can and will be able to dismiss his loquaciousness with a shrug, as she is bound to have a few peculiarities of her own that he will have to bear. He finds her enthusiasm and energy boundless and exhilarating. She will not resent his running her affairs provided he looks upon her as an equal and respects her opinions.

ROOSTER HUSBAND + SNAKE WIFE

The exuberant and intrepid Rooster man could brighten up the Snake's serious view of life and bolster her spirits as well. A prosperous union for both. They are both intellectuals but on different levels. She is serene, reflective and deliberate; he is overcharged with zeal and dauntless optimism. This union provides them with the opportunity to balance the scales and offset each other's excesses.

ROOSTER HUSBAND + HORSE WIFE

A smooth marriage is not indicated as these two strong-minded individuals are easily irritated by each other. He can be provocative and undiplomatic and will castigate her for her high living and lack of steadiness. But she is too sophisticated, witty and flamboyant to settle for the simple and hard-working life he has planned. The Rooster may have grandiose ideas but his methods are dependable and precise. In the opposite corner, the Horse may be more practical and realistic about her goals but she is unpredictable and inconsistent in her method of application. He cannot comprehend her changeable ways and she cannot abide his strict routine and obsession with facts and figures.

ROOSTER HUSBAND + SHEEP WIFE

The tough-minded Rooster has the stamina to match his taste for work and perfection. The Sheep is kind-hearted, emotional and dependent. He may patronize her need to cling to someone, but cannot be expected to put up with her self-pitying and indulgent ways. He can deal better with facts than with her tender feelings. She can understand his optimistic drive and ambitions, but may find him too cold, calculating and particular. She is genteel and easily hurt and could pack up and go home to Mama if he censures her too much or too often. The tolerance factor in this combination is very low.

ROOSTER HUSBAND + MONKEY WIFE

Most likely to result in a cool and defensive union unless both partners can alter their behavior suitably. The Monkey could have the annoying habit of grabbing what she wants and hanging on to it, oblivious of what others may feel. He is too rigorous and stringent to let her get away with this. She is not amused, on the other hand, by his skillful and parsimonious ways, nor impressed with his gift for oratory and debate. She possesses equal powers of rhetoric and will provoke him to anger. They tend to rub each other the wrong way. They will only cooperate when the inducement to do so is irresistible.

ROOSTER HUSBAND + ROOSTER WIFE

Both are virtuous personalities but this match could provoke an unhealthy "holier than thou" attitude between these contenders. They are both peevish and often obsessed with their own views and will not pay much heed to the opinions of the other. However, these two are also duty-oriented and have conscientious and responsible natures. Who knows, they may be able to relinquish some of their demanding ways to achieve common goals. Then again, both are argumentative and opinionated, and there may be endless discussions before they sign the Peace Treaty or agree to call a truce.

ROOSTER HUSBAND + DOG WIFE

No doubt both parties here have fine minds, value their integrity and are proud of themselves. However, in spite of their self-assurance and poise, they are also very outspoken. If the Rooster starts to nag and grumble about the Dog's frailties, she could respond by throwing harmony out the window and giving him some scalding rhetoric of her own. Both parties have sharp tongues and could hurt each other quite painfully. A workable relationship only if one of them is unselfish and sensible enough to entice the other to lay down arms.

ROOSTER HUSBAND + BOAR WIFE

The Boar is trusting and easygoing. She accepts things at face value and will politely skim the surface instead of offending others. The Rooster makes pointed accusations; he is the unrelenting private eye who has to get to the root of the problem even if it means upsetting everyone's apple cart in the process. The Boar is an independent thinker but is always receptive to suggestions, while he is observant about every detail. She would love to take his advice if only he could put a little sugar on it. She is prone to being naive and easily imposed on by others. She may have need of his sharp faculties. This could be the one common denominator of their marriage.

DOG HUSBAND + RAT WIFE

A union which could develop fairly well if they have strong mutual interests. They are both sensible and outgoing and could find contentment because of the lack of friction in this marriage. She may be more affectionate and thrifty but the Dog is reasonably easygoing and tactful enough to avoid bickering with her on unimportant issues. Both will try to give each other enough breathing space to ensure freedom of expression and movement about their house.

DOG HUSBAND + OX WIFE

Both are faithful and loyal and will take their conjugal duties seriously. Their difficulties could arise from the Ox's overbearing attitude and rigid opinions. The Dog prefers free speech and equality and may not humor the narrow-minded Ox for too long. The Ox, on the other hand, may resent the Dog's overdirect and outspoken ways; she can nurse grievances for a long time. They both shun pettiness and injustice, but are sometimes guilty of these faults themselves. A relationship that needs a lot of understanding and compromise.

DOG HUSBAND + TIGER WIFE

Both are idealistic by nature and have the same humanitarian interests. The Dog can be more objective and logical than the animated but hotheaded Tigress. He is thus able enough to advise her when she gets too emotional or impulsive. He is diplomatic and unbiased and will persuade her to see reason without touching any of her sensitive spots. The Tiger, on the other hand, is demonstrative, affectionate and honest with her feelings, which the Dog likes, and her sanguine disposition could liven up any relationship. They will feel completely at ease with each other. A well-suited match that should enhance this couple's unpretentiousness and generous personalities. A combination that will bring out the best in both.

DOG HUSBAND + RABBIT WIFE

A good and lasting match. The Rabbit is imaginative, charming and diplomatic. The Dog is straightforward but agreeable in manner. Both enjoy honest fun and entertainment, but will prefer activities that have useful purposes. They have innately cooperative spirits and will allow each other a fair degree of independence and assertiveness. She has a strong need for comfort and luxury, while he is less materialistic and more understanding. Both will have little difficulty in putting up with each other's peculiarities. A union that should bring out the best in each of the partners.

DOG HUSBAND + DRAGON WIFE

Each may have the wrong chemistry for the other. Their basic dispositions are uncomplementary and they may opt to disperse their energies in different directions. Both have leadership abilities but in totally different directions. The Dog loves cooperation and may resent the Dragon's audacious, high-handed and overpowering tactics. She may find him taciturn and erratic if she pushes him too much; the Dog has a reputation for being pugnacious and acidly sharp when hurt. Neither can conform easily to the other's wishes and this could only be a love-hate relationship at its best.

DOG HUSBAND + SNAKE WIFE

He is level-headed and open-minded but may still be puzzled by her mystique. She has a fair respect for his intelligence but is inclined toward more sophistication and luxury than the unmaterialistic can endure. Both lack the proper understanding to ever be totally enchanted with each other's personality, but may be realistic enough to have an amicable life together if each can accept the other for what he or she is.

DOG HUSBAND + HORSE WIFE

This will be a happy and fruitful match, as these two people have a sound understanding of each other's needs and deficiencies. The Dog is honorable and intelligent enough to work well with the capable Horse. He also admires her keen knowledge of timing and strategy, while she finds him reasonable and practical enough to depend on. They will both get the cooperation they seek and still be able to enjoy the degree of individualism and independence they require.

DOG HUSBAND + SHEEP WIFE

They may have strong or weak conflicts of interest, but this sort of union will make both partners less amiable than they normally are. She is too sentimental and her wistful ways will serve to irritate the logical Dog, who will be more curt and impatient than sympathetic. She is tolerant and unselfish when handled correctly, but in this case she may become withdrawn and dejected by the Dog's hardy and direct manner. In the final analysis, both may find that they have too little in common to bear the strain of their very different personalities.

DOG HUSBAND + MONKEY WIFE

A workable and fairly positive match if both are generous and forgiving enough to discount the other's frailties. The Monkey wife will admire the Dog for his sensible approach and logical outlook; no one knows the value of intelligence more than she. He, on the other hand, sees her as a capable go-getter and will appreciate her witty and charming personality. She is the more materialistic of the two and he is the more idealistic. She values tangible wealth. He puts his principles first. Together they could contentedly travel the middle of the road.

DOG HUSBAND + ROOSTER WIFE

A cool to moderate coexistence is in store for this couple. Both are discriminating and forthright souls who may be easily displeased with each other's faults. Normally, they may strive harder to be more agreeable, but this match could bring out their most offensive traits, making them willful and uncompromising. Both are too quick to retaliate when challenged and can be fierce fighters. The Dog is nice and easygoing only as long as you keep out of his hair. The Rooster is virtuous and equally sincere in her efforts, but she has much too rigid an outlook to suit the Dog. She will make him feel like she is out to reform him and he will never stand for that.

DOG HUSBAND + DOG WIFE

They are reasonably compatible. Both have the same warm and stable nature although the female of the species may be the more outspoken and critical of the pair. An idealistic and conscientious couple who will seek and value each other's opinions. Dogs are fairly conforming in marital relationships and will perform well when they desire harmony. No large problems in this union if they will consult and respect each other. They should always make joint decisions as neither can tolerate being left out.

DOG HUSBAND + BOAR WIFE

This couple may have quite dissimilar personalities but could still maintain a fairly agreeable relationship. He is dependable and sharp enough for her to rely on, while she is loving, uncomplaining and affectionate enough for him to have a comfortable feeling of togetherness. They are not averse to mutual concessions and will share whatever they have with each other. A union that will be happy because neither will need to harp on the other's weaknesses.

BOAR HUSBAND + RAT WIFE

There is a good measure of attraction between these two and they will strive to have a companionable and peaceful relationship. Both are outgoing, sociable and energetic and will probably center their life around their home, their friends and their mutual interests, which will include a good deal of entertaining. This couple will be drawn to active pursuits and have definite ideas about their involvements. She could be the more sensitive and prudent of the two, while he is positive but too conciliatory at times for his own good. He may have need of her counsel.

BOAR HUSBAND + OX WIFE

An acceptable union but unlikely to be a strong one. Their different outlook and behavioral patterns will engender underlying friction. As a rule the Boar is warm, generous and understanding, but the Ox lady may only notice his sensuality and love of extravagance and find him too immoderate for her needs. On the other side, the Ox's predilection for hard work and constant security and self-discipline may unnerve the Boar. He is jovial, gregarious and open and he works only to ensure his leisure. She is serious, systematic and rigid and finds contentment in her labors.

BOAR HUSBAND + TIGER WIFE

A warm and gratifying union, as each side has a strong desire to please the other. Both are affectionate, dynamic and progressive in their basic attitude and will complement each other. He is kind and understanding enough to cope with the unpredictable and exciting moods of the Tiger, while she finds him devoted, courageous and unselfish. The Tiger is usually repentant for her outbursts when she meets no opposition, and the Boar's good humor and compassionate ways will bring out the best in her and make her more compliant to his wishes.

BOAR HUSBAND + RABBIT WIFE

The Boar is courageous and dedicated enough for the quiet and well-mannered Rabbit. She is sagacious, resilient and subtle enough to impart some of her astuteness to him without his noticing. He finds her kind and cautious and will lavish on her both his affections and the luxuries she likes. The Boar is selfless enough not to seek more than the Rabbit can give and she will be happy to be the object of his attentions and generosity. Both could feel enriched by this union.

BOAR HUSBAND + DRAGON WIFE

A fairly successful relationship in which the gains will probably outweigh the losses. Both are ardent and forceful, although in different ways. The powerful Dragon wife could stimulate any spouse into action or break him in the process. The Boar is not averse to bending to the desires of his loved one and will be tireless in his efforts to achieve success and win her approval. They are evenly matched in energy and love of physical exertion. Their mutual flaw is that they are both too responsive to stimuli and could be easily carried away by enthusiasm and excesses. There may be no one to apply the brakes.

BOAR HUSBAND + SNAKE WIFE

The aesthetic Snake cannot stand the Boar's sincere but mundane and simple ways. He finds her too complex and secretive. The Snake is too highly evolved, ambitious and profound for the overindulgent and trusting Boar. She will not approve of his open and easygoing manners and will be aloof and unsympathetic to him. The Boar, in turn, will find the Snake's uncommunicative and coldly calculating attitude very disconcerting. Both will suffer from unfulfilled expectations and a lack of appreciation for each other's positive traits.

BOAR HUSBAND + HORSE WIFE

They are both pleasure seekers and have very sociable personalities and could benefit each other to a certain extent. She is imaginative and resourceful while he is dependable and good-natured. The Boar admires the Horse's animated and cheerful ways, and she finds his devotion and honest fortitude very pleasing. They both understand the value of compromise and will have an active and involved marriage without stepping on each other's toes. They will opt to live their life to the fullest. On the darker side, neither party will worry too much about tomorrow.

BOAR HUSBAND + SHEEP WIFE

A warm, intimate marriage for this couple. Both will give their best to the union and have a deep love and genuine concern for one another.

The Boar is sturdy, gallant and thoughtful enough to please the gentle and compassionate Sheep lady. She, on the other hand, will mother him and make him the object of her worship. He is sensual and simple and will interpret her possessiveness as true love and devotion. The Boar is generous and protective, and the Sheep will perform her best when she knows she is loved and appreciated, as she will be in this union.

BOAR HUSBAND + MONKEY WIFE

A fairly civil union, but they may not be really fascinated by each other's real personality. The Boar is too straightforward and scrupulous for the complicated Monkey. She has more pungent tastes and the Boar will definitely be too bland. On the other hand, while the Monkey is deviously charming, her basic intricacy and pretentiousness may prove too much for him. Both are bound to be irritated and bruised by the incapacities of the other. Still, they could make a go of this match if they can figure each other out and concentrate on their positive qualities.

BOAR HUSBAND + ROOSTER WIFE

Could turn out to be a feasible match if both parties make the proper concessions. There will be areas of disagreement, but both have the capacity to work out differences if they admire each other enough. The Boar may be too passionate and warm for the analytical and mentally inclined Rooster, while she is too argumentative and knowledgeable to follow or love him blindly. However, on the positive side, neither is too thin-skinned and criticism will slide off their backs like water. He is honest and accommodating and has a true need for her diligent and critical mind, and while she is capable and self-confident, she will have every need for the diplomacy and reliability of the affable Boar.

BOAR HUSBAND + DOG WIFE

A kind and agreeable relationship despite their differing attitudes toward life. Both are robust, open and honest and like doing their best whenever possible. However, the Dog could be aggressive and will not withhold her criticism if the Boar is too self-indulgent or lax in his duties. She is not as passionate as he, and may lack understanding of his large appetites and sensuality. Still, they could find common grounds for cooperation as the Dog has more insight than the Boar and will be loyal to him. Likewise, the Boar is tolerant and generous enough to forgive the Dog's peculiarities and see her as the trustworthy and noble ally she is.

BOAR HUSBAND + BOAR WIFE

A combination that could work out well if they can take the good with the bad. Being born under the same sign, both will be strong, courageous and modest, but they may lack direction and tenacity and may not be able to strengthen each other's weak points. Sincerity and goodwill without resolute and systematic organization could wreak havoc for two such well-meaning people. One of them will have to be unemotional and disciplined enough to face reality and adversity, otherwise their mutual love and loyalty will not be much protection for them.

Chapter 14
When Sun Signs Meet Moon Signs:
The 144 Combinations

ARIES

ARIES RAT: FIRE + POSITIVE WATER

A person with typical Aries veracity tempered by Rat craft and immense charm. A magnificently headstrong but progressive personality. Self-assured and always in full control of his faculties, he will plunge into a busy and involved life, with a tendency to being somewhat rushed and irritable. Well-read and boldly inquisitive, the Aries Rat mixes and mingles freely in all circles because of his vibrant sociality.

ARIES OX: FIRE + NEGATIVE WATER

A temperamental and adamant personality. The Buffalo is slow and sure; the Ram is self-possessed and arrogant. In this combination, both signs are not graceful with words and the result could be too much action and strength of will without enough tolerance. Still, this person looks before he leaps, as both animals here are surefooted and selfish about giving up territory staked out as theirs. The Aries Ox goes a long way by himself and seldom seeks aid or burdens others with his troubles. But if and when he decides to challenge authority, he can be intolerable.

ARIES TIGER: FIRE + POSITIVE WOOD

A fiery tempest that will neither wane nor blow itself out. Neither sign composing this combination is known for patience or forebearance. Superexciting and magnetic, the Aries Tiger or Tigress will have a life full of climaxes as he or she is most generous with exclamation points. One finds it hard to imagine this sort of personality at rest. A fireball of energy, he could dash about incessantly or suddenly lash out in fretful tantrums. Restless, innovative and notoriously brave, he is never short of friends—or enemies. Sensuous and wildly attractive, this person is bound for an eventful life because he will make every effort to take center stage.

ARIES RABBIT: FIRE + NEGATIVE WOOD

A domesticated Ram, genteel and with a beguiling calmness. This combination will produce a person with nerves of steel; always willing to bend in theory yet never quite doing it in actuality. The Ram's frankness is camouflaged by the Hare's carefully chosen words. A nicer and kinder Aries than most, with slower ways. You can expect him to be solicitous but firm; enthusiastic but given to biding his time. The peaceful but observant Aries Rabbit is assured of getting things done his way—in the end.

ARIES DRAGON: FIRE + POSITIVE WOOD

A bright torch who leads the way. Full of noblesse oblige. It is his birthright to shine and he will be eternally optimistic, blessed with mass appeal and contagious enthusiasm. Yet, this overrighteous soul could also be destructively domineering or marked with imperious self-confidence and reckless courage. He is the all-or-nothing man who marches into battle with all flags unfurled. When challenged on his royal rights, the Aries Dragon can be a fearsome beast.

ARIES SNAKE: FIRE + NEGATIVE FIRE

A person more profound and deliberate in stance. Criticizes with sharp finesse and could snub lesser beings into obedience. The Snake is wise and guarded while the Ram is expansive and has liberal views.

The Aries Snake applies his intelligence to everything he does. This astute combination could produce a prolific achiever. Here is a person in whom the plotter and the doer are happily wed.

ARIES HORSE: FIRE + POSITIVE FIRE

As one can see, this sign has too much active fire. The Aries Horse could be perpetually turned on. Yet the Horse could teach the Ram to run with grace and agility and not to use those horns so much. Witty, dashing and spirited, this person tends to overwork. He expresses himself brilliantly but often rashly. Dauntless and impatient, he will rush to start new ventures and be unpersevering in finishing them.

ARIES SHEEP: FIRE + NEGATIVE FIRE

A more submissive Ram but this may be for appearance only. He keeps his own counsel, and while looking ever so meek and mild, he may be terribly set in his ways. The aggressiveness in him is muted and buried—but it will surface when he feels threatened. Hence, a more controlled and patient personality, free of guile and treachery.

ARIES MONKEY: FIRE + POSITIVE METAL

Sounds off loud and clear like a brass gong. Blessed with an ease of expression, he takes it upon himself to sell himself and avidly promotes his ideas. The Aries Monkey is full of mental poise and balance. Swinging from one tree to another, he will participate in everything, in every sense of the word. He is unimpressed by restrictions and nothing will deter him from his plotted course. The Ram gives the Monkey unabashed honesty; he will look you straight in the eye with sincerity. What goes on in his brain could be a different matter. After he gives you that firm handshake—anything goes.

ARIES ROOSTER: FIRE + NEGATIVE METAL

Hard to ignore, impossible to dismiss and difficult to keep up with are the three phrases that characterize the Aries Rooster. When he is positive, he could be truly indispensable. When negative, you could have a full-fledged megalomaniac on your hands. Straight as a rod and thoroughly honorable in intent, this personality will make indelible impressions wherever he goes. He tells it like it is, and in the final accounting he remains faithful to his convictions. He has a very clear conscience.

ARIES DOG: FIRE + POSITIVE METAL

A poised and dedicated personality. Self-assured and warm-hearted, this person will be noted for his or her refreshing frankness that spells sincerity but not offense. A vivacious advocate of realism and honesty, the Aries Dog could be a real trooper when called upon to make sacrifices. He will seek emotional and spiritual fulfillment over material benefits. The Ram is full of drive and initiative, so the cynical Dog will regenerate quickly after disappointments.

ARIES BOAR: FIRE + NEGATIVE WATER

Sunny optimism and passion are the key words for this energetic combination. Here the Boar's easygoing nature could override that famous Aries temper and directness. A personality rich in raw sex appeal and expendable energy. Both signs are robust, rowdy and given to free and generous displays of affection. Sturdy and magnanimous, the Aries Boar is a veritable pillar of strength.

TAURUS

TAUREAN RAT: EARTH + POSITIVE WATER

A sign of enterprise and activity that blends with a love of security. The Taurean Rat is practical and companionable. He keeps in stride with the changes of his time and will have strong literary leanings. Money means a lot to this type of a person and his realistic soul teaches him early in life not to bank on anyone but himself. The Rat is amenable and clever with compromises, while the Bull is not too curiosity prone or given to misadventures, especially monetary ones. A person born in this combination could write or talk his way out of trouble, but he won't like to waste his money on legal fees. William Shakespeare was a Taurean Rat.

TAUREAN OX: EARTH + NEGATIVE WATER

A slow but extremely persistent climber. When dealing with a Taurean Ox, just bear in mind that he has four horns and eight hooves and this sort of armory is enough for anyone. The Venus personality of the Bull is sensuous, but both signs here are very definite about what they want. Orderly, practical and determined, the Taurean Ox can also be dictatorial and obsessed with self-enforced discipline. He expresses himself in plain, down-to-earth language and abhors flattery and fancy talk. When he is aroused, he could suddenly turn into a one-man stampede, and once he sets his mind to something, well, he could be about as open to discussion and as movable as the Sphinx.

TAUREAN TIGER: EARTH + POSITIVE WOOD

The otherwise stolid practicality and efficiency of the Bull will be lightened by vivacious feline humor and regality. An endearing and easy-to-relate-to Taurean or an unusually stable and intellectual Tiger, whichever way you want it. He or she is inclined to be a bit more traditional and conservative, but the Taurean reserve may be replaced by the Tiger's unpretentiousness and congeniality. Firm and methodical about carrying out his mission in life, this person will nonetheless be warm and appealing, and generous with his time and energy.

TAUREAN RABBIT: EARTH + NEGATIVE WOOD

A tactful Bull with more delicacy and contemplativeness. Both signs here are well-organized physically and mentally, although the Hare is definitely more keenly observant and placidly disposed. The Taurean Rabbit will not seek to impose his will upon others, but rather strive to convince them by his winning graciousness. Failing to win by diplomacy, he could withdraw into a stubborn sullenness. With the Bull's broad shoulders present here, the Rabbit may not shun the weight of heavy responsibilities.

TAUREAN DRAGON: EARTH + POSITIVE WOOD

Steady as the beacon of a lighthouse, this mundane Dragon will be endowed with heavenly might and practical goals. The normal Taurean predictability will be overshadowed by Dragon dazzle at times, and he is a bit short of guile and pretense. The Taurean Dragon will be distinctly attractive, although he tends to be an aloof and somewhat slow mover. He is always aboveboard, fair-minded and performance-conscious; a reliable soul who invests his time and energies wisely and in the right places.

TAUREAN SNAKE: EARTH + NEGATIVE FIRE

Could surpass us all for tenacity and durability. The Taurean Snake is a personality with both feet planted solidly in the ground. The two signs in this combination both subscribe to the belief that a bird in the hand is worth two in the bush, so a native of this solar-lunar mixture will be especially careful about money and not inclined to gamble. He is never plagued by doubts or fears. He believes in his own abilities and sails assiduously toward his destiny. He will be especially sensitive to music or the other arts and stimulants that affect his senses. He rarely has any regrets about his courses of action, and since both signs here need security, the Taurean Snake will know how to make hay while the sun shines.

TAUREAN HORSE: EARTH + POSITIVE FIRE

Here the normal Taurean steadiness and love of regularity may be colored by the rainbow moods of the flamboyant Horse. Still, both are conscientious in attending to their own needs and never hindered by overdeveloped scruples or deep self-analysis. A person born with this combination has a strong sense of security and quiet determination. He will be a quicker Taurean on one side or a slower horse on the other, but inevitably he will have a lively personality that will always respond to reason and sound argument.

TAUREAN SHEEP: EARTH + NEGATIVE FIRE

A strong-willed Sheep who clings too much to the past at times. The Bull is purposeful and blessed with fixed ideas about what he wants, which ideally curtails the Sheep's indecisiveness. However, the malleable Sheep is always open to suggestions the Taurean is not. This combination produces a character full of constructive common sense, calm persuasiveness and an unerring eye for beauty. The Taurean Sheep may be a lover of ease, but he will apply himself diligently to ensuring his personal comfort and security.

TAUREAN MONKEY: EARTH + POSITIVE METAL

The Taurean Monkey could be composed and businesslike on the surface and bubbling with fertile ideas underneath. The Monkey's presence here could polish the Bull's rough edges, making him more attractive. Taurus is of an impressively sound character, while the Monkey is famous for his flexible intellect. Together, they will build a person who will be ambitious, communicative and able to achieve mastery over his environment. The Venus child is earthy and faithful, while the Monkey is cooperative in spite of being preoccupied with his own interests. Consequently, the Taurean Monkey will be shrewd but honest, adaptable but steady.

TAUREAN ROOSTER: EARTH + NEGATIVE METAL

This combination of two such hard-working signs could give us a person who staunchly believes in Spartan denial (it's good for the soul, you know) or other such endurance tests. He will win hands down of course, while you droop with exhaustion; he does not know the meaning of the word fatigue. While both signs here are serious in outlook, the Bull will certainly have better control over his tongue than the Rooster. The end product may be a bit on the dry side, as both Bull and Rooster have a similar brand of laconic humor.

TAUREAN DOG: EARTH + POSITIVE METAL

The Taurean Dog is a cautious and stable character. He is easy to be with, as he will do his best to make you relax in his company. The Bull is more physical than mental, while the Dog can be dedicated and generous to others. Together, they will form a person blessed with great endurance and warmth of affection; openly honest and never too advanced in his or her thinking to stop and consider another person's point of view. Positive, active and cheerful of outlook, he will try his best to please, while keeping a sensible lookout for his own interests.

TAUREAN BOAR: EARTH + NEGATIVE WATER

Solidly built for reliability, the Taurean Boar can be as impregnable as a fortress when he wants to be. Otherwise, he is an affable fellow with large and lusty appetites. A person of this combination will do everything with mucho gusto, as both solar and lunar signs here are remarkably sensual and healthy. Patient and conscientious, the Taurean Boar will be a genuine friend and confidant. This combination produces a Bull who is more cooperative and a Boar favored with industry and perseverance.

GEMINI

GEMINI RAT: AIR + POSITIVE WATER

A tremendously energetic combination. Both signs have an unmistakable flair for words and hence this personality could be an indefatigable talker or writer. The Rat is careful where the Twins are carefree. This person tends to give his attention to too many different projects without being very selective about them and thus accomplishes less than he should in the end. No doubt, the Gemini Rat is innovative and exciting to have around, but his loyalties may change too quickly to be relied upon.

GEMINI OX: AIR + NEGATIVE WATER

The Gemini virtuoso widens the Buffalo's narrow-mindedness and gives him more humor and vitality. Yet, the Ox's lassitude should prove a blessing in this instance, as this person will be able to finish appointed tasks and not be balky with routine assignments. A responsible soul who will be able to regulate himself and make use of his sound visionary qualities as well.

GEMINI TIGER: AIR + POSITIVE WOOD

A spontaneous Tiger. One can almost hear his laughter crack the ice of any uneasy gathering. Quick and talkative, he can be an invaluable asset if he is not temperamental and too outspoken. A person born with this combination is bound to be an incessant mover, but in too much of a hurry most of the time. If he could sit and do some good planning before using his speed and inborn love of activity, he could be almost invincible.

GEMINI RABBIT: AIR + NEGATIVE WOOD

A quietly eloquent and vastly persuasive personality. The extemporaneous ways of Mercury's Gemini are joined here by the Hare's subtlety and discretion. A person of this combination will be smart and quick-witted. Both signs are fortunate enough to be able to assess the future trend of events, and hence the Gemini Rabbit is gifted with foresight. The Gemini in him discovers worthwhile ventures while the Rabbit devises the most feasible way to profit without investing too much labor.

GEMINI DRAGON: AIR + POSITIVE WOOD

The Gemini Dragon will be a hurricane of activity; fast, agile and fearless, he will be noted for his great "do-it-yourself" kind of efficiency. Mercury's child is sharp and clear-minded, while the Dragon never lacks the courage or determination to put his ideas to work. A person of this combination will be a great success if he pays more attention to detail, which both signs here tend to brush off too easily. With the Dragon's leadership and Gemini's ability to relate to people, this personality will enjoy a large and respected sphere of influence.

GEMINI SNAKE: AIR + NEGATIVE FIRE

Distinctively effervescent and poised, the Gemini Snake strikes quick and true. He is full of charm and an enigmatic dignity and never gives away his true motives. The Gemini Snake will be especially enchanting to the opposite sex. A person of this combination is never agitated to a point where he or she loses total control. Still, the Gemini Snake can be a kind of brinksman, taking things to the very edge as if to test his own judgment and reflexes. But this should be no great cause for alarm, as the Snake is usually sensible enough to balance off the volatile movements of Gemini.

GEMINI HORSE: AIR + POSITIVE FIRE

Combustible and highly inconsistent combination. The Twin's love of chameleon changes plus the Horse's penchant for constant mobility is combined here to the highest degree possible. The Gemini Horse is capable and lightning-fast with his reflexes. With this wit around, there will never be a dull moment. He moves at breakneck speed, covering a lot of ground, but never going deeper than the surface. Easily infatuated and just as fast to lose interest, this solar-lunar mixture personifies Mercury incarnate.

GEMINI SHEEP: AIR + NEGATIVE FIRE

A versatile and creative combination. The sheep's good taste and refined manners coupled with Gemini's wit and humour should strike a congenial balance. With Mercury's influence here the Sheep personality loses some of that sentimentalism and acquires more of Gemini's love of action and practical outlook on life.

GEMINI MONKEY: AIR + POSITIVE METAL

Although this combination will never produce a deep, soul-searching type of personality, this could be a sign of genius. The Gemini Monkey is the epitome of versatility, as both signs can and will achieve things that seem utterly impossible and spout out ideas by the dozen. Mercury's Twins are deft and alluring, while the Monkey is the intrepid magician. A person born under this combination is inventive and self-reliant; he probably devised every shortcut in the book.

GEMINI ROOSTER: AIR + NEGATIVE METAL

Here Gemini's inconsistency will be ameliorated by Rooster efficiency and love of precision. He is a sporty fellow who speaks his mind with matter-of-fact candor and can get to the point without much ado or fear of reprisals. The Gemini Rooster is still touchy about criticism and will swerve at the slightest blow to his ego or opposition to his views. The Rooster in this combination is bound to be more colorful. A finger-snapping, hustle-bustle soul—full of life, good intentions, organizational talent and practical aspirations.

GEMINI DOG: AIR + POSITIVE METAL

A Dog of rapid movements and a multitude of talents. Blessed with star quality, this personality could be an excellent entertainer, as he or she will project a natural and likable image to the public. Gemini's mercurial spirit is quick to adapt to changes and is easily fired by enthusiasm and excitement. The Dog is appealing in his modesty and consideration. But this person may also suffer because he or she tries to live up to expectations not of his own making.

GEMINI BOAR: AIR + NEGATIVE WATER

The Twins' whirlwind activities will sometimes leave the poor Boar lightheaded in this combination. But while the Boar invests goodwill and honesty in this bargain, Mercury will provide initiative, stimuli and quick logic. The Gemini Boar will be a sociable and very popular problem-solver. He sees the whole picture with scientific clarity, yet never leaves out the humane aspects in his final consideration. He will want life to be spicy and is at his best where there is a frequent change of scenery.

CANCER

CANCERIAN RAT: WATER + POSITIVE WATER

A deeply intuitive and secretive personality. The Cancerian Rat is a veritable well of emotions. The Rat's outgoing personality here could enliven and lessen the Moonchild's strong inhibitions or shyness. In this combination we find a person not easily lead astray by impractical aspirations. Things have to be tried and found true before the Cancerian Rat gives his trust. He is only relaxed in familiar surroundings. Both solar and lunar signs here are concerned with domestic affairs, and this personality will like to have a close-knit family life besides accumulating wealth and material possessions.

CANCERIAN OX: WATER + NEGATIVE WATER

A person born with this combination will not be half as amiable as he looks. But he will be thoughtful and considerate in spite of behaving like a motherly dictator at times. The Cancerian Ox is not a sacrificial goat and will cause a furor if his rights are trampled on. Here the

Buffalo will not allow the Crab to become too affected by his emotions, while the Cancerian influence on the Ox will definitely diminish some of that regimental grit. This person may turn out to be a very good listener who can be firm and understanding at the same time.

CANCERIAN TIGER: WATER + POSITIVE WOOD

An offbeat Crab, full of feline surprises, sparks and ardent love songs. All sizzling jealousy and possessiveness up front, but soft as butter underneath. The Cancerian Tiger is amorous and incorrigibly roman-tic. An avid party-goer. He can burst into laughter or tears without much provocation. Generally, a person belonging to this combination will be most helpful and considerate because of the Crab's kind-heartedness and the Tiger's lively and optimistic temperament.

CANCERIAN RABBIT: WATER + NEGATIVE WOOD

The Cancerian Rabbit could be a tentative and withdrawn personality for whom changes or having to let go of things is a traumatic situation. He makes few lasting relationships during his entire lifetime and will bare his soul only to those precious few. He likes to carefully assess situations from a vantage point located a safe distance from trouble. And, although he is psychic and blessed with extraordinary vision, he tends to be mainly devoted to his own problems, maintaining a laissez-faire attitude toward others. Although he can be dependable and sympathetic, the Cancerian Rabbit is also given to romantic illusions and idyllic dreams and should guard against intense brooding and self-pity when things fail to go his way.

CANCERIAN DRAGON: WATER + POSITIVE WOOD

Here sensitive charm and dignity are joined. The Cancerian Dragon will not be as militant as other Dragons but will have the quiet and regal bearing of authority. The Dragon is idealistic where the Crab is deep and searching. Impressions made upon this type of person will be slow but infinitely more permanent. With the Moon's cool disposi-tion, this Dragon could be a less keyed-up performer. He will also have the Dragon's strength in developing the acquisitive instincts of the

Crab. Life with him or her could be pleasurable, as the Cancerian Dragon is responsive and tolerant.

CANCERIAN SNAKE: WATER + NEGATIVE FIRE

This personality could possess a mysterious and highly enchanting nature, somewhat like the shimmering reflection of the Moon on a placid body of water. He seeks permanence, fame and strong material security, yet is bound by the Snake's illusory qualities and Cancer's inhibited nature. He will love to have his family and lots of people around him even if they are parasitic and imposing. The Moonchild is protective and dependent on love, while the Snake half of this person is defensive, suspicious and paranoid about failure. He could well be very successful, but will he learn to be completely happy and at home with his complicated inner self?

CANCERIAN HORSE: WATER + POSITIVE FIRE

An active but calmly collected personality. Although he is refined and in tune with his environment, the Cancerian Horse is still subject to a myriad of moods and caprices. This person will not be as self-sacrificing as Cancer with other lunar signs, but he or she will still have tasteful preferences and a loving nature. The Horse's presence here insures that this personality will be more outgoing and less inclined to take life too seriously. The Crab won't be so clinging, as the Horse knows where to let go. The result is a character polished in speech and manners, with a safety valve to protect himself against overinvolvement.

CANCERIAN SHEEP: WATER + NEGATIVE FIRE

Here we find a character of deep piety, filial devotion and love of children. The Cancerian Sheep is a feminine combination. Consequently, he is easily hurt, quick to retreat and passive in attitude. Timorous and sensitive to discomforts and deprivations, this sort of person thrives on opulence and conjugal harmony. Despite being plagued by his frothy inhibitions, the Cancerian Sheep will be largely unselfish and will take great interest in his home and domestic duties.

He is also a patron of the arts. Definitely not a solitary soul, he or she will need and have a lot of friends and family members around to keep him happy.

CANCERIAN MONKEY: WATER + POSITIVE METAL

A home-loving, modest Monkey with unerring fiscal abilities and a good eye for investments. He may have rich tastes and prefer sumptuous and elegant decor for his surroundings; he will like to show his degree of success by his artistic and expensive possessions. This sort of a person will also be found installing multiple gadgets around his home to eliminate irksome everyday chores. Yet behind his demure Cancerian appearance, this Monkey will still maintain his indisputable intellectual prowess and will enjoy matching wits with the most able of opponents.

CANCERIAN ROOSTER: WATER + NEGATIVE METAL

A careful, motherly and efficient personality with warm, demonstrative manners. The Cancerian Rooster is always genuinely helpful, but still you will note the aggressiveness of the Chicken shining through. For once, the orderly Rooster's good intentions will be expressed and applied with Cancerian kindness and good taste, thus winning him support and endorsement on all fronts. In this combination, Cancer's passive tenacity is linked to the Rooster's active perseverance. This person will be difficult to defeat, as he will allow nothing to hinder him from achieving his goals.

CANCERIAN DOG: WATER + POSITIVE METAL

The acute sensitivity of the Crab is intertwined here with the internal balance of the Dog. This personality will not be too rash or emotional and will be able to maintain his equilibrium and fair-mindedness. In spite of the Dog's sharp tongue, this sign will be a keen appreciator of beauty and purity. The Cancerian Dog may have discriminating tastes, but is less materialistic. Thus, a person of this combination will display a natural affection for others and establish noble standards for himself, while living a refined but moderate life style.

CANCERIAN BOAR: WATER + NEGATIVE WATER

The two signs constituting this combination are emotional and given to the pursuit of physical pleasure and luxuries. The Boar is highly sexed and easily dissipated by overindulgence; the Crab, while more aesthetic in outlook, is only constructive when he can relinquish his hold on things no longer essential to him. Both Crab and Boar have lovingly generous natures and are very impressionable. But then, while the Moonchild votes for quality and stability, the Boar is in favor of quantity and rapid progress. If the positive qualities of both solar and lunar signs can be brought together in the personality here, he will no doubt find love, wealth and contentment.

LEO

LEO RAT: FIRE + POSITIVE WATER

The Rat is perceptive and a strong believer in getting real value for his money. The Lion checks the Rat's avarice and makes this personality less calculating. The Leo Rat is aristocratic, impetuous and involved in everything. Daring and proud, he will love freedom and be very democratic when called upon to lead. This trustworthy person will not neglect the details or the financial side of matters. Leonine integrity coupled with the Rat's presence of mind and sagacity will make a person born with this combination magnetic, appealing and loquacious.

LEO OX: FIRE + NEGATIVE WATER

A warm yet slightly impersonal person dignified in appearance. The Leo Ox could also be dramatic and pompous at times, as the Lion's ego does take up a lot of room. Here, the Buffalo's sternness and uncompromising outlook will serve only to reinforce the Sun sign's indomitable will. But the Lion spreads his largesse and radiance onto the otherwise celibate-looking Ox, and this person will be far from dull. A respectable and strong personality, the Leo Ox will have the ability to command effortlessly.

LEO TIGER: FIRE + POSITIVE WOOD

A fiery personality that could scorch disrespectful onlookers or others who dare take him or her for granted. A bundle of roars and claws, the Leo Tiger never fails to draw the crowds. Capable of depth and variety in his emotions, this person can be torrid, sulky and magnanimous all in one breath. He tends to act superior, especially when he is unsure of himself. The Leonine Tiger has very strong recuperative powers, both mentally and physically. And when he or she loves, it's all, all the way.

LEO RABBIT: FIRE + NEGATIVE WOOD

A majestic Hare with fine qualities for leadership although somewhat self-centered in reality. He will have the charisma to sway the masses and the luck to get him through the trials in his life. This combination links aggressiveness with cool discretion and a person born under these signs will not advocate war openly. He knows how to make himself immensely popular and will possess the knack of doing the right thing at the right time. Both solar and lunar signs here indulge in their leisure activities seriously, and this personality may pursue illicit and expensive hobbies secretly.

LEO DRAGON: FIRE + POSITIVE WOOD

A magnificent, breathtaking personality who will loom over us, larger than life, and who is truly convinced of his right to rule. The Leo Dragon is a commanding performer who will keep his guns loaded all the time. The Lion provides the already bombastic Dragon with more dynamite than he can use, so this personality can be very willful and difficult to manage when others do not yield him right of way. However, he never carries grudges and when he makes explosive statements, well it's just his way of clearing the air. In such a double regal sign, this person is blessed with good fortune, as he will always try to keep his promises and is noble and chivalrous to the less fortunate.

LEO SNAKE: FIRE + NEGATIVE FIRE

Life is lined with success and tragedy for the Leo Snake because of his or her great intensity and refusal to take second place to anyone. At his best, this person will be a radiant example of grace, intelligence and elegance. He needs a great deal of love and understanding to bring out his virtues and will perform lavishly when admired. However, he is also inclined to be spoiled, selfish and conceited, as a result of having too much attention poured on him or of being given his way too often. His warmth and sincerity only emerge if he is allowed to lead a quiet life and forget himself by helping others.

LEO HORSE: FIRE + POSITIVE FIRE

With such a sunny disposition, this personality rarely has shadows of doubt about anything. Idealistically ambitious, passionate and true, the Leo Horse surges forward in an optimistic but sporadic fashion. He will be impulsive and given to grand gestures. He needs many emotional outlets to release his pent-up energies. A generous and sporty individual, the Leonine Horse is expressive and loves physical exercise.

LEO SHEEP: FIRE + NEGATIVE FIRE

The assertive Lion will ease the Sheep's shyness and make him bold and high-spirited. The Leo Sheep will be respectable and will strive nobly to live up to confidence placed in him. Less pessimistic and not easily cajoled by criticism, this sort of person can stand on his own two feet and win the approval he seeks. A more independent Sheep, fortified by Leo's will and strong character, he will never be lacking in warmth.

LEO MONKEY: FIRE + POSITIVE METAL

A personality fused by two signs of towering ambition and sound intelligence. The Lion is authoritative but never underhanded or mean. This should curtail the Monkey's trickery, although the Monkey could be a splendid alter ego for this stately soul and add the Midas touch to his undertakings. The Leo Monkey will be classy and self-reliant. He or she could be cheeky or audacious with a tendency to pry into the affairs of others, but this will be mostly out of curiosity, not malice.

LEO ROOSTER: FIRE + NEGATIVE METAL

The Lion's generosity here should hopefully subdue the Rooster's penchant for hair-splitting. Still, both signs are strong and masterful and could be hell bent on success. The Rooster can attend to mundane matters with devotion and steady application, while the Lion has his heart set on glory. A person of this mixture could have all the real assets to reach the pinnacle of power, but one cannot help feeling that he is a little too commanding and superior to have around.

LEO DOG: FIRE + POSITIVE METAL

The Lion's august appearance here could brighten the warm yet pensive outlook of the Dog. With these two signs in him, this person will possess a strong moral fiber and is very sure of himself. Endowed with a safer and saner judgment than most, he can make decisions which are usually above reproach. He hates injustice and will never betray any trust placed in him. The Lion is captivating while the Dog is realistic. This person will elect to take the middle of the road and is not naive about the high cost of success.

LEO BOAR: FIRE + NEGATIVE WATER

A gregarious Boar with refreshingly natural humor and some excesses to boot. Gifted with irrepressible vitality, the Leo Boar will put zest into everything he does and will relish hard work compounded by equally hard play. Because his emotions are usually expressed in red hot tones, he is dramatic and could claim the theater as his favorite habitat. This personality is most unselfish, never hypocritical and will have a kind of childlike faith that brings out the best in people he deals with.

VIRGO

VIRGO RAT: EARTH + POSITIVE WATER

These two active signs make up a superindustrious soul with a natural aptitude for investigating things. The pure-minded Virgo will be made more jovial and delightful by the Rat. This person is bound to be extremely inquisitive and will explore every option open to him or her before making a move. The Virgo Rat will be an ingenious and studious soul with limitless capabilities if he knows how to hold his tongue.

VIRGO OX: EARTH + NEGATIVE WATER

The Virgo Ox is shrewd, phlegmatic and quite infallible in his own dogmatic mind. It does not matter how much formal education this sort of person has, he will never stop assimilating knowledge and bettering himself throughout life. He will also hate being in crowded or noisy places as it offends his monastic soul and love of quiet concentration. Need someone to set down every letter of the law? No one should be better qualified than he. Very strong and just as systematic, this person emphasizes rigid discipline and will never hesitate to take wrongdoers to task.

VIRGO TIGER: EARTH + POSITIVE WOOD

Because the Virgo is reserved and analytical whereas the Tiger cannot keep his feelings safely hidden, the Virgo Tiger will be less spontaneous but still sparkling—in a neat, orderly manner. These solar and lunar signs could bridge to form an exacting but humane soul who is cautious with his choice of words. With the Tiger's color and daring and Virgo's self-control, this personality could taste the best of both worlds.

VIRGO RABBIT: EARTH + NEGATIVE WOOD

A virtuous but solitary soul who will do whatever needs to be done with a minimum of fuss. Both the Virgin and the Hare believe in being organized and careful. This person will never purposely seek to offend. He believes too much in protocol. He will have all the facts thoroughly checked to his satisfaction before accusing anyone. The Virgo Hare also loves to deliberate but in a quiet, factual manner. Here, at last, the Rabbit won't mind being loaded by responsibilities if it proves financially rewarding.

VIRGO DRAGON: EARTH + POSITIVE WOOD

Both signs here have total confidence in themselves and are knowledgeable, although the Virgin is the more realistic and plodding of the two. This person will have a great thirst for learning and perfection. He has to shine and could turn very resentful when opposed. He will not give up easily and sometimes will not give up at all. Both signs in this combination have many sterling qualities and the Virgo Dragon will be admirable for his sure strength and character. Yet he is guilty of overkill and acts of unmitigated zealousness when he sets off to right some wrong.

VIRGO SNAKE: EARTH + NEGATIVE FIRE

Virgo's eye for detail and love of organization plus the Snake's ability to shield his feelings and conduct clandestine maneuvers will surely turn this personality into a secretive but extremely aware person. Scholarly, fiercely dedicated and thoroughly work-oriented, a person born with this combination could chain himself to a fixed goal until he succeeds. While the rest of humanity bogs down with the rigors and struggles of daily life, the Virgo Snake will seem immune to conventional wear and tear, as he can block everything out of his mind once he concentrates. Vices? None, unless you consider being autocratic, unemotional and ruthlessly efficient as such.

VIRGO HORSE: EARTH + POSITIVE FIRE

Virgo makes the Horse more predictable and subdued in his passion. His motions are bound to be better calculated and rehearsed. Although the Virgo Horse's reflexes are slower, he will still be sharp and alert though of a less boisterous nature. The solar Earth sign here could put out some of the Horse's flame, but the outcome could be beneficial as it will provide fertile ground for a more responsible person to grow in.

VIRGO SHEEP: EARTH + NEGATIVE FIRE

The Sheep is elegant and full of niceties but a bit of a spendthrift. The Virgin is more somber and much more careful with finances. Here, in this combination, we could find the Sheep practicing the virtues of thrift, self-denial and cold resolve. The congenial Sheep will be more resolute if the positive qualities of both are enhanced. Otherwise, we may have one of those smart souls who will love "to teach"—but not "to do."

VIRGO MONKEY: EARTH + POSITIVE METAL

The Virgin is a diligent and competent worker while the Monkey's guile will provide the ideal catalyst to put Virgo's administrative talents to work. The Virgo Monkey will be scientific and inventive. Blessed with an exploratory mind and computerlike memory, he will be a successful and avid businessman, making sure and winning bets. A critical person, he will compare and categorize endlessly, providing practical answers of his own wherever necessary.

VIRGO ROOSTER: EARTH + NEGATIVE METAL

An incredibly secure fowl who has both feet anchored deep in the ground. Because both signs here are virtuously eccentric, he could puzzle us with his unlikely preferences and perfectionism. A clear and logical thinker, he excels in mental tasks. He is the perpetual student, and on any subject that is his field you can put your encyclopedia away and trust him to be the absolute authority. A walking library of facts, he is seldom wrong and will meticulously register every bit of information for the benefit of posterity. A lover of charts and graphs, he is incurably performance-oriented. On the negative end, remember, both signs here have the peculiar pastime of faultfinding.

VIRGO DOG: EARTH + POSITIVE METAL

An academic and responsible soul. Two such fretfully caring signs could combine to produce a worrier, overly concerned with the woes of humanity. The sum of their admirable qualities could be much reduced when it comes to total appeal. For although the Dog is more even in temperament, he will be inhibited by the industrious and straitlaced Virgo in him. Unprejudiced and spiritual, the Virgo Dog will be steady and unworldly. Virgo's excellent mental powers and the Dog's neutrality may produce an able legal executor.

VIRGO BOAR: EARTH + NEGATIVE WATER

The sensual and generous Boar should redeem the Virgo personality from too much heavy or monotonous work. Yet the Virgin's deep intellectual qualities could assist the trusting Boar in making sound decisions. The Virgo Boar commits himself less willingly despite his modest and kind appearance. This combination produces a reliable person who is able to identify with the group while remaining sensibly honest to his convictions. The Virgo's economic aptitude here is joined to the Boar's luck.

LIBRA

LIBRAN RAT: AIR + POSITIVE WATER

An exciting personality, bubbling like soda water with life and vivacity. The Balance loves society and harmonious relations as does the Rat and both signs are born charmers. The Libran Rat is bound to be very flexible and understanding. Yet a person born under this combination will not lose the Rat's love of economy or Libra's knack for joint ventures. Because of these qualities, he will possess a sharp eye for beauty matched by a keen nose for bargains.

LIBRAN OX: AIR + NEGATIVE WATER

The Libran Ox will not be extremely stubborn nor tyrannical, for Venus's child opts for comfort and compromise. The Buffalo's rigidness is curbed a good deal here, although one is also assured this personality will not have that strong Libran need for dependency. Cheerful and not exacting in outlook, this Ox will make friends easily while maintaining high standards about whom he chooses to model himself after. An Ox who loves the good life, he won't plan on working too hard without in-between bouts of leisure. Trust the Libran Ox to enjoy the fruits of his labor.

LIBRAN TIGER: AIR + POSITIVE WOOD

A fanciful but good-humored Tiger with the enticing manners of

Venus's Libra. Both signs tend to procrastinate, so onlookers may be left to sigh anxiously while this subject changes his mind frequently or fails to sort out his preferences altogether. However, the potent Tiger is forceful once he sets his mind on something and can be good-hearted and hard-working to boot. With Libra's graciousness, this Tiger will stalk his prey with fascinating artistry.

LIBRAN RABBIT: AIR + NEGATIVE WOOD

A skittish but lovable soul, the Libran Rabbit will have the Hare's clear mind and can appreciate the aesthetic value of things. Both solar and lunar signs here are adept at weighing pros and cons. This subject will not relish being tied down permanently, so despite his immense capabilities at forming wide-ranging congenial relationships, he is twice shy about long-term involvements. While he is definitely not a power grabber, the Libran Rabbit will still be a levelheaded and sensible soul. A well-mannered subject who never fails to exhibit good taste and discretion in speech and movements.

LIBRAN DRAGON: AIR + POSITIVE WOOD

An erect and sprightly soul, not at all fearsome. This is the non-belligerent type of Dragon. Dimpled and benign, he has an earnest and guilt-free personality. The Balance is tipped here toward the Dragon's compelling magnetism, yet although the Libran Dragon has a lot of drive, he won't be as dependable as other Dragons. As both signs in this combination have genuine and sincere personalities, you can expect this subject to be endowed with wide-eyed honesty, unintentional frankness and a minimum of inhibitions.

LIBRAN SNAKE: AIR + NEGATIVE FIRE

A tantalizing combination. Easy to relate to and endowed with impeccable taste, the alluring Libran Snake is *muy simpatico* indeed! He may be an enigmatic thinker, but he takes care to express himself in more conventional ways. A person of this combination wavers less, what with the Snake's steadfastness and patience. He will certainly be able to enamor people with his subtlety and wit. Cool and very desirable, he can be pleasure-bent and may rely too much on popular consensus to act independently.

LIBRAN HORSE: AIR + POSITIVE FIRE

Libra is even more sunny and kind-humored here and will express himself expertly when linked to the quick and ever youthful Horse. This person will be less selfish and more cooperative. Yet, while the Libran Horse is a vacillating diplomat in the affairs of others, he can be a keen negotiator for his own self. And in spite of his unpredictability and apparent glibness, he will be a capable producer as he knows on which side his bread is buttered.

LIBRAN SHEEP: AIR + NEGATIVE FIRE

The Libran Sheep loves attention and sympathy. Approval and friendship are of utmost importance to him. He or she may look as fragile and exquisite as bone china, but there is a certain restiveness and built-in resilience in this person. An authority on art forms and beauty, he has a superb sense of balance and color usage. The Libran Sheep is inclined to be cultured, refined and possibly fastidious in his dress and grooming. His very receptive nature causes him to pause too long and too often, tallying up votes and gathering opinions tirelessly. If he cannot capitalize on his talents through the forceful management of others, he may end up being a fence-sitter.

LIBRAN MONKEY: AIR + POSITIVE METAL

Artful with words, polite and mindful, the angelic Libran Monkey has a smile that promises paradise. Although what he eventually delivers may or may not be up to par, the trappings are splendid and no one in his right mind could possibly pass up this delightful package. Yes, he will evaluate and exploit situations to his advantage, but he is also not adverse to taking others in on a partnership basis. The enterprising Monkey here will have Libra's democratic cooperation and find more acceptance than he normally would.

LIBRAN ROOSTER: AIR + NEGATIVE METAL

The Balance gives the Chicken's exacting nature great equilibrium. We will have a Rooster here who will take to feathering his nest with eider- down and expensive perfume. He is an intellectual who loves comfort and is smooth in delivering his lines, and there may be little if any room for argument. Although he is still likely to be particular and observant as all Roosters are, Libra will give him better ability to comprehend the views of others, thus resulting in a person less critical over trifles and much more animated and happy. He will have higher popularity ratings than Chickens of other varieties.

LIBRAN DOG: AIR + POSITIVE METAL

The Dog is not one to weave underhanded or intricate plots, while Venus's child is not a troublemaker and would prefer to stay in everyone's good graces, too. This kind of person will receive good reviews by just being himself. His honesty and equanimity will make him a just and able arbiter, even if he may seem a bit leftist at times. Libra's peaceful disposition and the Dog's charity toward the less fortunate will make this subject a sort of social worker who not only genuinely sympathizes but will feel obligated to help.

LIBRAN BOAR: AIR + NEGATIVE WATER

Two agreeable signs unite here to form a very magnanimous and unselfish person. Sensitive and artistic Libra is given the Boar's sustaining stamina and noble character. The Libran Boar will be not only gentle and tolerant but very much alive when it comes to sensuality. His patient and faithful exterior may conceal inner ambitions and secret aspirations that are hard to guess. Rich but mellow like good red wine, he is loving, sentimental and constant in love.

SCORPIO

SCORPIO RAT: WATER + POSITIVE WATER

A scheming, intense and fantastically potent Rat. The Rat is competitive by nature, and here Scorpio will strengthen his willpower and avarice. Efficiency is at top level here. Starched aprons for the lady Scorpio Rats and overalls for her male counterparts, as both signs in this combination are hard-working and productive, although the

Scorpion is less verbose. If he had the power, he would not hesitate to wipe out his adversaries with the stroke of a pen. A good writer but an even better politician.

SCORPIO OX: WATER + NEGATIVE WATER

A personality gifted with the Buffalo's armor and the deadly sting of the Scorpion. Never doing things by halves and quick to retaliate, he will tread fearlessly into the deep waters his sign represents. Endowed with an intractable and very demanding ego, this subject will be an outstanding religious leader or simply a rake. He could use all his energies upholding the law or going against it.

SCORPIO TIGER: WATER + POSITIVE WOOD

Full of thrills and skills, the Scorpio Tiger has sex appeal and glamor enough for ten ordinary mortals. Proud and self-confident, he will undertake ambitious projects with the endurance of the Scorpion and the optimism of the Tiger. He has strong incendiary qualities—to the fighting spirit of the Tiger is added the Scorpion intensity. As sure as death and taxes, he will have to take revenge, even if it's only a few playful scratches now and then to remind you not to take him or her too lightly (as if we dare).

SCORPIO RABBIT: WATER + NEGATIVE WOOD

A secretive and recalcitrant personality. Pluto's child is deep and the Hare's modest and soft appearance provides excellent cover for Scorpio's strong emotions. This person disciplines himself admirably but could have a deadly temper and unforgiving heart if you cross him. Still, the Rabbit knows how to preserve his dignity with feigned acquiescence when necessary. An erotic and penetrating nature covered by a spotless reputation. The Scorpio Rabbit is sometimes at a loss between the tugs of Pluto's passion and the Hare's calm intellect and love of harmony.

SCORPIO DRAGON: WATER + POSITIVE WOOD

A lusty, plotting Dragon who could be most explicit about his likes and dislikes. Here we find Scorpio's compelling intensity matched with the Dragon's awesome powers. This combination could be detrimental to the subject's personality if he allows it to lead him to gross excesses. Both lunar and solar signs here are oversupplied with strength and commanding magnetism. Under all that devastating charm, make no mistake, he is as hard as nails. As for the female, one is strongly reminded of that nursery rhyme that goes, "When she is good, she's very, very good, but when she is bad—she's horrid!"

SCORPIO SNAKE: WATER + NEGATIVE FIRE

Skeptical, skeptical combination. The Scorpio Snake will possess great depths of emotion and be a cunning tactician. Cloaking his feelings with prudishness, he may prove to be quite inscrutable. Ambitious and performance-oriented, he soaks up knowledge like a sponge and is adept at interpreting the slightest insinuation. Whatever arouses his curiosity will be examined with no costs spared. Self-contained and ultrasecretive, you won't catch him handing out explanations. Honestly, he cares little about idle gossip, but it is worth remembering that he is not to be taken lightly, for hell hath no fury like a Scorpion Snake scorned!

SCORPIO HORSE: WATER + POSITIVE FIRE

Scorpio has the definite fixity that could coax the Horse to apply his strength strategically. Here is a Horse who lacks the casualness and cheerful spontaneity of other stallions; yet, though he may be serious, he won't be grim. He will still resist being bound to repetitive chores. Not at all a transparent fellow, he may be darkly handsome and penetrative in nature because of that mysterious Scorpion air. He could be difficult to reason with when he is hell-bent on going his way.

SCORPIO SHEEP: WATER + NEGATIVE FIRE

The sober by-product of this Water and Fire mixture is a personality strong of mind and body, but graced with a delicacy of expression and creativity that could fool the most experienced hands. He listens to his intuitions, his loved ones and finally to public opinion—in that order. But whatever else Scorpio's plots may have planned, the Sheep puts a limit on the price he will pay for success. He won't like to deliberately hurt others or gloat over his victories. Scorpio is a good cosign here for the Sheep, as it prevents this subject from wallowing in self-pity and forces him to act on his own more often.

SCORPIO MONKEY: WATER + POSITIVE METAL

The devious imp plus Pluto's self-love and intensity will produce a personality who truly exists for his own pleasure. Scorpio's stealth keeps him wedded to an uncompromising way of thinking. Submissiveness and consideration are not his chief virtues. Yet the Scorpio Monkey can be indispensable, efficient, attractive, clever and most aspiring. He will work hard for what he wants but could be pitiless to those looking for a handout. The Monkey is positive and captivating, but also incorrigible when it comes to getting his way. Both signs here are masterful at retaliation; he will have to even the score—or die trying.

SCORPIO ROOSTER: WATER + NEGATIVE WATER

Such fortitude and stamina! This combination is made up of two strong, individualistic and high-minded signs. Abrupt and to the point, the Scorpio Rooster abhors compromise. Don't even hint at it. It means defeat to him and he is never *ever* going down as a quitter. Since this personality sets out to win, he usually does, although his methods won't win him hordes of friends. Never mind, he may prefer proud isolation to yielding even a single inch of ground. Scorpio's watery currents bring out the sleuth in the Rooster and little if anything escapes this commanding investigator.

SCORPIO DOG: WATER + POSITIVE METAL

Powerful, dedicated and energetic, this person will display the Dog's righteous spirit and Pluto's deep insight. The Scorpio Dog likes to honor his promises but Scorpio here could be detrimental to the liberal Dog's nature. Pugnacious when stirred, and sparing with words, this person can be willful and relentless in the face of defeat. Because he believes in absolute commitment, the Scorpio Dog will serve God or the Devil with equal fervor. But he will never have two masters.

SCORPIO BOAR: WATER + NEGATIVE WATER

Lavish with his affections but very much set on gratifying his own wishes first, this hefty Boar is his own man—or woman. Sensuous and power-conscious, he will unabashedly pursue his ambitions. A smart Boar, he knows how to compromise, though often at the expense of others. He can be very emphatic about his rights in spite of his outward generosity. Still, one sees no lack of admirers queueing up for the pleasure of his company. But do watch out for that vengeful streak.

SAGITTARIUS

SAGITTARIAN RAT: FIRE + POSITIVE WATER

A serendipity dancer—the Sagittarian Rat is sleek and speedy with the Archer's aim and the Rat's opportunistic insight. Sagittarius is Jupiter's bold and proud son and the Rat effuses charm and brilliance. This personality will be accommodating and cheerful. He has great joie de vivre coupled with a strong hold on reality. His luck comes from paying heed to his splendid hunches. He is a clever judge of situations. Blessed with great presence of mind, he will not flounder when faced with an emergency. A person of this combination loves to be in the thick of company.

SAGITTARIAN OX: FIRE + NEGATIVE WATER

The Archer uses the Ox's god-given authority with more finesse and goodwill. The Sagittarian Ox is still heavy-handed, but will certainly make up for his stubbornness by having exquisite yet functional tastes. A more guided sort of perfectionist, this person is realistic but has more flair and style. Looking for the good in others and planning how to salvage hopeless situations brings him the most happiness and success. The Ox is a strong helmsman, and the Archer's vibes and showmanship are above par. He can conduct flawless rescue operations and will probably be an excellent entrepreneur. Aristocratic, genuine and solidly straightforward, his devotion is usually well placed.

SAGITTARIAN TIGER: FIRE + POSITIVE WOOD

This person is extremely alert and his vigilant reactions are likely to be accurate. An upright, energetic and expressive being, the Sagittarian Tiger has few inhibitions. He loves to dispense with formalities and nothing deters him from getting to the heart of the matter once his curiosity is aroused. Fiery wit and colorful manners will typify a personality born with this combination. He could be didactic and moralizing, but he has too much intelligence and elegance to ever really be coarse.

SAGITTARIAN RABBIT: FIRE + NEGATIVE WOOD

A gallivanting Hare and far from moody. Mixing and mingling freely with all colors and creeds, he will possess the ability to understand the incomprehensible—or at least he will make every attempt to see the views of the opposition. His futuristic outlook can be attributed to the crystalline vision of both signs here. Open, mild-mannered and quietly perceptive, he rarely becomes agitated to the point of losing that splendid composure. A diplomat's dream, he can be calculating and bold without appearing too outspoken. The Rabbit needs the Archer's buoyant spirits, and Sagittarius in turn could fare well with the Hare's love of harmony and discretion.

SAGITTARIAN DRAGON: FIRE + POSITIVE WOOD

Pleasant, jovial, warm, forward and also somewhat opinionated, the Sagittarian Dragon is swift and faithful and will abide no deception. Both signs here are always ready for action. Masterful and impatient, the Sagittarian Dragon thrives on involvement and will participate in whatever action abounds. His interests are sure to be numerous and varied. He often offends by his pointed speech, but he does so without malice, unaware that his arrows have struck close to the heart. A noble and unselfish fellow, he shows his true worth when he comes forward to help when no one else will stick up for you.

SAGITTARIAN SNAKE: FIRE + NEGATIVE FIRE

Here the Snake is lighter, freer and more relaxed, with a cultivated air of nonchalance. Fashionable, informed and dashing, he will also have a lesser sense of duty because of Sagittarius's love of freedom. You won't find him or her chained to the workbench. He or she has too much class, and besides, both signs here have lofty ideals and love success and applause—although in different ways. The Snake is tenacious and careful and bides his time. The Archer strikes when the iron is hot and never hesitates to forge his destiny by action. The outcome of this union produces a wise but unshackled man or woman.

SAGITTARIAN HORSE: FIRE + POSITIVE FIRE

A personality who loves to live life at a feverish pace. Not a weary bone in his body, brilliant and daring, he is forever on the go. The Archer's sign could be disruptive to the Horse here: too much speed, spirit and wit without enough perseverance. A person with this combination relies on his intuition a great deal and tends to work himself into a nervous state by taking on more than he can handle or by letting his fertile imagination get the better of him. However, he is very sports-oriented and exercise is the ideal outlet for his accumulated pressures. The Sagittarian Horse not only speaks but acts his mind with absolute conviction.

SAGITTARIAN SHEEP: FIRE + NEGATIVE FIRE

A well-meaning and philosophical Sheep with a wide-angle view of coming trends. Direct and honest, he is still likely to shun irksome details or dirty work. The Sagittarian Sheep will love to explore new heights and present startling theories. This sort of person is more athletic than emotional. He can laugh off his mistakes and take constructive criticism well. Endowed with fashion sense and good taste, he will be able to innovate new styles with aplomb. Confident in his powers, he will be more outspoken than other Sheep.

SAGITTARIAN MONKEY: FIRE + POSITIVE METAL

The Monkey gives sustaining fortitude and organizational talent to the high-minded Sagittarian. This personality will possess both integrity and an impregnable mind, in spite of that fancy-free image he projects to throw us off. A clever and intelligent manipulator, he never reveals his real angle until he is sure of clinching the deal. A Sagittarian Monkey is the lucky and dynamic conjuror produced by the combined forces of aristocratic Sagittarius and the ingenious Monkey.

SAGITTARIAN ROOSTER: FIRE + NEGATIVE METAL

Ambitious, talkative and active, with the decisiveness common to the two signs present here, the Sagittarian Rooster sets his sights very high. Don't argue with him unless your patience is infinite, for he could carry on a debate from here to eternity to prove his point. But since both signs are scrupulously honest, he makes a poor liar. Don't ask him for the truth unless you can stand to hear it. In spite of his undisguised frankness, he can be quite selfless and will not hesitate to volunteer his help if he feels you need it. Sagittarius gives the Rooster more dignity here and a surer aim.

SAGITTARIAN DOG: FIRE + POSITIVE METAL

A playful, adventurous yet respectable Dog. Swift, open and sincere, he will be well-liked for his considerate ways and sensible outlook. Informal and warmly personal, he shows his feelings without pretense. Levelheaded and realistic, he is quick to respond and is precise in speech and manners. A notable keeper of confidences, he rarely squirms or falters under pressure. This solar-lunar union produces an expansive and thoughtful personality.

SAGITTARIAN BOAR: FIRE + NEGATIVE WATER

A candidate for the good citizen award. This combination produces a person with considerable humor and large appetites. Both signs here are noble but naive, although the Archer could be more blunt about announcing his wishes. Jupiter's bounty and the Boar's luck are heaped upon this subject because of his trusting and uncalculating nature. One can count on the Sagittarian Boar to share his last cent with a friend. Neither sign succumbs to despair easily, so this person will be made of sturdy stuff, perhaps even a bit thick-skinned. Yet when he achieves success, he won't hoard his money. He will dole it out and somehow everyone will benefit from his good fortune.

CAPRICORN

CAPRICORN RAT: EARTH + POSITIVE WATER

Sociable, steady, resourceful. A consummate hoarder, he labels, catalogs and takes stock of possessions endlessly. Don't laugh—come rainy weather, he may have cornered all the umbrellas on the market. The Capricorn Rat is wise and careful. He will be less mobile and adventurous than other Rats. Faithful and tactful, he likes to form permanent relationships. With the secure Capricorn inside him, this Rat is less likely to take chances or gamble. Whatever else he is, you can be sure this fellow takes out a lot of insurance.

CAPRICORN OX: EARTH + NEGATIVE WATER

A serious marriage of two slow but sure signs here produces a personality made of granite that will withstand the tests of hard times and adversity. His preconceived notions are often inflexible, and his righteousness overpowering. Harsh but extremely self-sufficient he sequesters the lighter side of his nature and wills himself to climb the loftiest cliffs with nary a word of complaint. Although he may be tender and selfless toward those he loves, he is rarely demonstrative with affection. This Spartan subject is simple and deliberate. He will be able to bear twice the responsibilities others find hard even to think about. The Capricorn Ox will surely rise to the very top of the mountain—but with clenched fists, no doubt.

CAPRICORN TIGER: EARTH + POSITIVE WOOD

The result of this combination will be a captivating but less headstrong and impetuous Tiger. No doubt, he or she will still have that strong temper, but Capricorn's influence should see that this force is applied correctly. Linked to the Mountain Goat, this Tiger is not so restless as normal and is inclined to be less of a radical. He does not like sudden changes and can be relied upon to take his vows seriously. A dutiful Tiger who won't mind hardships or menial tasks if they develop his abilities. The Capricorn Tiger will not be entirely led by his heart as Tigers of more combustible combinations are.

CAPRICORN RABBIT: EARTH + NEGATIVE WOOD

A scion of society and firm subscriber to fixed hierarchical values, the Capricorn Rabbit is usually blessed with a fortuitous life while the Goat in him still takes nothing for granted. He will know how to invest his time and money wisely. The Hare's docility is toughened by sinewy Capricorn resolve, and this person will display a passion for sound strategy. He will neither form nor change opinions readily. Both signs have a similar calm disposition. The Rabbit in him is never above negotiation, while the Goat is as sure-footed as ever.

CAPRICORN DRAGON: EARTH + POSITIVE WOOD

The sureness of the Mountain Goat and the unquenchable aspirations of the celestial Dragon. Both signs have ample powers for leadership. The resultant personality will be realistic, doubly hard-working and entirely self-assured. Exceptionally forceful and commanding, he could move mountains by his colossal power of will. He spares no one, least of all himself, in his drive for accomplishing difficult tasks. The Capricorn Dragon will be more athletic and muscular than cerebral. He loves his privacy, too. Respect that "Do not Disturb" sign whenever it appears on his door. He really means it!

CAPRICORN SNAKE: EARTH + NEGATIVE FIRE

Brainy and aloof, staid and pious, expertly elusive in playing his game—the Capricorn Snake is a veritable Rock of Gibraltar. Since neither sign is too extroverted, this person's passions will run very deep. With a remarkably high level of endurance, he can wait out his enemies with the patience of Father Time. An avid learner, his grand visions will be realized through careful planning and stern stick-to-it-tiveness. The Capricorn Snake is never caught second-guessing anything.

CAPRICORN HORSE: EARTH + POSITIVE FIRE

The Mountain Goat's most welcome gift to this combination is consistency. The Horse should have more permanent and reliable qualities because of it. Both signs in this match spur the subject toward continuous activity and industry. Responsive but careful to check the sources of his information, the Capricorn Horse likes to mind his own business while tuning in on the nuances others give out. A less carefree spirit, the Horse here will lend speed and grace to Capricorn's solid resolve. This person will know how to set his priorities and be able to accomplish much.

CAPRICORN SHEEP: EARTH + NEGATIVE FIRE

Here the noncommittal and pliable Sheep comes under the steady guidance of the Mountain Goat. Hence, this person is more certain of what he wants and will not hesitate to make his own decisions. Because of the good fortune and benevolence the eighth lunar sign brings to him, the Capricorn Sheep will be handsomely rewarded for the hardships and deficiencies he copes with. Less content to stay in the background, this kind of Sheep will take an active role in shaping his own destiny—and we won't be hearing so many complaints either.

CAPRICORN MONKEY: EARTH + POSITIVE METAL

Both signs here are coordinated and competent, although the Monkey is delightful where the Goat is staid and honest. Here, Capricorn has access to the Monkey's gift of mental maneuvers and lively imagination, while the Monkey revels in the unwavering forcefulness the Goat brings. The result is a quiet and diligent personality, still clever but not as audacious in manner.

CAPRICORN ROOSTER: EARTH + NEGATIVE METAL

A person born with this combination excels in thoroughness, efficiency and a total lack of pretense. Neither sign in this match is known for malleability, so the Capricorn Rooster will resist all attempts to remake him. However, the Rooster is less flamboyant here and perhaps more tight-lipped, though still given to exercising his rhetoric without much forewarning. Rarely ruffled, this person will be a neat and exact creature who abides no nonsense or any deviation from the law.

CAPRICORN DOG: EARTH + POSITIVE METAL

The Capricorn Dog is likely to be generous and benevolent but also given to careful and systematic rituals of his own. He attaches a great deal of importance to the welfare of his family. The Dog is neighborly and a lover of all humanity, but the Mountain Goat should be able to assist him to watch out for himself, too. This person looks after his own interests without appearing selfish or greedy. With the Dog's reason and fairness, Capricorn is less stubborn. Above all, this person is true to himself. When faced with having to state his stand on a controversial issue, you can be sure he would prefer to be more accurate than kind.

CAPRICORN BOAR: EARTH + NEGATIVE WATER

A sinewy, cautious Boar with towering ambitions. Both solar and lunar signs here do not fear facing obstacles, although this conservative person has great respect for the wishes of others. Punctilious and hard-working, the Capricorn Boar will have the Pig's good faith and the Goat's "better safe than sorry" mentality. No pie-in-the-sky dreams for this conscientious worker. The Capricorn Boar upholds tradition with pride and does not skirt responsibility when rules have to be enforced.

AQUARIUS

AQUARIAN RAT: AIR + POSITIVE WATER

A match that could produce a bubbling or babbling brook. Cheerful and versatile, this aerated water personality is crystal clear in expressing himself and needs variety and freedom in everything he does. The Aquarian Rat is less acquisitive and values his personal relationships more than financial ones. Impatient and audacious, he can be rebellious. Armed with sharp perception and gifted with enticing charm, he can usually convince others to dance to his tune. He makes amends for his uneven moods by giving his allegiance to good causes and serving others without expecting rewards.

AQUARIAN OX: AIR + NEGATIVE WATER

The belligerent qualities of the Buffalo are altered here by the cool and airy ways of the Uranian sign. Nonviolent but nonconforming, too, the ebullient Aquarius will teach the stiff Ox that he must sometimes stoop to conquer. The Water Bearer is too intelligent to resort to the brute force Buffalos employ when they are vengeful. Likewise, this subject will have enhanced vision and social graces. He is less predictable than other Oxen and not above defying public opinion by trimming the rules to suit his tastes.

AQUARIAN TIGER: AIR + POSITIVE WOOD

A provocative Tiger with the courage and grace to carry out his wildest dreams. Transparent and free of any guile, it would be nice to know and love him. However, he rarely lets relationships get too settled or sets himself down long enough for you to study him properly. He is up and about, getting in and out of predicaments with a parodoxical penchant for puzzles. A publicity lover, the Aquarian Tiger is very communicative and given to cheerfully adjusting regulations to his advantage. Independent and unstable, he is ruled by colorful ideals and forever led on by great expectations. His mind and spirit are as free as the wind. It is impossible to ever contain him and one should never even try.

AQUARIAN RABBIT: AIR + NEGATIVE WOOD

An optimistic nature with an exploring mind, this subject will be neither oversensitive to injury nor quick to anger. The personality brought together by these two signs is able to project himself splendidly and promote understanding between other people by his psychic insight into their character. Both solar and lunar signs here pick up brain waves and vibrations of impending events and decode them expertly. The Aquarian Rabbit has reliable premonitions. However, where the Water Bearer is open-minded and too liberal about progress, the Hare mitigates this impulsiveness because he hesitates to leave familiar settings or trade in his old lamp for a new one. But, by and large, the Aquarian Rabbit is more engrossed in the world around him than in his own self.

AQUARIAN DRAGON: AIR + POSITIVE WOOD

The catalytic effect of this combination is a person with clarity of expression backed by an authoritativeness that is difficult to ignore or challenge. The Aquarian Dragon is forever changing and improving; an individualistic and constant expander of modes. Deceit is anathema to the shining Dragon, while the breezy Aquarian wins distinction for his ability to deal with people and tough situations. This person can be sudden and unorthodox, but never cruel or scheming. Both signs here can forgive and forget, although the Dragon is warlike when thwarted, whereas the Water Bearer is more broad-minded and brotherly.

AQUARIAN SNAKE: AIR + NEGATIVE FIRE

With open and airy Aquarius blowing on him, the Snake is not very subtle here. This person is more cheerful and bright and rarely broods over circumstances he cannot alter. He shifts his direction as the situation warrants and is buoyant in outlook. He has a free and easy attitude and is occasionally erratic in his thinking. Yet he is also prone to nervous troubles if he cannot release his tensions. With the Snake's influence, he is also susceptible to jealousy and will recede inward when upset. Otherwise, he should find wide acceptance, as this sort of person has the telepathic ability to convey his wishes without making deliberate efforts to influence others.

AQUARIAN HORSE: AIR + POSITIVE FIRE

An enthusiastic personality, full of wanderlust and caprice, he may always have his bags packed for some real or imaginary journey. The Aquarian Horse lives half in the present and half in the colorful future of his magic rainbow. The one thing he never dwells morbidly on is the shadowy past, and with his record for surprises, he may definitely have one. Optimistic and jaunty, one could truly say that his cup runneth over with love of life and involvement. Given to searching for truth, the Horse and Uranus-ruled Aquarius speed on, surrounded by crowds and commitments to keep mind and body well occupied.

AQUARIAN SHEEP: AIR + NEGATIVE FIRE

Too much moderation here. Both signs are friendly and tolerant, given to intuitive pursuits and altruistic activities. Freedom-loving Aquarius may refuse to conform and so this mild-seeming person may be inquisitive and unconventional. The good-natured Sheep is sensitive and he could possess the Water Bearer's deep well of knowledge and the Sheep's ability to bring situations to a peaceful solution. The Aquarian Sheep does not watch his popularity ratings too avidly. Self-denial is quite alien to him and he would rather have his fun now and pay later. With the Sheep's ability to gather sympathy after the fact, he may not have to pay at all.

AQUARIAN MONKEY: AIR + POSITIVE METAL

A spicy character never at a loss for words, the Aquarian Monkey combines the astounding intellect and the agility of the Monkey and the ample generosity of the Water Bearer. Both signs have a streak of willfulness and impertinence, so don't expect this person to fall obediently in line. Cerebral yet playful, sincere yet tricky, forceful yet complicated, he is the sum total of Aquarian restlessness and Monkey magic. The Aquarian Monkey is also likely to be ultramodern, flexible and probing because of the eager Monkey's tactics and the Water Carrier's thirst for knowledge.

AQUARIAN ROOSTER: AIR + NEGATIVE METAL

Not at all your run-of-the-mill Rooster. He is not as plodding as usual and his clock may be a bit too advanced; he's ahead of his time. But the Aquarian Rooster will still have the Rooster's directness, or genuine honesty as he likes to term it. When he speaks, he speaks, regardless of the furors he may cause. Actually, he relishes being different and even shocking at times. Because the Rooster sign helps this person to persevere and Aquarius has a futuristic outlook, the Aquarian Rooster will be able to draw up far-ranging plans and understand the future needs of people. He investigates with the candor of a child and the thoroughness of a scientist. Here is a Rooster with a constant axe to grind, who is eternally busy with his fact-finding missions.

AQUARIAN DOG: AIR + POSITIVE METAL

The strongly individualistic Dog is here made more movable, adaptable and daring by the Water Carrier's sign. Invariably rich in humor, he never refuses to lend a helping hand or say a kind word. When dark clouds gather, this person is a crusader in the truest sense of the word. Yet he never stays long enough in one place for the grass to grow under his feet, and although he is never intolerant, he does not have many intimate relationships either. He may be absentminded when he wraps himself up in his ideas. He tends to neglect the old camp for the new. An expert at instigating reforms, he is universalistic in outlook and will never knock anything without trying it first.

AQUARIAN BOAR: AIR + NEGATIVE WATER

The Boar is amorous by nature and has considerable strength of character. As Aquarians can be candid, reckless and defiant, this personality will certainly stir one's imagination. His didactic qualities are well masked behind that boisterous exterior. A trend-setter, he is never content to play a fixed role. This sign either makes delightful ripples or strong, splashing waves. Happy, prosperous and popular in spite of his shortcomings, the Water Bearer's broad outlook is joined to the Boar's spirit of cooperation and brotherhood.

PISCES

PISCES RAT: WATER + POSITIVE WATER

A very pleasing personality, as the Piscean is melodious and psychic and the Rat well versed in taking care of his family and interests. A subject formed by the combination of these two signs will always be able to demonstrate his creativity, even if he is shy and not desirous of facing the public. He could be a prolific writer because of the Fish's deep appreciation of human emotions. The natural aggressive and acquisitive tendencies of the clannish Rat are subdued to a fair degree, leaving a less aspiring person of peaceful inclinations. The person will value home and security before all else. Meditative, resourceful, sensitive but productive, the Pisces Rat will get straight A's for deportment.

PISCES OX: WATER + NEGATIVE WATER

Prim and proper, the Pisces Ox will have a mystical and retiring nature marked by strong inhibitions. Yet people are drawn to him despite his reticence because he exudes a certain feeling of security and will display the Ox's knack for being able to control his own environment. His reserved ways and quiet mannerisms only emphasize his strength and trustworthiness. Solemn, but with Pisces's gourmet tastes, he will also use the Ox's ability to achieve financial stability. As genuine as 24K gold and absolutely honest, the Pisces Ox will still have an ego that bruises easily, partly because of the Fish's sensitivity and partly because the Ox will refuse to tolerate any disrespect to his person.

PISCES TIGER: WATER + POSITIVE WOOD

The serene Pisces could do wonders for the dramatic Tiger personality here. Genteel, but not pliable, the Tiger will exhibit a calm inner nature and his liveliness will be reduced to a sparkling yet poetic level. The Piscean Tiger shields his or her claws and uses human psychology effectively to gain his or her objectives. The Fish is active and assertive here, while the Tiger relaxes and finds less conflict in life. But then, it's never safe to assume that the big Cat will ever allow himself to be put down too often. The Pisces Tiger may purr more than he roars, but nonetheless, he does roar.

PISCES RABBIT: WATER + NEGATIVE WOOD

Imaginative and impressionable, the Pisces Rabbit is a picture of gentility, beautiful manners and soft words. A poetic soul, dependent on others, he will be ingeniously artistic, clever and very fastidious. Yet despite his modest and unassuming appearance, he does not lack foresight or confidence. Actually, the low profile here could conceal an observant and astute mind, and one more selfish and caring about his creature comforts. He will work hard to stabilize his existence and to deflect any problems and conflicts onto others. Noncommittal in his pleasant and agreeable way, the Pisces Rabbit has a certain amount of narcissism.

PISCES DRAGON: WATER + POSITIVE WOOD

This amiable-looking mortal will have indomitable willpower. The Dragon's spirit provides ambition and a sense of adventure to the otherwise timorous Fish. This subject could act forcefully but with due restraint and consideration. Pisces is beneficial to the Dragon here, and although this person may blow hot and cold in one breath when he is unhappy, he rarely finds it necessary to go overboard as Dragons of more fiery matches do.

PISCES SNAKE: WATER + NEGATIVE FIRE

With gracious calm and fluid manners, the Pisces Snake conceals his wisdom and psychic powers well. He may be ineffectual and dreamy at times, but he always makes a good appearance in public. The Snake is intense, passionate and lucid while the Fish is deep and silent. A person of this nature is easily hurt by callous gestures and tends to nurture love and friendship with unfathomable emotions. The Pisces sign compensates for the Snake's ruthless determination by being compassionate, and his watery reserve brings forth surrealistic dreams and brilliant observations.

PISCES HORSE: WATER + POSITIVE FIRE

The soul of gallantry and finesse, this person is more subtle and receptive to the moods of others. Pisces patience will act as a tranquilizer on the Horse's mobility and exaggerated mannerisms. Maintaining a steady pace and reserve in resorting to action, this conspicuously conventional creature will not have the Horse's quick sense of urgency or the Fish's flaw of relying too much on the throb of his heart. He is a refined mixture of speed and sensitivity, neither too fast nor too slow, neither too efficient nor too sentimental.

PISCES SHEEP: WATER + NEGATIVE FIRE

Tedious and fussy, but still delightfully attractive, thoughtful and entertaining, the Pisces Sheep often ends up with the biggest piece of pie because of his generosity and kindness. He can also be sentimental and maudlin when he goes to an extreme. A lover of quiet pastoral scenes, stained-glass windows, organ music and lofty cathedrals, the background is a much safer and happier place for the Pisces Sheep to inhabit. Here he can meditate, as solitude brings out the best in his character.

PISCES MONKEY: WATER + POSITIVE METAL

Cool as a cucumber, delicate as the scent of lavender and intricate as a maze, the calculating but innocent-looking Piscean Monkey will be the perfect middleman or woman—benefitting from all the buyers and sellers of the world with unparalleled ease. The Monkey is naturally charming and Pisces is never outdone when it comes to casting mystic spells. The Monkey's Metal contains the Fish's mercurial sentimentality and gives his talents more form and substance.

PISCES ROOSTER: WATER + NEGATIVE METAL

A peace-loving personality with an exacting but cooperative character. The tough moral fiber of the virginal Rooster is all that it should be here, but Pisces, with his love of public relations, always manages to present a prettier picture. A less taciturn Rooster with no dogmatic inclinations, he could put by his staple diet of routine and methodical plodding and maybe even live a little. The conservative and gentle Pisces Rooster should have no difficulty obeying the rules, but he will see to it that his pattern of life is interwoven with equal amounts of rest and work.

PISCES DOG: WATER + POSITIVE METAL

Brave but deferential, the Piscean Dog will not be combative. The Fish's sign makes the Dog much less defensive and vigilant. He prefers security, serenity and comfort, although he still remains attentive to the needs of others. Lovely and disconcertingly attractive in his retiring way, this restive Dog is quite happy with the Fish's in-depth understanding of self, and he is less interested in indulging in outward conflict.

PISCES BOAR: WATER + NEGATIVE WATER

The Fish has the essential instincts for survival and a quiet confidence in his ability to comprehend the human mind. The Boar has vast reserves of energy and a positive mental attitude that makes everything possible. A combination of these two signs could produce effective and harmonious results if both play their parts well. Both Boar and Fish seem always able to find support when they need it, and this person will be able to muddle through with unbelievable success. Totally devoted to his loved ones, he lavishes affection upon them and will have worthy as well as unworthy friends who take advantage of his goodness. But confrontation is not his cup of tea. He treasures his personal relationships, and should matters come to a head, he prefers to settle out of court.

On the following pages are details of Arrow books that will be of interest.

Learn more about what is ahead for you and your loved ones, friends and business associates!

SUPER HOROSCOPES 1985

Arrow publish an individual *Super Horoscope* book for each of the twelve signs of the Zodiac, which is a candid, complete and individual forecast for the year. Each of them details the particular sign's dominant characteristics, with a character analysis, yearly and daily forecasts, and moon tables, as well as sections on signs of the Zodiac and the planets of the solar system.

THE BOOK OF CHINESE BELIEFS

Frena Bloomfield

Earth magic, ghost weddings, passports to the after-life: the spirit world of the Chinese exists side-by-side with everyday reality, and affects every aspect of Chinese life from diet and decor to getting married or opening a business.

Frena Bloomfield has lived and worked in Hong Kong and has talked in depth to many practitioners of the magic arts. *The Book of Chinese Beliefs* is a fascinating introduction to a rich culture where the dead are ever-present and even the siting of a house or village is governed by the laws of earth magic.

RELIVING PAST LIVES

Helen Wambach

An Egyptian scribe, a peasant girl in the pre-Christian world, an English housewife in the eighteenth century . . .

Lives separated from our own by time and by space – but all experienced in the present, by ordinary men and women, under the astonishing method of hypnotic regression. Some remember violent lives and brutal deaths, others lives of quiet domesticity. Peasants, priests, soldiers and teachers – voices of our pasts talking to us across the centuries.

At last, the incredible truth. The irrefutable facts. The indisputable proof. In *Reliving Past Lives*, the actual case studies of a respected clinical psychologist lead to one simple, devastating conclusion: reincarnation.

'Absorbing . . . the evidence is very impressive indeed'
New Statesman

'An astounding casebook' *Northern Echo*

TEST YOUR OWN SUPERMIND

Your hidden powers and how to use them

David Adams

Telepathy, ESP, telekinesis, precognition, psychic healing —
are they paranormal powers possessed by the fortunate few —
or mental skills which are latent in all of us?

In this astonishing book psychologist David Adams presents
the evidence that has convinced even the most sceptical
scientists that such powers exist — and shows how you can
unlock the secrets of your own supermind and use the powers
that lie dormant within you.

TEST YOUR OWN SUPERMIND is based on detailed case
histories, reports of investigations and scientific research into
every aspect of the paranormal: and contains exercises that
enable you to tap your hidden powers and put them to work.

YOUR PSYCHIC WORLD A-Z
An everyday guide

Ann Petrie

Everyone is psychic.

Everyone has the ability to develop extrasensory perception, but few know what to do with it.

Taking examples from everyday life, this book looks at the efficiency of your energy and your love, and presents a whole new perspective on the psychic world.

It explains *why* certain unusual or uncanny situations occur, and how to handle them in ways most beneficial to you and those around you.

This guide tells you what to do if you — Meet a ghost, a ghoul or a poltergeist; Feel you've been cursed; Fall in love at first sight; Remember places you know you've never been to before; Have dreams that come true; Need to protect yourself from psychic attack — plus many more pieces of essential advice on relating to the psychic world around you.

Ann Petrie is a psychic-astrologer who combines her gifts in a unique way in writing, broadcasting and counselling.

BESTSELLING NON-FICTION FROM ARROW

All these books are available from your bookshop or newsagent or you can order them direct. Just tick the titles you want and complete the form below.

☐	THE GREAT ESCAPE	Paul Brickhill	£1.60
☐	A RUMOR OF WAR	Philip Caputo	£1.95
☐	SS WEREWOLF	Charles Whiting	£1.50
☐	A LITTLE ZIT ON THE SIDE	Jasper Carrott	£1.25
☐	ART OF COARSE ACTING	Michael Green	£1.25
☐	UNLUCKIEST MAN IN THE WORLD	Mike Harding	£1.25
☐	DIARY OF A SOMEBODY	Christopher Matthew	£1.25
☐	TALES FROM A LONG ROOM	Peter Tinniswood	£1.75
☐	LOVE WITHOUT FEAR	Eustace Chesser	£1.95
☐	NO CHANGE	Wendy Cooper	£1.75
☐	MEN IN LOVE	Nancy Friday	£2.50

Postage _____

Total _____

ARROW BOOKS, BOOKSERVICE BY POST, PO BOX 29, DOUGLAS, ISLE OF MAN, BRITISH ISLES

Please enclose a cheque or postal order made out to Arrow Books Ltd for the amount due including 15p per book for postage and packing both for orders within the UK and for overseas orders.

Please print clearly

NAME ....

ADDRESS ....

....

Whilst every effort is made to keep prices down and to keep popular books in print, Arrow Books cannot guarantee that prices will be the same as those advertised here or that the books will be available.